PRAISE FOR STEPHEN DANDO-COLLINS'S

SEVEN AGAINST THEBES

"Yet another scorching and enthralling epic from the pen of Stephen Dando-Collins, the modern age's foremost dramatizer of ancient Greek and Roman history. Enough turmoil, blood, and tears for six books!

"The real story of how Oedipus came to unknowingly kill his father, sleep with his own mother, and thus beget his own brothers and sisters, contrasts graphically with the commonly held misconception, fostered by Sigmund Freud, that he committed incest semi-consciously. The subsequent unfolding of gigantic events resulting from this freakish accidental union makes absorbing reading, and involves the lives of so many legendary names—Oedipus, Creon, Jocasta, Antigone, and the numerous gods, kings, heroes, and beautiful women who throng the pages of Greek mythology.

"Stephen Dando-Collins brings his vast knowledge of the many sources of the times—the writings of Aeschylus, Sophocles, Euripides, Seneca, and subsequent scholars and playwrights—to reveal the events leading up to the ill-fated and bloody assault on Thebes in his usual clear and graphic style, while explaining in his scholarly notes how he has extrapolated the most likely true events from the many entangled versions handed down through the ages.

"This tale of the 'original magnificent seven' is a far more complex and tragic narrative than that related in the cinematic age, but still it's a shame that Yul Brynner and Steve McQueen aren't around to play the heroic leads!" —**Robin Hawdon, British playwright and author of** *Almost Famous* **and** *The Land, the Land*

"With impressive and thorough attention to detail, Stephen Dando-Collins's *Seven Against Thebes* brings the ancient world into fierce action. He shows the all too human emotions, motives, and clashes of these Bronze Age men, who may—or may not—have lived more than three millennia ago, in a thrilling and astonishingly relatable way. By puzzling through the different variations of the myth, corroborating them with geographies, biographies, poems, artwork, archaeological evidence, histories, and more, he manages to expertly stitch together the remains to bring to life the incredibly important and foundational ancient myth of Thebes." —**Anya Leonard, founder and director of Classical Wisdom, author of *Sappho: The Lost Poetess***

"Why only (and this) Seven fighting against the great ancient city of Thebes? Read all about it in Stephen Dando-Collins's latest mythographic extravaganza, squarely based as it is on the complex multiplicity of enthralling ancient written sources." —**Paul Cartledge, A.G. Leventis Professor of Greek Culture emeritus at Cambridge University and author of *Thebes: The Forgotten City of Ancient Greece***

SEVEN AGAINST
THEBES

ALSO BY STEPHEN DANDO-COLLINS

SEVEN AGAINST
THEBES

THE QUEST OF THE ORIGINAL
MAGNIFICENT SEVEN

STEPHEN DANDO-COLLINS

TURNER

PUBLISHING COMPANY

Turner Publishing Company
Nashville, Tennessee
www.turnerpublishing.com

Seven Against Thebes: The Quest of the Original Magnificent Seven

Cover and book design by William Ruoto

Library of Congress Cataloging-in-Publication Data

Names: Dando-Collins, Stephen, author.
Title: Seven against Thebes : the quest of the original magnificent seven / Stephen Dando-Collins.
Description: Nashville, Tennessee : Turner Publishing Company, [2023] | Includes bibliographical references and index.
Identifiers: LCCN 2022044643 (print) | LCCN 2022044644 (ebook) | ISBN 9781684428922 (paperback) | ISBN 9781684428939 (hardcover) | ISBN 9781684428946 (epub)
Subjects: LCSH: Seven against Thebes (Greek mythology)—Fiction. | LCGFT: Mythological fiction. | Novels.
Classification: LCC PR9619.3.D242 S47 2023 (print) | LCC PR9619.3.D242 (ebook) | DDC 823/.914—dc23/eng/20221024
LC record available at https://lccn.loc.gov/2022044643
LC ebook record available at https://lccn.loc.gov/2022044644

Printed in the United States of America

"There is a saying among men: a noble deed should not be buried silently in the ground."

—Pindar, fourth-century BC Theban poet, *The Odes*

My name, Stephen, is Greek in origin. It means "crown." And behind every crown there is a queen. In my case, her name is Louise. She is my wife, my rock. For forty years she has marched at my side, in sunny times listening to my tales of life and death from long, long ago, and in the darkest of times when our world has been shaken by words you never want to hear. Always there, never faltering. This book is for her.

CONTENTS

PREFACE

This work is an exploration of myth, legend, and origin stories that passed down through many generations, initially sung in verse and later committed to written form via histories and ancient poems and plays, to arrive at a historical narrative concerning one of the greatest military adventures of all time. This adventure was equal in the minds of Greeks and Romans with the siege of Troy as told in Homer's epic *The Iliad*, an event which it predated by a generation. And while the story, like *The Iliad*, has mythical elements, there is no factual, historical, or archaeological reason to suggest that the military campaign described in this story did not take place much as described.

In the 13th century BC, a quarter of a century before the Trojan War, seven Greek warrior heroes went against the Greek city of Thebes to restore one of their number to the throne of his father, the famous King Oedipus. Several children of those seven heroes would later take part in the siege of Troy.

The basic *Seven Against Thebes* story would be mirrored by Akira Kurosawa's 1954 Japanese movie, *Seven Samurai*, which in turn inspired John Sturges's star-packed 1960 Hollywood Western classic *The Magnificent Seven*. The seven principal characters in both movies bear a strong resemblance to the seven champions in *Seven Against Thebes*—the ethics-driven leader down on his luck; his brother-in-arms and first recruit; the inexperienced younger man wishing to prove himself; a traumatized fighter who dreads his impending death; and three hardened and skillful fighters who join the expedition with varying motives.

Horst Bucholz's young character Chico is *Seven Against Thebes*'s Parthenopaeus, youngest member of the Seven, while Robert Vaughn's troubled Lee mirrors Amphiaraus, and Hippomedon seems to have become James Coburn's weapons expert Britt. Steve McQueen's character Vin, who had a penchant for explosives, resembles fire-bearing Capaneus.

Neither *Magnificent Seven* screenwriter William Roberts or Walter Bernstein admitted to having been influenced by the *Seven Against Thebes* story. Neither did Akira Kurosawa. Yet the similarities in basic quest and characters seem to make those similarities more than coincidental. But, of course, in the films the writers reversed the emphasis of *Seven Against Thebes* by telling the story of the seven leading defenders, not the seven leading attackers, of the town.

The unsatisfying 2016 remake of *The Magnificent Seven* did away with much of that original *Seven Against Thebes* characterization—which the remake's writers were apparently oblivious to, just as this most recent version changed the setting and all the characters' names, while also substantially changing the plot from the original film.

The last time a retelling of the *Seven Against Thebes* story was committed to English in an original telling was when English poet John Lydgate wrote his own version of the epic in the 1420s. In the Afterword of this book, I explain how and why I have used the available ancient sources for my interpretation of the *Seven Against Thebes* story to create a plausible telling of history, while also providing credible motivations that are offered or suggested by the Greek and Roman writers.

Most ancient writers attributed the influence of the gods to many aspects of the story. In rendering a narrative that approximates the historical facts, I have attributed all the decisions taken by the leaders on both sides to the ambitions, egos, foibles, and superstitions of mere mortals, with the outcomes dictated by the culmination of those decisions; when it came to drought, epidemic, and earthquake, I credit Mother Nature.

I commence the book with the story of Oedipus, who famously

killed his father and married his mother. Oedipus was the father of the leader of the Seven, and his encounter with the riddling Sphinx outside Thebes would result in his becoming king of Thebes, setting up the eventual conflict between his sons that led to the Seven going against Thebes. To modern minds, the story of the Sphinx and her riddle veers into fantasy; but as I will point out later in this book, there is a contemporary example that suggests that the Sphinx may actually have been a clever female highway robber, not a mythical beast.

So let us begin the tale as the storytellers of Thebes began telling it thousands of years ago, with Oedipus on the road from Delphi, deeply troubled by a prophecy he has received from the Pythia, the oracle of Apollo; and, as he approaches the intersection that would change his life, he is intending to turn away from the road to home and flee . . .

LIST OF PRINCIPAL CHARACTERS

COMMANDERS OF THE ARGIVE ARMY

Adrastus, King of Argos.
Mecisteus, deputy and brother of King Adrastus (not originally part of the campaign).

THE SEVEN

Polynices of Thebes. Son of Oedipus, late king of Thebes.
Tydeus of Calydon. Son of Oeneus, late king of Calydon.
Amphiaraus of Argos, "The Prophet." Son of Oecles of Arcadia. Cousin and brother-in-law of King Adrastus.
Capaneus of Argos, "Torch." Son of Hipponous. Grandson of Iphis, late king of Argos.
Hippomedon of Mycenae, "Horse Ruler." Son of Mnesimachus, grandson of Talaus, late king of Argos, cousin of King Adrastus.
Eteoclus of Argos. Son of a peasant, grandson of Iphis, late king of Argos.
Parthenopaeus of Arcadia, "Cub." Son of Talaus, late king of Argos, and female warrior Atalanta.

COMMANDERS OF THE THEBAN ARMY

Eteocles, King of Thebes, son of Oedipus and brother of Polynices.

Creon, deputy and uncle of Eteocles, uncle of Polynices, brother of Queen Jocasta, and brother-in-law of Oedipus, late king of Thebes.

THE SEVEN DEFENDERS OF THE GATES OF THEBES

Eteocles, King of Thebes, defender of the Hypsistan Gate, against Polynices.

Melanippus, son of Astacus, defender of the Proetid Gate, against Tydeus.

Lasthenes, son of Oicles, defender of the Fountain (Homolid) Gate, against Amphiaraus.

Polyphontes, son of Hipponous, defender of the Electra Gate, against Capaneus.

Hyperbius, son of Oenops, defender of the Ogycian Gate, against Hippomedon.

Megareus, son of Creon, defender of the Neistan Gate, against Eteoclus.

Actor, another son of Oenops and brother of Hyperbius, defender of the Boreas Gate, against Parthenopaeus.

THE OFFSPRING

Alcmaeon, son of Amphiaraus.

Aegialeus, son of King Adrastus.

Thersander, son of Polynices.

Diomedes, son of Tydeus.

Sthenelus, son of Capaneus.

Polydorus, son of Hippomedon.

Promachus, son of Parthenopaeus.

Euryalus, son of Mecisteus.

Amphilocus, also a son of Amphiaraus.

Medon, son of Etoclus

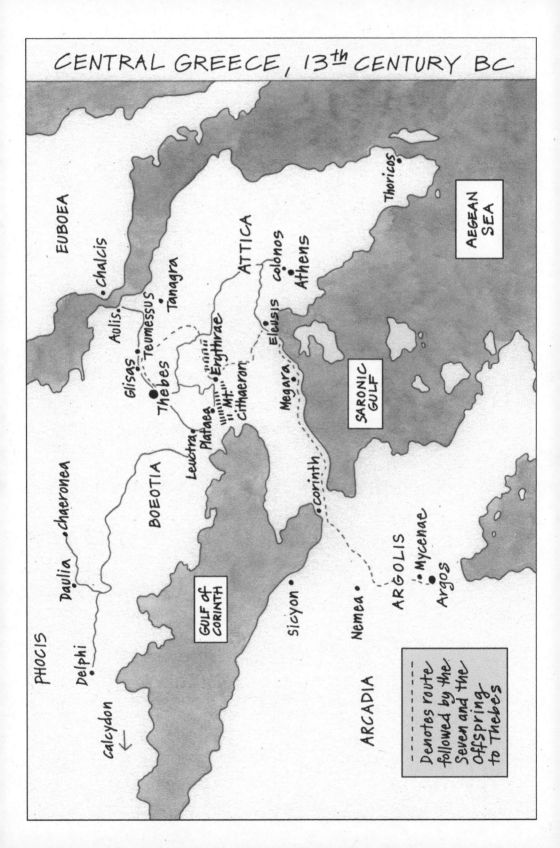

CENTRAL GREECE, 13ᵗʰ CENTURY BC

EUBOEA

AEGEAN SEA

Thoricos

ATTICA

Colonos
Athens

Chalcis

Aulis

Teumessus

Tanagra

Erythrae

Eleusis

SARONIC GULF

Glisas

Thebes

Mt. Cithaeron

Megara

Leuctra

Plataea

BOEOTIA

Corinth

Chaeronea

Daulia

GULF of CORINTH

Sicyon

Nemea

Mycenae

Argos

ARGOLIS

PHOCIS

Delphi

Calcydon

ARCADIA

- - - - Denotes route followed by the Seven and the Offspring to Thebes

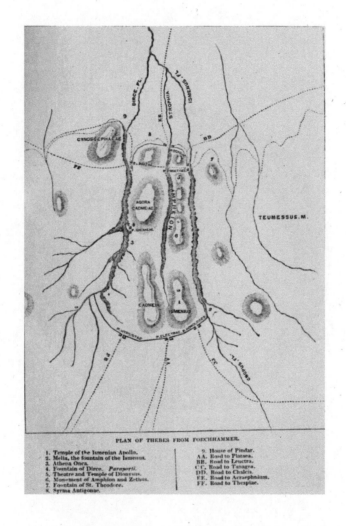

PLAN OF THEBES FROM FORCHHAMMER.

1. Temple of the Ismenian Apollo.
2. Melia, the fountain of the Ismenus.
3. Athena Onca.
4. Fountain of Dirce. *Paraportii.*
5. Theatre and Temple of Dionysus.
6. Monument of Amphion and Zethus.
7. Fountain of St. Theodore.
8. Syrma Antigonæ.

9. House of Pindar.
AA. Road to Platæa.
BB. Road to Leuctra.
CC. Road to Tanagra.
DD. Road to Chalcis.
EE. Road to Acræphnium.
FF. Road to Thespiæ.

Map of Ancient Thebes. From Topographia Thebarum
Heptapylarum, P W Forchhammer, 1854.

Oedipus and the Sphinx, classical Greek illustration.
Bridgeman Images.

A Campanian Neck-Amphora depicting Capaneus
climbing his ladder to set the Theban gate tower alight.
Bridgeman Images.

Etruscan urn depicting Polynices and Eteocles killing each other.
Bridgeman Images.

Nineteenth-century engraving showing the Seven taking their vows over the body of the sacred bull. Bridgeman Images.

Oedipus and daughter Antigone flee Thebes.
Bridgeman Images.

Bust of Greek dramatist Aeschylus, who wrote the play
Seven Against Thebes. *Bridgeman Images.*

Bust of Greek dramatist Sophocles, who wrote the play Oedipus Rex. *Bridgeman Images.*

Thebes in 1878, showing no trace of its ancient walls or gates. The Cadmea was on the hilltop upper right.

SEVEN AGAINST
THEBES

1.

OEDIPUS AND THE RIDDLE OF THE SPHINX

In the district of Phocis in central Greece during the Age of Heroes, a tall, well-built young man trudged wearily along a dusty road that passed through the hills, heading east. His hair was brown, his tawny-red beard neatly trimmed to a point. He was draped with a rough woolen cloak fixed at the shoulder with a simple bronze brooch. A broad-brimmed farmer's hat shaded his head from the baking Greek summer sun. On his left hip hung a long, slim sword in a plain scabbard of wood and leather, which was suspended from a baldric hanging over his right shoulder. A leather bag over the other shoulder contained a few personal possessions. And, like most pedestrians of this age, he walked with the aid of a long, stout wooden stave.[1]

The young man was called Oedipus. This name, meaning "swollen feet," had been given to him by his parents King Polybius and Queen Merope of Corinth. They had never shared with Oedipus their reason for giving him this name. For all he knew, it was connected with some tradition of his mother, a highborn native of Doris, a small mountainous kingdom located north of Phocis. Polybius had apparently set aside his first wife Periboea because she could not give him children, so he and his second wife Merope had doted on this boy, their only child, as he was raised in prosperous Corinth as a prince and heir to Polybius's throne. Then, after he officially reached manhood at age sixteen, something occurred that shook Oedipus's world. Just recently, at a banquet in Corinth, one of the diners had become drunk and offensive.

"You are not the true son of your father Polybius," the diner had declared to Oedipus.[2]

Others present had brushed this off as the wine talking; but Oedipus, who looked little like either his father or his mother, had been so troubled by the man's claim that he had told his parents about it. They had been furious at the accusation and took their anger out on the man who had uttered it, punishing him with banishment. For a time, that had made Oedipus feel better. But the memory of the claim had haunted him, so he decided to take action to either definitively quash or verify the accusation.

Like all Greeks, Oedipus worshipped a pantheon of gods in which Apollo, son of king of the gods Zeus, was the god of sun and light and patron deity of song, dance, poetry, healing, hunting, and prophecy. And like those Greeks who could afford it, Oedipus had decided to make a pilgrimage to Delphi in Phocis, home of the famed Oracle of Delphi. There, each summer, a priestess who served Phoebus Apollo—Bright Apollo as he was known because of his connection with the sun—would offer answers to questions put to the prophetic god. Most people asked Apollo about their futures, but in Oedipus's case, the question would be about his past: "Is Polybius my true father and sire?"[3]

Fearful of his parents' reaction, he had told them nothing of his quest and had traveled to Delphi in secret. Instead of driving in a chariot, as was the habit of Greek nobles, Oedipus had gone on foot. Instead of taking an entourage of servants, he had gone alone. And instead of wearing his finest outfit, he had worn the clothes of a common farmer. All this he did to preserve his anonymity so that no one would recognize him and report to King Polybius at Corinth that his son had paid a visit to Apollo's mouthpiece.

What he dreaded most was the question from his parents: "What did you ask of Apollo?" For he could not lie to the parents he loved and would have to confess to the king and queen that he harbored doubts that Polybius was truly his natural father.

At the town of Delphi on the southern slopes of Mount Parnassus, Oedipus had joined the long line of supplicants on the Sacred Way, the road that zigzagged up the dry, rugged mountain slope to the massive, rectangular, colonnaded Temple of Apollo that sat on a small plateau overlooking the valley below. There, his offering of gold was deposited in the Treasury of Apollo by the priests of the temple—men who, as well-to-do Greeks, were selected for the prestigious priestly post.

A local woman was chosen by the priests to serve as medium between Apollo and the thousands who came to Delphi's mount each summer to have their questions answered. She was called the Pythia, because, according to myth, it was at Delphi's Castalian Spring that Apollo had killed the monster Python, freeing a prophetess it had imprisoned. The Pythia sat in a cave beneath Delphi's Temple of Apollo, breathing in vapors that rose through a fissure in the rocks. She famously gave her replies in verse form, and those verses could often be cryptic and require interpretation.

Oedipus had taken his turn descending into the cave beneath the temple, where he found the seated Pythia, a mature woman, awaiting him. A priest then required the pilgrim to pose his question. Just a single question was permitted. The Pythia had gone into a trance-like state, and before long she recited an answer to the question. An assistant sitting close by recorded her words in ink on vellum, which he handed to Oedipus, who was led back up into the light of day as he scrutinized the lines.

He had been expecting his reply from the depths to involve, like many issued by the different Pythias over the centuries, a riddle that required deciphering. Oedipus enjoyed a good riddle. But the prophecy the young prince received shocked him. It had nothing to do with his past. It was all about his future: "You are fated to defile your mother's bed. You will show to men a brood at which they will not be able to look. You will be the killer of the man who fathered you."[4]

Oedipus had attempted to make sense of all this, wondering what it had to do with his question. Some of the Oracle of Delphi's predictions proved so cryptic that they would defy deciphering until after the event or events they described took place, and it was only then that the true meaning would become apparent.

Racking his mind for a hidden meaning to his prophecy without success, Oedipus left Delphi in a daze. As he walked, he decided that, to thwart the prophecy, he could never return to Corinth. He reasoned that if he never again set eyes on his father King Polybius, he could not kill him. To protect his father, he had to avoid the possibility of ever again being in the presence of Polybius. Oedipus would have to take himself as far away from Corinth as humanly possible.

By the time he was several miles into his trek, Oedipus had made up his mind to take himself, via the road to Daulia, to the northeast coast of mainland Greece. There, he would acquire a boat. Having grown up in Corinth, a maritime city, he had been taught to sail and to navigate by the stars. "By the stars alone," he would later say, he intended charting a course to some faraway land where Polybius could never be expected to set foot. In that way, the oracle's prophecy could never be realized.[5]

As Oedipus topped a rise, ahead he could see a valley crossroads where three roads intersected. One road was his own, the west-to-east road from Delphi. Of the two other routes branching off from the intersection, one followed a river northeast to Daulia, then went on to Orchomenus, Chaeroneia, and the coast. The other road ran due south for several miles before turning sharply east and running toward far-distant Leuctra. He had used this latter route on his way from Corinth to Delphi.

Studying the scene, Oedipus saw, coming up the Leuctra road toward the crossroads at a walking pace, a chariot drawn by a pair of colts. A herald walked ahead of the chariot, bearing a staff. A driver and a passenger occupied the chariot, while two servants walked behind. It eventuated that Oedipus reached the intersection just a little ahead of the chariot and the herald preceding it.

"Make way there!" called the herald as he approached Oedipus. "Stand aside for my master!"

Oedipus, in no mood to be ordered around by a servant, stood his ground at the commencement of the road to Delphi, right in the path of the chariot. The driver, clearly intending to take the Delphi road, was forced to come to a halt where the three roads met.

"Stand aside, I said!" cried the steward, shoving Oedipus from the middle of the road.[6]

All things about Oedipus's character could be described as quick. He was quick to learn, quick to act, quick to decide, quick to judge, quick to accuse. Most of all, he was quick to anger. Like an erupting volcano, his temper now rose. Part of Oedipus's upbringing as a boy had involved training with all manner of weapons. These included the wooden staff, which, wielded with skill, could inflict blows that were both painful and fatal. Now, he swung his staff with his right hand, smashing it down on the back of his assailant's skull, where it connected with a loud crack. Eyes rolling and dropping his own staff, the steward crumpled to the ground.

Now Oedipus walked on, intending to pass to the left of the stationary chariot and keep going, taking the road to Daulia to the northeast. But as he drew level with the car, the passenger rose up from his bench seat. Tall, well dressed, aged in his forties, the man was of similar build to Oedipus, but his hair and beard were beginning to silver. His clothing was plain and unadorned. In his hands he wielded a goad, a long wooden cattle prod with a forked end, which led Oedipus to believe the man must be a well-to-do farmer.

"Rogue! Villain!" cried the passenger. "Take this!" Before Oedipus could protect himself, the fellow smashed the goad down on top of his head.

Oedipus staggered away, head in pain, ears ringing. But within seconds, instinct and rage combined to drive him into offensive action. Turning back to the chariot, he swung his staff with both hands. Catching the standing passenger in the midriff, the blow knocked the man from the chariot and onto the road, where he laid on his back. This spooked the chariot's two horses, which reared up on their hind legs, and for the moment the driver was fully occupied in trying to control them.

Both of the servants who had been trailing the chariot were armed with sheathed swords. Yelling incoherently, the younger of these men drew his weapon and ran at Oedipus, who deftly stepped to one side just as the servant swiped at his head with his sword. Then, in a fluid movement, Oedipus swung his staff, cracking the fellow across the back as he passed, sending him sprawling, facedown, to the roadside.

Turning to face the second servant, who had not moved, Oedipus readied his staff to defend against another attack. But he saw a strange look in the eyes of this middle-aged man. The servant's eyes dropped to Oedipus's sandaled feet—to his ankles, which had been scarred since birth. Elevating his gaze, he again looked Oedipus in the face. For a long moment they confronted each other, before the servant turned and fled back along the road to Leuctra, casting aside his sword as he ran, then throwing off his cloak so he could run faster.

In the roadway, the floored steward had not moved, but the owner of the chariot was striving to sit up, grabbing at his stinging ribs as he did. In the chariot, the driver was bringing his colts under control. At the roadside, the first servant was getting to his feet, still with sword in hand, and turning to face the man from Corinth.

The outnumbered Oedipus reckoned that if he did not act quickly, he would be a dead man. Casting aside his staff, he drew his sword; then, before the young servant could strike him, he ran him through the chest with his blade. In the chariot, the driver had let go of his reins and drawn his sword. Jumping down to the ground from the rear of his vehicle, this man swung wildly at Oedipus, who simply ducked aside and then plunged the sharp and bloodied tip of his own sword into the man's stomach. Dropping his sword and clutching the site of the wound, the driver staggered back against his chariot. This was enough to again spook the horses and set them in motion. Dashing forward, they took the driverless chariot away, up the Delphi road, as the driver collapsed onto the roadway.

Only the owner of the chariot remained to be dealt with. He had struggled to his feet and now drew his sword. Without a moment's thought, Oedipus strode toward him, knocked aside the man's proffered blade, then slashed him across the throat. With eyes bulging and blood jetting from his neck, the man sank to his knees and toppled forward onto his face.

Now, as Oedipus stood in the middle of the crossroads with bodies all around him, rage gave way to reason. He had just killed several men. Who would believe he had done it in self-defense? No witnesses must be allowed to remain to accuse him. The chariot's owner would soon drown in his own blood. The steward had died the instant Oedipus had cracked his skull. But the first servant and the driver remained alive. Standing over each man in turn, Oedipus slashed their throats, quickly dispatching the pair of them. There remained only the second servant, the older man who had fled. Deciding that he must catch and kill the man to prevent him identifying the killer of his master, Oedipus set off after him, jogging along the road to Leuctra in the fellow's wake.[7]

How long Oedipus pursued his quest to overtake and kill the last remaining witness to the killing at the crossroads, not even he would recall. But at solid walking pace, the journey would have taken him two to three days—although, in his haste, he may have walked through some of the hours of darkness. After passing out of Phocis and crossing the flatlands of Boeotia, he reached Leuctra without overtaking the fleeing servant.

From Leuctra, a road ran south to Plataea and Mount Cithaeron. From there, a traveler could take roads heading southwest to Corinth or southeast to Athens. He had used this route, in reverse, on the journey from Corinth to Delphi. Another road ran east from Leuctra, to the city of Thebes, from where another easterly highway known as the Chalcis Road led to Aulis, a small port on the Euripus Strait controlled by Thebes. At the strait, Oedipus might hire a boatman to ferry him the three miles across the water to the more populous city of Chalcis, on Euboea, Greece's largest island. There, he should be able to find a boat to continue his flight.

With escape and survival ever present in his mind, for a time Oedipus considered this plan. Yet it was possible his quarry had taken the road to Plataea. Deciding to be safe rather than sorry and make every effort to eliminate the witness of the killings at the crossroads before he did anything else, Oedipus set off along the road to Plataea. It took two days of solid walking to reach this city, without spotting his quarry.

After spending the night at Plataea and deciding the pursuit was now pointless, Oedipus reverted to his previous plan of reaching the sea. Now he had two reasons to sail away: his desire to avoid ever again seeing his parents and thus to defy the prediction of the oracle, and the need to escape any connection with the killings at the crossroads in Phocis.

So he took the road from Plataea to Thebes, via which he could reach the sea at Aulis. After several hours, the road entered a chain of hills before emerging onto the Theban plain. Once the road topped a rise and began to slope down to the plain, Oedipus saw that ahead, in the middle of the plain, rose the walled battlements of a city, with round stone towers housing its gates. Within the city there were several hills, with the tallest, a flat-topped hill in the south, housing a formidable walled citadel. This was the city of Thebes, fabled birthplace of the hero-god Heracles.

As Oedipus was taking in this sight, he heard the flapping of wings. Then, to his astonishment, a mighty beast dropped from the sky, landing on the road in front of him. The beast possessed the body of a full-grown lioness with the head of a snake on the end of a long tail. Powerful eagle wings spread from the shoulders. And yet the head was human, with short hair and the face of a beautiful woman. For a moment, Oedipus was frozen with shock.

"Traveler, do you know who I am?" the beast asked. As she spoke, she revealed teeth as sharp as daggers.

Oedipus could barely find his tongue. "I, er . . ."

"I am the Sphinx, guardian of the road to Thebes. To pass me by and enter the city, travelers must answer a riddle. Answer correctly and you will be free to go." Her voice was seductive, but her flashing teeth sent a message of unmistakable threat.

Oedipus strove to remain calm. He quickly banished his first instincts, that of fight or flight. Neither option was viable against such an agile adversary, which could take to the air or leap on him with equal ease if he either ran or attempted to use his staff or sword. He had heard of Sphinxes. Most Greeks had. But in his recollection, they were supposed to only live in Egypt and were exclusively male. According to some Greeks, Sphinxes were related to Cerberus, the multi-headed dog that stood guard over the entrance to Hades. To be honest, Oedipus had thought tales of Sphinxes that ate humans the sort of monster myth invented by mothers to frighten their children into not straying far from home. Now, as his initial disbelief gave way to rationality, he felt oddly honored to come face to face with a Sphinx. How many men could claim that?

"Well?" asked the Sphinx. "What say you, traveler? Don't you have a tongue?"

"What . . ." He cleared his throat. "What if I chose not to enter Thebes, and turned back the way I came?" he asked, attempting to sound unafraid.

"Answer my riddle correctly, and you will be free to go wherever you wish. An intelligent man like yourself should have no difficulty solving the riddle." She swished her tail; and as she did, a forked tongue shot from the snake head on the end of it.

"What if I failed to answer the riddle correctly?"

"In that case, I would seize you by the throat, suffocate the life out of you, then tear you limb from limb and feast on your flesh. It has been some time since my last meal. You have come along at just the right time."

"How many travelers prior to me have answered the riddle correctly?"

"Not one." She smiled again, flashing her teeth. "But they were not you. Do you have what it takes to match wits with me?"

"If I were to answer the riddle correctly, what guarantee do I have that you would permit me to pass?"

"I am many things, traveler, but a liar I will never be."

"A riddle, you say?" Oedipus's favorite riddle was this: There are two sisters. One gives birth to the other, and she in turn gives birth to the first. Who are the two sisters? As Oedipus had quickly deduced, the sisters are Day and Night. If he could master that brain-teaser, could he not master the Sphinx's riddle? Not that he had any choice in the matter. Both he and the Sphinx knew that his life depended on his doing what no man before him had done.

"Would you like to hear my riddle?" she asked.

"Why not?" he responded, striving to sound confident.

"Then proceed to my riddling roost above." She indicated a rocky ledge on the hilltop behind him. "Go ahead. I will be right behind you."

Oedipus walked up the hill, hearing the footfall of the Sphinx padding along right behind him. Below the ledge there was a flat-topped boulder, just high enough to make a comfortable seat for him. Strewn around the ground were the whitened bones of countless travelers whose journey had ended here.

"Take a seat," said the Sphinx, as she sprang up onto the ledge and sat on her haunches, looking down at him.

Oedipus seated himself on the boulder, crossed his legs, and looked up at her. "Let's waste no more time," he said. "Go ahead, give me your riddle."

"My, you are a confident fellow," she said, impressed. "Others before you have attempted to delay the inevitable."

"*Your* inevitable defeat can only be delayed so long," he responded.

She laughed. "You are shaping up to be a worthy adversary indeed. I shall enjoy our contest as much as its outcome." She suddenly looked serious—deadly serious. "Very well. Are you ready?"

He nodded. "Give me your riddle."

"Which creature has one voice and yet becomes four-footed, then two-footed, then three-footed?"

He pursed his lips, then asked, "How long do I have to solve the riddle?"

"Take as much time as you wish between now and sunset," she replied. "I am in no hurry."

"Can I ask questions? Will you give me a clue?"

She shook her head. "No questions, no clues. You are permitted just a single guess. Get it wrong once, and you will pay the penalty."

He repeated the riddle to himself. "Which creature has one voice and yet becomes four-footed, then two-footed, then three-footed?" Resting his right elbow on his raised thigh, he stroked his beard with the fingers of his right hand as his mind went to work. He pondered whether the answer might involve a mythological beast, perhaps even a Sphinx, only to quickly dismiss the possibility—when would a Sphinx or any other mythological creature become three-legged? Then it occurred to him that the first words of the riddle were in fact a clue. Apart from Sphinxes, which creatures had a voice? Birds and animals made sounds, but they could not be described as possessing a voice. Humans alone had a voice. But how could a man have four legs, then two, then three? And then an image of an infant entered his mind, first crawling, then pulling itself to its feet. Oedipus smiled to himself.

"Why do you smile?" asked the Sphinx, intrigued.

"I have the answer," he announced.

The Sphinx looked shocked. "So soon? Take your time, traveler. Don't be in a hurry to die."

"No, I have the answer to your riddle," he replied with assurance.

"Very well. It's your choice. What is your answer?"

"The creature is man, who walks on all fours as a baby, then walks on two feet as an adult, then uses a walking stick in old age."

"No!" cried the Sphinx. "This cannot be! No man is as smart as me! No man could possibly solve such a clever riddle!"

"I did," said Oedipus matter-of-factly.

The Sphinx rose up, let out a pained howl, then threw herself from the ledge, landing down the slope on her head, clearly trying to dash out her own brains in her despair. Oedipus jumped up, drew his sword, and scrambled down the rocky incline to where the Sphinx laid on her back, legs in the air, looking up at him. She was still alive. With two hands, Oedipus swung his sword and cleaved the Sphinx's pretty head from her barbarous body.[8]

For a time he sat on a rock, looking at the decapitated Sphinx, as blood oozed from her severed neck. The ordeal had drained him of energy. As the sun began to set behind him, he looked toward the distant Thebes. Was it possible that the servant who had evaded him at the crossroads in Phocis had come from this city, had reached it just ahead of him, and was now raising the alarm? If the fellow came from Thebes, he would have been aware that the Sphinx patrolled this road and intercepted unwitting strangers. That being the case, the servant would have taken steps to avoid and slip by her. To Oedipus's mind, this scenario was unlikely but not impossible. After his near-fatal encounter with the Sphinx, it was better to again be safe than sorry, Oedipus told himself.

So, despite being tired, hungry, and thirsty, he spent the night on the hillside overlooking the road, waiting to see if a party of armed men came hurrying from Thebes, led by the escaped servant and bent on finding Oedipus the murderer in Phocis or beyond. But no one came out of Thebes and passed along the road below Oedipus. The next morning, deciding that the servant could not have gone to Thebes, Oedipus picked himself up and trudged down the road to the city, feeling positive and intending to stay no more than a night before continuing to the coast along the Chalcis Road.

He left behind vineyards that covered the lower slopes of the hills; then, on the flat of the plain, he passed through fields of barleycorn dotted with farmers' stone huts. Closer to the city, stock grazed contentedly on a riverbank. As he drew nearer to Thebes, Oedipus saw that his road from Plataea, considered the main road to Thebes, led to the most central of three gates in the city's southern wall. He joined the tail end of a line of local farmers who were going into the city, carrying their produce on asses and in carts.

Thebes was a long, narrow city, its high protecting walls tracing a shape not unlike the head of a Grecian spear. In the south, the wall curved gently outward. Up the western and eastern sides of the city, the walls followed two streams, south to north. On the western side flowed the more substantial Dirce, named for the wife of the early Theban ruler Lycus and mother of the twins Amphion and Zethus, who both became kings of the city. The eastern wall followed the Ismenus, a stream named for an earthly son of Apollo. In the north, these two waterways curved elegantly to the spear point, where the Ismenus joined the Dirce, which continued to flow north.

Three roads led to three gates in the southern wall—on the left the road from Leuctra, on the right a road from Tanagra, with the middle road running from Plataea. Round stone towers flanked each gate, with pedestrians and vehicles passing through the double gates to enter or leave the city. The gateways were just wide enough to allow the passage of a single wagon, cart, or chariot, or three horsemen riding abreast. A gatekeeper by the open gate looked Oedipus up and down suspiciously and stepped into his path, using a staff to bar his way.

"Halt!" cried the gatekeeper. "What do you want here, stranger?"

"Where can I wash and secure food and drink?" Oedipus asked.

"You are covered with blood," said the gatekeeper. "What's the cause?"

Oedipus looked at his clothes, his arms, his hands, his legs, his sandaled feet. All bore a coating of sweat and dust combined with dried blood—from the crossroads fight and from his decapitation of the Sphinx. "I met a beast on the road here," Oedipus replied, "and was forced to kill it."

"A beast? What manner of beast?"

"You will never believe it, but it was a Sphinx. A vicious creature! She posed me a riddle, expecting me to fail the test. But I gave the correct answer and took off her head with my sword."

The gatekeeper eyed him with disbelief. "You killed the Sphinx? You? Where is the beast now?"

"She lies dead, in two parts, below a ledge above the road west, over yonder." He nodded back the way he had come.

The gatekeeper called over a longhaired child of ten or so. "Boy, run up to the Cadmea at once and inform our lord Creon that there is a stranger at the Electra Gate who claims to have slain the Sphinx. Tell him I await His Excellency's instructions."[9]

Wide-eyed, the boy dashed away, following the broad cedar steps that rose up the southern side of the hill occupying the southern part of the city. On all sides but the southern slope, the hill possessed steep, rocky, cliff-like sides. In addition, to the east and west, deep gullies made access to the hill even more difficult. It was an admirable site for a citadel.

With the messenger's departure, the gatekeeper directed Oedipus to a nearby fountain outside the city wall. This fountain was located next to a sanctuary to Zeus Hypsistus (Zeus Most High), which gave the nearby Hypsistan Gate its name. Once Oedipus had washed his bloodied and dusty face, hair, arms, legs, and feet, he returned to the gatekeeper to await the outcome of the message sent up to the Cadmea by way of the boy. As he waited, Oedipus looked beyond the open gate to the broad city streets.[10]

The people he saw inside Thebes all looked somber and subdued. Some women were even crying. "Not a smile do I see, not a laugh do I hear," he said. "Instead, I hear women sobbing. What is the cause of such gloom?"

"All of Thebes is in mourning, stranger," the gatekeeper sadly revealed. "Yesterday we learned that our king, Laius, was waylaid and killed on the road by robbers."

"That is terrible," Oedipus returned. "Your king, you say? Killed by robbers?"

"As chance would have it, King Laius was on his way to Delphi to ask Loxias what we should do to rid Thebes of the Sphinx." Loxias was another name for Apollo, used reverently by those Greeks who didn't wish to utter his name in vain. "And here you say that you have killed the Sphinx!" the gatekeeper continued. "Our prayers have been answered!"

Oedipus shrugged. "All I did was solve a riddle," he said modestly. "Who is this Creon you have sent to?"

"Creon is brother-in-law of the king. Laius left him in charge during his absence. For the moment, Creon is serving as our king, until the Governors of Thebes decide on a successor to King Laius."

A little while later, a crowd of bearded men descended on the Electra Gate. Hurrying down the cedar steps from the Cadmea came a short, handsome, regal-looking man in his thirties followed by a throng of Spartoi, as the elders of the city elite were known, all talking excitedly at once.

"Is this the fellow who says he killed the Sphinx?" demanded the leader of the group.

"One and the same, my lord Creon," the gatekeeper replied with a bow of his head.

"What name have you, fellow?" Creon asked Oedipus, taking in the tall stranger with bloodied garments.

"Oedipus of Corinth at your service, my lord," said Oedipus with a weary smile and a bow. "I seek only food and drink and a place to lay my head for the night. I will then be on my way again."

"No, no, no!" Creon exclaimed. "The man who rids Thebes of the privations of the Sphinx deserves to be richly rewarded. But first, tell me, where does the body of the Sphinx lie?"[11]

Oedipus pointed to the distant slope, and Creon delegated men to go at once to the spot. Chariots were sent for, and soon several of the vehicles were speeding away from the city with dust spewing from beneath their wheels.

In the meantime, Creon and the elders of Thebes flocked around Oedipus and enthusiastically conducted him up to the

Cadmea. This citadel had been built by the founder of Thebes, King Cadmus. A native of Phoenicia in the Eastern Mediterranean, Cadmus was the son of Phoenician king Agenor. Cadmus had arrived here on the Theban plain some centuries earlier with an invading Phoenician army. Driving out one local tribe and incorporating another into his ranks, Cadmus had built the hilltop stronghold that bore his name. Over time, the city of Thebes had grown below the Cadmea. To begin with, Cadmus had not even spoken Greek; but not only had he learned Greek, he had also taught the Greeks how to commit their language to written form.

In the colonnaded Audience Hall at the center of the Cadmea, food, drink, and bowls of rosewater for washing were brought to Oedipus, and his hosts stood watching with beaming smiles as, embarrassed by the attention, he refreshed and fed himself.

The men delegated to investigate the death of the Sphinx returned. As they walked in, one man, Thebes's high priest of Zeus, carried the Sphinx's head aloft on the head of a spear. "It is true!" he cried. "The beast is slain!"

Cheers filled the hall.

"You, Oedipus," declared Creon, "are the savior of Thebes." Already, Creon was thinking about matching this handsome young man with his sister Jocasta, the widow of King Laius, which would relieve him of the responsibility of caring for her.

"Such a brave man deserves to be our king," said Astacus, one of the most senior and respected of the city elders elected to the body known as the Governors. Astacus, as it happened, secretly disliked Creon, and he had no desire to see him permanently reign as king of Thebes. In Oedipus, this unassuming young fellow, Astacus saw a potential king he could flatter—and manipulate. "Have we not always advanced those who advance Thebes?"

"I would most certainly give him the hand in marriage of my sister Jocasta, widow of King Laius," said Creon, attempting to slow the momentum of this sudden push to crown the stranger.

"Will you take the throne if it is offered, Oedipus?" asked Oenops, another of the elders who numbered among the Governors, and who, like his friend Astacus, had no wish to see Creon remain in charge of the city.

"Well . . ." Oedipus began, a little dazed. As the Theban elite crowded around, patting him on the back and shaking his hand, it occurred to Oedipus that a king would stand above suspicion should the story of the killing of the farmer and his servants at the crossroads in Phocis ever emerge. "Is the throne of Thebes offered?" he asked.

Creon called above the hubbub, "Those of the Governors who are in favor of hailing our savior Oedipus the new king of Thebes, raise their hand."[12]

Amid loud acclamation, and carried forward on the wave of excitement generated by the news that Oedipus had rid Thebes of the predations of the Sphinx, every single Governor apart from Creon raised his hand. This surprised Creon, who clearly had no idea how disliked he was by the Spartoi. A cunning man—a quality that contributed to his lack of popularity, but a far from perceptive one, which also counted against him—he had put the question to the vote to take the steam out of the rush to crown the stranger king. Instead, his plan had backfired on him. To save face, he too now raised his hand, making the vote unanimous.

Oedipus was also surprised. All of a sudden, he had gone from a man about to go on the run to a man about to be handed a kingdom.

2.

OEDIPUS LEARNS THE TRUTH

For two decades, Oedipus reigned as King of Thebes, ruling wisely and humanely, and his people thanked the gods for it and for him. The population of Thebes at this time was smaller than that of Oedipus's hometown of Corinth, which boasted ninety thousand residents. Thebes was a relatively small city with a population of some ten thousand, its realm modest but prosperous. Yet, as word spread throughout Greece and beyond that its new king Oedipus had solved the riddle of the Sphinx and slain the beast, freeing Thebes, the king and his city had won a level of respect and renown usually reserved for larger, more powerful rulers and realms.

The story of Oedipus, the Sphinx, and the riddle spread throughout Greece and entered Greek folklore. For several years after the event, wise men came from afar to hear from Oedipus's own lips the riddle posed by the Sphinx, with all confessing that, in his place, they would not have come up with the correct answer. Not that Oedipus was flattered by the attention—all this was in the past, which he wished forgotten.

From his parents King Polybius and Queen Merope at Corinth, Oedipus heard not a word. Knowing how much they loved him, he suspected they were broken-hearted that he had apparently deserted them and his birthright as heir to the Corinthian throne and accepted the lesser Theban throne. For his part, still terrified by the prophecy that he would kill his father, Oedipus was determined to never set eyes on Polybius again and did nothing to create even the possibility that it might happen. Consequently, he made no attempt to contact the parents he loved.

As Creon had promised, he gave his widowed sister Jocasta in marriage to Oedipus once her period of mourning following the death of her first husband Laius came to an end. Oedipus never laid eyes on his bride until their wedding day. He was told she was a beauty, as her name Jocasta, meaning Shining Moon, suggested. And a beauty she was. Just a teenager when she had married Laius, she was now in her late thirties and was Oedipus's senior by some fifteen years. But that did not concern Oedipus. He fell in love with Jocasta the moment he saw her, and she with him.

Oedipus was told that Jocasta and Laius had just one child, a boy, who had died within days of his birth. It was thought by courtiers of Thebes that Jocasta must have become infertile after that, so there was great rejoicing among Thebans when she subsequently produced a brace of sons with Oedipus, an heir and a spare, followed by a pair of daughters.

The first son they named Polynices, which means "much strife." This name was intended to advertise the fact that, after much strife, Thebes was free from threat and once more a safe and prosperous place and that the royal house of Thebes was leaving behind its strife-torn past. The next boy, who arrived a year or so later, was a beautiful baby. His parents called him Eteocles, meaning "truly glorious." After a gap of several years, the couple's first daughter came along. They named her Antigone, or "worthy of one's parents." A few years later, the second daughter arrived. Oedipus and Jocasta named her Ismene, meaning "knowledgeable," in the hope that she would grow to become an intelligent woman.

Oedipus adored his children, who developed different and distinct characters. By the time his first son Polynices left his teens behind, he had grown into an athletic but quiet, thoughtful youth. Polynices's handsome younger brother Eteocles was somewhat vain and extremely competitive, hating to lose any contest in which he competed, from riding to wrestling to spear-throwing.

Once Oedipus's daughters reached their early teens, their protective, possessive father considered them still too young to be marriage material, even though Greek women were frequently given in marriage at that age. Antigone was Oedipus's favorite child. She had her mother's beauty and was bold and firm in her opinions. But Antigone's strongest quality was her solid loyalty to family and friends. If one term could describe Antigone, it was "dutiful." Her younger sister Ismene was the beauteous image of her mother but was more inward-looking than her sister. Unlike many beautiful girls, Ismene wasn't outgoing and didn't seek to flaunt her beauty. She was content to sit at a spinning wheel all day and had no real mind of her own. If one term could characterize Ismene, it was "timid."

The children were lovingly indulged by Oedipus, but they learned to never test his patience, of which he had little. In fact, only recently, his sons had incurred his wrath. For the twentieth anniversary of their father's reign, they had arranged a public banquet. Oedipus had reluctantly agreed to the banquet. On the night of the celebration, Polynices and Eteocles had their father served his food on the treasured ancient silver table of King Cadmus and delivered his wine in a gold cup. The king had erupted in rage, admonishing his crestfallen sons in front of the entire court: ostentation was something Oedipus never wished to be accused of. Modesty in all things was his credo.

After this well-intentioned misjudgment, in an attempt to make up for their error, Polynices and Eteocles had gone the other direction entirely some months later. This was following a major sacrifice to the goddess Athena. For the first time, Polynices and Eteocles had served as the most senior of the seven naked priests who oversaw the sacrifice of a he-goat to Athena at the city's altar of Athena Onca. Following the animal's sacrifice, the brothers had deliberately sent their father the rump of the beast for his table, thinking he would prefer a modest cut—the shoulder was considered the prime cut and had traditionally been sent to the kings of Thebes on these occasions. When Oedipus was served the rump, he again publicly erupted with anger. Did his sons not know by now, Oedipus raged, that tradition was as important to him as modesty?

This same year, events were coming to a head that would change the lives of all Thebans, but most particularly and dramatically those of Oedipus and his family. The previous autumn, the usual October rains had failed to fall. By the spring, drought was gripping Thebes and her fertile farmlands. For months on end, no rain fell. Rivers and streams ceased to run. The city's deep artesian wells continued to provide for the people of Thebes, but there was no water for crops or animals. The barleycorn crop perished, grapes withered on the vine, and flocks died in droves.

And then, a plague hit the people of the city. Before it was over, perhaps a thousand Thebans would be dead. The sickness began with a headache and was followed by an ugly rash on the face and body and then by fever. If the patient lived to the seventh or eighth day, they would develop diarrhea. If that did not kill them, they might survive but sometimes with long-term effects such as paralysis or blindness. As the sun beat down through Sirius's Dog Star days that summer, food and water rationing became necessary in the city. It was during these days of restrictions that Polynices and Eteocles made their blunder in bringing out Cadmus's silver table and the gold cup at their father's anniversary celebration.

To protect his family, Oedipus barred them from having contact with commoners. When it was absolutely necessary to meet with the city elders, he did so outside the palace, on its steps, in the open air. In the late summer, begged by the elders to apply his famed wisdom to finding a solution to their predicament, Oedipus sent Creon, his brother-in-law and chief counselor these past twenty years, on a mission to Delphi. There, Creon was to ask the oracle what Apollo required Thebes to do to rid itself of the double pestilence that was gripping the city and her people.

As summer drew to a close, there was no word from Creon. The time had elapsed when he might reasonably have completed his journey to Delphi and returned. Oedipus began to worry that his royal envoy had failed to reach the Pythia before she withdrew from her subterranean place of prophecy until the following summer. Was Creon too afraid to return with his mission unaccomplished? Just as Oedipus was beginning to despair of an answer from the oracle, word reached him in the Cadmea when he was in his bed one night that a delegation of Theban city elders was outside the palace, demanding an audience.

When the bronze double doors opened and Oedipus emerged from the palace in his nightgown, flanked by a pair of armed soldiers of the Cadmean Guard, he found the delegation awaiting him, kneeling on the lowest of the broad palace steps. The delegation was made up of boy priests of Apollo and older priests of other deities, all of them members of Spartoi elite families. Some bore burning torches, others toted olive branches to show that they had come in peace. On the warm night air rose the sweet scent of burning incense and the wails of mourning wives, mothers, and daughters, from the city below. All day, Thebans had sat in the city's marketplaces chanting prayers, while countless others had made offerings at the shrine of Apollo on the Ismenium Hill and at the two shrines of Pallas, god of wisdom, within the city walls.

The Spartoi delegation was led by Thebes's high priest of Zeus. "Oedipus, glorious king in all our eyes," the high priest began, "forgive us for rousing you from your sleep, but can you give your desperate people a promise of relief? You have been our savior before. Can you not save us now? Whether you know what we must do through the whisper of a god or have it in your own power to offer the remedy, tell us now, we beseech you, before it's too late."[13]

"You haven't roused me from my sleep," Oedipus said to put their minds at ease. "Be assured, my children, I have wept many tears and have turned over in my mind innumerable possible solutions as a consequence of our city's problems. The sole remedy I personally could alight upon was to send Creon, my own wife's brother, to the Pythia at the Temple of Bright Apollo, to learn by what word or deed I could save this town. Yet it troubles me what Creon is doing. He delays, strangely, beyond the time that I would have expected him to return. But when he comes, I will be no true man if I don't do as the god requires."

"But Creon comes," said the priest.

"He comes?" Oedipus responded with surprise. "Now?"

"I received a message that he was asking to be admitted to a city gate," the priest advised. "See now, the guards at the gate to the Cadmea signal that he is coming up the steps to us as we speak."

Looking to the heavens, Oedipus cried, "O, lord Apollo, may Creon bring us bright fortune!"

The Cadmea gate was opened, and Creon, dusty and tired, walked to join the party at the bottom of the palace steps. On his head he wore a crown made from bay leaves, a traditional adornment for a messenger bearing glad tidings, which immediately buoyed the hopes of all present.

"Creon, prince, my kinsman, son of Menoeceus, what news have you brought us from the god?" the king hopefully inquired.

"Good news!" Creon wearily declared, passing through the delegation and climbing several steps to stand a little below Oedipus. "Believe me, even the most unbearable troubles will end in perfect harmony if those troubles find the right solution."

"But what does the oracle say?" Oedipus impatiently returned. "So far your words make me neither pleased nor afraid."

Creon nodded to the delegation. "Would you hear what I have to tell you while they are present, or shall I hold my tongue until we go inside?"

"Speak before us all. The interests of all the people come before my own."

"Very well, I will tell you what I heard from the god."

The king and the Spartoi pricked their ears to hear what came next.

Creon said: "Our lord Bright Apollo bids us to drive out a defiling thing that this land has harbored. While it continues to be harbored here, the land cannot be healed."

"What is the defiling thing?" Oedipus demanded. "And by what religious rite can we cleanse ourselves of it?"

"By banishing a man or by bloodshed, as it was by bloodshed that the curse was brought upon our city in the first place."

"And who is the man?"

"I should explain that King Laius was lord of our land before you became pilot of this state," Creon explained.

"Of course. Although I never saw him myself. What of it?"

"Laius was murdered. And the god clearly requires us to wreak vengeance on his murderers, whoever they may be."

With the Spartoi bursting into animated conversation among themselves, Oedipus rubbed his chin thoughtfully as the task set by Apollo became clearer—although it seemed a nigh-impossible task. The king raised his hand for silence, then asked Creon: "And where on earth are they, these murderers? Where shall the faint trail of this old crime be found?"

"In this land of Thebes, so says the god," Creon replied. "What is sought after can be caught. Only that which goes unwatched escapes."

"Here, in Thebes?" Oedipus mused. "Was it in a house, or the field, or on strange soil, that Laius met his bloody end?" He knew the answer to this question, having been told on his first day in Thebes that Laius had been killed on the road to Delphi. But Oedipus was a man consumed by guilt, and for years he had experienced sleepless nights as he was racked by nightmares in which he relived the confrontation with the men at the crossroads. For he knew that he was as much a murderer as the robbers accused of killing King Laius. Worse than that, deep down, Oedipus harbored a nagging doubt about that day. So now he pretended to have forgotten all about the circumstances surrounding the death of Laius.

"It was on a visit to Delphi," Creon answered. "After which he came home no more."

"And was there no one to tell of the crime? Was there no companion on his journey from whom details might have been gained, and used?" Oedipus asked.

"All were killed but for one who fled in fear," Creon replied. "So dreadful was the experience, he was able to tell us only one thing for certain that he saw."

"And what was that?" Oedipus asked with intense interest. "One thing might be a clue to many others. From small things hope can grow."

"He told me at the time he brought the news that robbers met and fell on them. Laius wasn't killed by one man, but by many hands."

"Why, if the robbers came from Thebes as the god says, did they travel so far to attack Laius in Phocis? And how did they know he was taking the road to Delphi? Unless bribes were paid here for the information . . ."

"Such things were surmised at the time," Creon acknowledged. "But once Laius was slain, our thoughts almost immediately turned to other things, and no one rose up to avenge the late king's death."

Those other things Creon was referring to were the arrival at Thebes of Oedipus on the day after the report of Laius's death was received; the overwhelming excitement at the news that Oedipus had slain the Sphinx; and the rush to install Oedipus as the new king of Thebes.

Upon reflection, Creon had acted poorly in failing to press Oedipus to send a party to immediately seek and retrieve the body of his brother-in-law Laius, for funeral rites and cremation. Without those rites, the Greeks believed, Laius's soul couldn't be ferried by Charon the ferryman across the rivers Styx and Acheron to the Underworld and the Afterlife. In truth, Creon had disliked Laius—a cruel and vicious man, and a pedophile to boot. Laius had raped and abducted the youth Chrisippus of Pisa, son of Laius's own benefactor Pellops no less, and brought the boy to Thebes once he claimed the throne. There Laius had made the youth share his bed—in preference over Creon's sister, Laius's wife and queen, Jocasta. Angered by this, Creon had been more than happy to let the body of the widely despised Laius rot and go without the benefit of holy rites, condemning his soul to wander, lost, over the Earth.

In fact, many years after this, it would emerge that the body of Laius was discovered at the roadside by travelers from Plataea, who were on their way home from a visit to Delphi. They took the bodies of Laius and his attendants with them to their city, where the king of Plataea paid for them to be cremated with due rites, their identities remaining unknown. There their ashes would lie, in an unmarked strangers' grave, forgotten until after the death of Oedipus, when the truth of what had happened at the crossroads subsequently became broadly known and the people of Plataea put two and two together.

A search party had eventually been sent from Thebes by King Oedipus in an attempt to locate Laius's remains, at the insistence of Laius's widow Jocasta. But this was only after her marriage to Oedipus, a considerable time after Laius's death. By then, the bodies of Laius and his companions had been taken to Plataea and interred. You might ask why no one from Thebes asked at Plataea if Laius's body had been found. There were two fundamental reasons for this not occurring. Firstly, Plataea was a long way from Phocis. The city of Leuctra was much closer to the site of Laius's death, and inquiries would have been made there by the Theban search party. Secondly, Plataea was a rival city to Thebes, a close neighbor bordering Theban lands that was at times in conflict with Thebes over territory. No self-respecting Theban would have lowered himself to ask the Plataeans for anything.

On the other hand, as much as Creon was at fault in this issue, Oedipus had acted equally poorly in failing to immediately order the retrieval of his royal predecessor's remains and to order a search made for the perpetrators of the crime. He could have questioned the sole survivor of Laius's party for descriptions of the murderers, and sought them out. But instead, he had let sleeping dogs lie. It was as if Oedipus had wanted the whole matter of Laius's death to be forgotten as quickly as possible, so that all Theban focus was placed on his reign. But now, with the matter being aired in front of the priests, and with the gods involved, if Creon wanted to attempt to track down the band of robbers said to be responsible for Laius's death, Oedipus was prepared to accommodate him.

"Very well," said Oedipus now, "I will start afresh and shine light into dark corners." Whatever Oedipus's faults, he was a faithful and fearing worshipper of Apollo; and if Apollo now required a manhunt, a manhunt Oedipus would give him. "Worthily has Apollo, and you, Creon, bestowed this task on the people of Thebes, and you will find me united with you in seeking vengeance." He turned his attention to the delegation below. "On your feet, all of you. Go summon all the city elders to this place at once, and tell the people of Thebes that their king intends to leave nothing untried in the quest for the truth. And with the help of Apollo, the return of our good health will be made certain, or we shall die in the attempt."

Oedipus and Creon went into the palace, Oedipus to await the mass meeting, the exhausted Creon to accept the king's invitation to use the palace's guest quarters for the night rather than immediately return to his home in the city below. In the meantime, it did not take long for all the members of the Spartoi to climb to the Cadmea and gather at the foot of the palace steps as their king had commanded. Once they had assembled, kneeling on the lower steps with their most senior members to the fore, Oedipus reemerged through the grand palace doors, fully dressed now and wearing a golden crown. He addressed them from the top of the steps as they knelt before him amid a sea of sputtering torches.

"Citizens, you have prayed," he began, "and in answer to your prayers I say: Listen to what I ask of you now and act on my words, and relief will come to our city. If any one of you knows who killed Laius, son of Labdacus, I ask him to tell me all now. I was a stranger to the deed and wouldn't get far trying to trace the facts alone and without a single clue. If such a man is afraid to speak through the fear of incriminating himself, I say: Don't let that stand in your way. All you will suffer for your part in the crime will be banishment out of this land of Thebes, unharmed."

The assembled Spartoi burst into conversation among themselves, questioning each other about the identity of the man their sovereign was bent on finding.

Oedipus let them talk; then, when it was apparent that no one was going to volunteer himself, he raised his hand; and when silence returned, he continued. "Alternatively, if anyone knows that the murderer is a foreigner, from another land, don't keep silent—I'll pay that informant a reward for the information and also give him my heartfelt thanks."

Below, men were shaking their heads. No one seemed to possess the information he sought. Either that, or they were intent on keeping it to themselves.

Certain that someone must know something and impatient with his audience now, Oedipus said, "If any one of you, through fear, attempts to protect a friend or themselves with their silence, I command that no one in this land is to give them shelter, to speak to them, or even offer prayers for them. Anyone who does so is a partner in the crime. This is the defiling thing, as the Pythian oracle has only now revealed to me."

This declaration had many in the audience turning to each other with surprise.

"I solemnly pray," their king went on, "that the life of the evil murderer, whoever he may be, and whether his hidden guilt is lonely or has colleagues, meets an evil end. And I swear to you, if that man is found under my own roof, may I suffer the same punishments that I now call down on others! If anyone should disobey me in this, I pray that the gods send them neither the harvest of the earth nor the fruit of the womb. But for all of you loyal descendants of Cadmus to whom my measures seem wise and just, may justice and all the gods be with you, always."

Again the Spartoi burst into conversation.

"Majesty," called Oenops, one of the most senior and respected of the Governors, silencing the others, "on my oath I'm not the murderer, nor can I point to he who is. But surely it was for the bright shining god to tell us who could have carried out the deed?"[14]

"I understand what you say," Oedipus returned, "but no man on earth can force the gods to do what they choose not to do."

"Then what seems the next best thing for us to do?" Oenops asked. "If there is a third course of action, don't hesitate to reveal it."

"Well, I know that our lord Teiresias is the prophet most like our lord the bright shining Apollo. From him, a searcher for the truth might learn the answers he seeks."

"I have already followed that path," said Oedipus with irritation. "At the suggestion of Creon, I twice sent a man to fetch Teiresias, but he didn't come. I'm surprised he isn't here with you all now. It's as if he is afraid to come."

The prophet had in fact been summoned with all the rest, with messengers sent to his house. Now, as Oedipus spoke, there was movement to one side. "Ah," said Oenops, "here at last they bring the god-like prophet. If the truth lives in anyone, it's in him."

Two Cadmean guards bearing lanterns escorted a shuffling old man and a boy to the fringe of the gathering. The boy, of ten or eleven, with hair to his shoulders as was the custom for all Greek boys, acted as a crutch for the tall gray-haired man, who walked with eyes staring sightlessly ahead and with one hand on the boy's shoulder and a staff of tough and resilient cornel wood in the other hand.[15]

The son of a shepherd, Teiresias had, according to a legend accepted as fact by many Greeks, famously been transformed into a woman by the goddess Hera for seven years. Later, after his return to manhood, blindness claimed him and he developed the skill of seeing into the future, into the past, and into the hearts of men. Reputedly, the gods sent messages to him via the songs of birds, and this was how he divined the future and the past. The boy brought the aged prophet to the foot of the palace steps, where they halted. There, the child dropped to his knees, but Teiresias remained standing, with one steadying hand on the head of his young assistant.

"Teiresias," said the king, "you know all things, in heaven and in earth, and despite your blindness you will know that a plague haunts this land. You, great prophet, are our last hope, our only protector and savior. Use whatever skills you have, and rescue yourself, rescue the state, rescue me!"

"How should I do that?" asked the blind man.

"You will also know, even if the messengers didn't tell you, that the bright god answered our question to him by revealing that for the plague to be lifted from us, the slayers of Laius must be either slain themselves or banished from this land."

"I knew this well," the old man replied, nodding slowly. "But let us forget it. I should not have come."

"What?" Oedipus returned with surprise.

"Let me go home. It will be easier for you, and for me, if you permit me to go."

"Your strange words are offensive to this state that nurtured you. What are you withholding, Teiresias?"

"You speak when you shouldn't. I don't want to make the same mistake." The old man patted the boy on the head to indicate that he wished to depart, and the youth came to his feet.

Oedipus was becoming increasingly frustrated. "For the love of the gods, don't turn away if you know things!" he cried. He dropped to one knee. "We all implore you on our knees!"

Seeing this, the boy again knelt.

"Yes, you are all ignorant of the facts," said the prophet with a sigh. "But I won't share my painful knowledge with you."

"What are you saying?" Scowling, Oedipus regained his feet. "You know the secret but won't share it with us? Is that it? You plan to turn your back on us and destroy Thebes?" Oedipus's fury was rising. "Speak up! You would make a stone angry!"

"Rage if you must, as fiercely as you know how. But I'll say no more."

It was now that two of Oedipus's traits, his quick temper and his quickness to judge, combined to fuel an outburst. "I'm so angry, I won't hold back what I'm thinking," he declared. "Be aware that it seems to me that you must have played a role in the plotting of the murder and were guilty of the crime, short of having committed it with your own hands." This brought gasps from the listening audience. "Had you not been blind, I would have said this affair was all your doing."

As a murmur of disbelief ran around the Spartoi, old Teiresias finally lost his restraint. "You want the truth?" he exclaimed. "Very well. I call on you to abide by your own decree, and from this day speak neither to me nor to any of those assembled here." He stabbed a finger in the king's direction. "*You* are the accursed defiler of this land, Oedipus!"

Again the gathered Spartoi gasped.

Oedipus's eyes narrowed. "You think you can escape what's coming to you with such a brazen accusation, old man?"

"The truth is my protection," Teiresias calmly countered. "And I say that you are the murderer of the man whose murderer you seek. I also say that you have been living in sin with your nearest relative but are unable to see what woe has befallen you."

Oedipus, for all his wisdom, was human. And like most humans, he placed self-preservation before all other things. In his confrontation with the Sphinx, he had preserved himself with his agility of mind. That same quality drove him now. After Teiresias had accused him of murder, Oedipus, sensing that his audience could not bring themselves to believe that such a revered and holy man could have murdered anyone, sought a fresh target for his defensive venom.

"Was this your idea to accuse me, or Creon's?" Oedipus demanded.

This brought new gasps from the gathering, combining surprise and disbelief.

"No, Creon is no danger to you," Teiresias retorted with growing contempt. "You are danger enough to yourself."

Now, incandescent with rage, Oedipus prowled back and forth at the top of the steps, talking to himself, convincing himself. "Yes, trusty Creon, my old friend Creon, has crept up on me, yearning for my power, recruiting as his accomplice this scheming juggler, this tricky quack, who only has eyes for profit." He halted and returned his attention to Teiresias. "Come now, where have you proved yourself a prophet? When the beast watched our roads, did you say anything that could free these people? The riddle required a prophet's skills, but none were you found to possess. I, Oedipus the ignorant, silenced her when I seized on the answer with the use of my wits. And it is I, Oedipus, you are trying to oust, so as to stand beside Creon's throne. Well, you will *both* regret your zeal in trying to remove me!"

While this had been going on, the worried elders had been talking among themselves in hushed tones. Now, one of their number, Astacus, attempted to intervene on behalf of the gathering. "Wait! To our way of thinking, both this man's words and yours, Oedipus, have been uttered in anger. This isn't what we need. What we need is a way to meet the requirements of the god."

"A king you are, Oedipus," said Teiresias, sounding calm once more. "But I owe my loyalty to Loxias, not to you or to Creon. And I deserve a right to be heard and defend myself."

The men of the Spartoi all voiced their agreement to this, and expressed their desire to hear Teiresias speak.

"You have taunted me with my blindness, Oedipus," Teiresias continued, "yet you are blind to the misery that surrounds you. Do you know what stock you spring from? You have been an unwitting enemy of your own family. The double lash of your mother's curse and your father's curse will drive you from this land with dreadful haste and with darkness descended on eyes that now can see. And a host of other unimaginable ills will level you. So go ahead, heap scorn on Creon and on my message, but no man will be crushed more miserably than you!"

"Must I take this from him?" Oedipus called to the gathering. He glared down at the prophet. "May ruin befall you! Go, this instant. Back, away, to where you came from! Remove yourself from my door."

"I wouldn't have come if you hadn't called me."

"I never realized you would utter such foolishness."

"You think me a fool? And what of your parents?"

Oedipus frowned. "What of my parents? Wait . . . who was it that fathered me?"

"This very day will reveal the secret of your birth, and bring your ruin."

"You always speak in riddles!" Oedipus exclaimed.

"Aren't you the one who is skilled at unraveling riddles?" Teiresias taunted him.

"You find fault in that skill?"

"It was that skill that brought you to Thebes, and brought you undone."

"Yet I saved this city."

Realizing that this rancorous back-and-forth was going nowhere and that nothing more could be achieved, Teiresias said, with a sigh, "Then I will go, as you have bidden me. Boy, take me away."

As the prophet's assistant again resumed his feet, Oedipus raged: "Yes, take him away! While you remain, Teiresias, you are nothing but a hindrance to me, nothing but trouble. Once you are out of my sight, you will no longer annoy me."

"I leave you with this parting message," said Teiresias. "The man you seek, the murderer of Laius, is here, but he is not a native Theban. A blind man who has sight at present, a beggar who is currently rich, he will make his way to a strange land, feeling his way with his staff. He will be found to be both the brother and father of his children, the son and husband of the woman who bore him, heir to his father's bed, shedder of his father's blood. Think on that, and, if you find that I am wrong, *then* you can say that I have no skill in prophecy."

Oedipus watched as Teiresias was guided away by his young assistant, and the Spartoi erupted in conversation among themselves. But then the elders fell silent. Oedipus became aware that someone had come from the palace and was standing to his right at the top of the steps, commanding the attention of his subjects. It was his brother-in-law Creon, who had been lurking just inside the palace doors for much of this time, listening to the exchange between king and prophet, and taking in Oedipus's accusation that he had colluded with Teiresias in the murder of Laius.

"Fellow citizens," Creon began, "having learned that King Oedipus lays dire charges against me, I am here, and I am indignant! I would rather not live another day if I must bear such blame as this, that I am a traitor to this city, a traitor to you and to my friends."

"What gall!" cried Oedipus.

Astacus the elder, trying to excuse his king, called: "Perhaps, Creon, the accusation came as a result of stress and through anger, rather than being heartfelt."

"Yet he also accused me of counseling the prophet to utter falsehoods."

"That was said," Astacus agreed, "but I don't know why."

"This from the proven assassin!" Oedipus exploded. "The man who would rob me of my crown!"

Creon turned to Oedipus. "And is this charge laid against me with a steady eye and a steady mind?"

"Come, now," said Oedipus with a snort; "in the name of the gods, tell me, was it cowardice or foolishness you saw in me that induced you to plot my overthrow? Did you think I wouldn't be aware of your stealthy plan and couldn't ward it off? What a foolish attempt for a man without followers or wealth! For both are required to seek a throne."

"In answer, allow me a fair reply, then judge for yourself once you are fully informed," Creon said.

"I have no time for lectures from you!"

"If you think stubbornness without sense a gift, you aren't so wise after all."

Oedipus ranted: "If you think you can wrong a relative and escape the penalty, you are mad!"

"If that were true, you would be right," Creon agreed. "So, tell me: Precisely how is it you think I've wronged you?"

"Did you, or did you not, advise me to send for the prophet Teiresias?"

"I did. And I still think it was a wise course."

"Was he skilled as a prophet in the days of Laius?"

"He was as skilled then as he is today, and equally honored."

"Did he mention me at the time of Laius's death?"

"No."

Oedipus raised his hands. "Then, if he was so skilled, how is it he made no accusation of murder against me then but does so now?"

Creon could only shrug. "I don't know. And without any knowledge in the matter, it's best I remain silent."

"Yet you do know something—that, had Teiresias not conferred with you, he would never have accused me of being Laius's murderer!"

"Did he tell you that? You know as much as I do about this. Come, be reasonable . . ." Creon, striving to be conciliatory, moved to approach Oedipus.

"You are a false friend!" Oedipus declared, backing away.

"That is not true, as you must know in your heart," Creon said, hurt. "I don't seek your throne. Never have I yearned to be a king. It's against my nature. I have always been faithful to you. Send to the Pythia at Delphi and ask what message she sent back to you in my hands and determine whether I have lied to you about what she said. Next, if you find after due investigation that I have conspired with the prophet on anything, take me out and kill me. But don't rush to condemn me on some vague accusation. A just man learns the truth in the fullness of time: he doesn't label a man a scoundrel in a day."

"What he says is true, Majesty," called Astacus from below. "Those who are quick to judge stand on uncertain ground."

Oedipus, glaring down at Astacus, shook his head. "When the stealthy plotter is quickly moving in on me, I must be quick in my defense. I must strike first."

"What would you do with me, then?" Creon demanded with a quaking voice, finally losing his composure. "Banish me from my homeland?"

Oedipus's eyes were blazing now. "No, I desire your death, not your banishment!"

This brought not a gasp from the listening elders, but a groan.

"You are resolved not to believe me?" Creon asked.

"You haven't persuaded me that you are worthy of belief."

"And I find you no longer sane!" Creon cried. "You are no longer fit to rule!"

"Do you hear him, Thebes?" cried Oedipus, opening his arms to the audience. "From his own lips!"

"Thebes is my city too, not just yours," Creon countered.

At this point, a woman burst out through the open palace doors. It was Jocasta, wife of Oedipus and sister of Creon. Servants, hearing the king and his chief counselor trading increasingly bitter verbal blows, had rushed to rouse the queen from her bed so that she might intervene. She came in bare feet, with a gown wrapped around her and with her long dark tresses, let down for the bedroom, cascading below her shoulders. It was an appearance she would never normally reveal to any but her closest family, but the urgency of the moment trumped both pride and vanity.

"Wrongheaded men!" Jocasta cried, stepping between the brothers-in-law. "Why have you raised such a row! Aren't you ashamed, with your country so sick, to stir up personal troubles?" Taking Oedipus by the arm, she said, "Come, go into the palace. And you, Creon, go home."

"Sister," said Creon, "Oedipus your husband has threatened to do dreadful things to me."

"Yes," Oedipus countered, shaking free of his wife's grasp, "for I have caught him, Lady, working evil, by evil arts, against me."

"May I perish accursed," Creon returned, "if I've done anything you've accused me of."

"For the love of the gods!" exclaimed Jocasta. "Believe him, Oedipus, for my sake and for the sake of all those here. You've heard his sacred oath."

"Listen to her, Majesty, please," Astacus implored from below.

"What would you have me do, Astacus?" Oedipus demanded.

"Respect this man who has never been disloyal, and who now gives you his strong oath. You should never use an unproven charge to condemn a friend."

"In that case, you seek *my* destruction or exile?"

Astacus's face dropped. "No, Majesty! In front of all the gods, may I meet the worst possible doom if I have entertained any such thought! But my unhappy soul is worn enough by the withering of the land for our sorrows to be crowned by this dispute between you two."

Oedipus, seeing all the elders nodding in agreement with their colleague, threw his hands in the air. "Then let him go, though I'm surely doomed to die or be thrust from this land by my own decree if you were to believe that I know more than I do about this whole affair. But note that it's your lips, not his, that move my compassion."

Creon was shaking his head. "Sullenly you give in, just as you lose all sense in your anger." He looked to his sister. "It must be difficult for a wife to bear a nature such as this."

"Leave me in peace!" Oedipus raged. "Be gone!" Swinging on his heel, he strode toward the palace doors.

"I'm going," said Creon with a sigh. He raised his voice. "I may have found you blind to the truth; but in the eyes of all these, I am innocent." Turning, he descended the steps, made his way through the kneeling elders, and disappeared into the night.

"My Lady," called Astacus, as the elders began coming to their feet, "join your man in the palace. Console him."

"I will do so," Jocasta replied, "once I've learned what lies behind all this."

"Blind suspicion on one side," said Astacus with a sigh.

"And wounded pride on the other," added his comrade Oescus.

"The fault was on both sides?" Jocasta nodded in confirmation of her own thought. "And what is the story behind it all?"

"With our land so troubled as it is," Astacus responded, "I think the matter should rest where it ended." He turned to join the other elders, who were taking their leave. To Oenops he said in a lowered voice, shaking his head, "This from the king who previously set our beloved country on a safe course when it was beset by troubles."

Oedipus had halted at the open palace doors. "See what you have done," he snarled at Jocasta as she hurried to join him. "For all your good intent, all you achieved was to blunt my purpose."

"In the name of the gods, will you tell me the cause of such a surly temper?" she implored. Taking his arm again, she steered him in through the palace doors, which the guards closed behind them.

"I will tell you, Lady," said Oedipus as they slowly crossed the palace forecourt, arm in arm, "because I trust you above those people outside. The cause is Creon and the plots he has laid against me."

"Go on," she urged. "Can you tell me clearly how the feud began?"

Stopping, he turned to face Jocasta, then replied, his voice quavering with emotion. "He says I'm guilty of spilling the blood of Laius." Creon had not actually said this. But, finally, Oedipus was admitting to himself that a suspicion lurking within his own heart for decades, but which he had dismissed every time it reared its head in his quietest, darkest moments, could actually be true—that the nobleman he had killed at the crossroads had been Laius.

"What? He says that?" Jocasta scowled. "Where did he come by this? Through his own knowledge, or through the hearsay of another?"

"He has made a rascal prophet his mouthpiece, while keeping his own lips entirely pure." Now, in his wild desperation to convince his wife that he was innocent of a horrible crime, Oedipus was accusing Creon and Teiresias of colluding against him.

"A prophet?" Jocasta laughed to herself. "Then acquit yourself of any such charges."

"But . . ."

"Listen to me, and comfort yourself in the knowledge that no mortal being shares in the godly science of prophecy. I'll give you pithy proof of that. A prediction came to Laius once—not directly from Bright Apollo himself but through his priests at Delphi—that Laius was doomed to die by the hand of his own child, the son who sprang from him and me."

Oedipus's eyebrows raised with surprise. "Truly?"

"Now, the story goes that Laius was murdered one day *by foreign robbers*, at a place where three highways meet." At this point, Jocasta began to choke up and her eyes took on an absent glaze. "My child was not fully three days old when Laius pinned its ankles together so that it could not crawl, and had it thrown by the hands of others on a trackless mountain. But it was all-powerful Apollo who chose to ensure that the baby wouldn't become his father's killer, that Laius's greatest fear, of being murdered by his own son, could not be realized." Focusing back on Oedipus once more, she declared: "So, you see, that's how accurately the messages of human fortune-tellers map out the future! Ignore them. Whatever the gods want, they bring to pass." Now she realized that the blood had quickly drained from Oedipus's face. "Husband," she asked, "what's wrong?"

Oedipus had paled. "Did I hear correctly?" he asked. "You said that Laius was killed where three highways meet?" He had been told that the murder had taken place at a crossroads, which he had taken as meaning a fork where one road became two.

"Yes, that's what we were told at the time, and nothing has occurred since to change it."

"And where did this take place?"

"In Phocis, where roads meet from Delphi and Daulia."

Oedipus shuddered. It was as if he had just taken a sword to the heart. "When, exactly, did this occur?" he asked, his voice almost a whisper now. His greatest fear, long secreted and suppressed, was being realized.

Frowning, she replied, "The news was spread in Thebes very shortly before you became king."

Oedipus sank to his knees, and, looking to the night sky above, cried, "Oh, Zeus, what have you done to me?"

Jocasta, afraid now, laid her hands on his shoulders and pulled him close, protectively, as a mother protects her child. "What is it, Oedipus? Tell me!"

"Not yet." He looked up at her with beseeching eyes. "First, describe Laius. How old was he?"

"Laius was tall, of middle age, with gray lightly strewn through his hair. In build and appearance, he was not unlike yourself."

"Oh, woe is me!" he cried. "I think I've been laboring under a dreadful curse, without knowing it."

Seeing fear in his eyes, Jocasta began to tremble. "What are you saying?"

"I'm beginning to suspect that the prophet may be able to see the truth after all! But answer me one more question."

"You only have to ask it."

"Did Laius go as a private person, taking a small force with him, or did he go as a prince, accompanied by many armed men?"

"There were five of them in all, one of them a herald. And one chariot, with Laius the passenger."

Oedipus groaned, then said, "Everything is clear now. Who was it that gave you all these details?"

"A servant—the sole survivor who came home."

"Is he close at hand, in the palace, now?"

"No. As soon as you became king, he came to me, took my hand, and begged me to send him from his post in the palace to the pastures, to the flocks, so he could be far out of sight of the city. He had formerly been a shepherd, you see. Despite being a slave, he was worthy of a much more important position than that, but, although thinking it an odd request, I did as he asked."

"Send for him, without delay."

"That's easily done. But why?"

"Come." Pulling himself back to his feet, he took Jocasta by the hand. Walking on unsteady legs, he led her to a stone bench usually occupied by visitors awaiting an audience with the king, and the pair sank down beside each other. Oedipus then proceeded to tell Jocasta a story he had never previously related to a living soul. He told her of the prediction he had received at Delphi that he would kill his own father and lie with his mother, and of his determination to defy the prediction by never returning to Corinth. He then told Jocasta of his meeting and deadly fight at the crossroads in Phocis. He didn't have to spell out to Jocasta what this could mean. Either, by some awful coincidence, two parties of four men had been killed at much the same time at a crossroads in Phocis, one by robbers, another by Oedipus, or there had been just a single bloody encounter.

Numb with shock at first, Jocasta found her tongue. "When the servant, the sole survivor, makes his appearance, what do you propose to do with him?"

"If his story tallies with yours, that Laius was killed by a robber gang, then I will stand free of guilt. But if he names just a single lonely wayfarer as the killer, then beyond doubt I was that man."

Unprepared to believe that Oedipus had killed Laius, Jocasta shook her head. "The fellow can't take back what he said, about the band of robbers. He said it before the entire city, not just to me. Even if he were to change his story, the prediction from Delphi was that Laius would die by the hand of his own son. How can that be, when his only son died on the mountainside? If I were you, Oedipus, I would have nothing more to do with prophecies of any kind."

This seemed to make Oedipus feel better. "What you say makes sense," he told Jocasta, coming to his feet. "But nevertheless, send someone to fetch the peasant."

"I'll send for him with the dawn. And fear not, I'll do nothing without your approval."

The following morning, at dawn, as Oedipus slept, Jocasta rose and dressed. While her hairdressers coiffed her hair in plaits wound around her head like a crown, she dictated a message and dispatched a messenger to a distant Theban farm below Mount Cithaeron, on the southern border of Thebes's lands. Jocasta, wearing myrtle garlands and attended by one handmaid holding an olive branch festooned with myrtle and another carrying burning incense, went to the palace's altar to Lycean Apollo, the household god of Theban royals.

Kneeling before the altar, which stood at the top of steps in an alcove off the palace's forecourt, Jocasta offered this prayer: "Oedipus's mind being in turmoil and being unable to help him with my counsel, I come to you, Lycean Apollo, in the hope that you will find a way of ridding us of the disease. For now we are all afraid, seeing him afraid, just as those who see fear in the helmsman of their ship become afraid." As she solemnly laid the tree branch on the altar, she heard voices behind her. Turning, she saw a visitor, an elderly stranger, talking with the doorman by the doors that were opened to the world with each sunrise.

"I come with an important message for King Oedipus," said the old man. "Where shall I find him?"

"The king is within," said the doorman, "but there is the queen, the mother of his children." He pointed to where Jocasta was still on her knees.

The messenger advanced toward the alcove of the household shrine. Jocasta, rising up, came to meet him.

"May you always be happy in a happy home, my Lady," he said, "since you are Oedipus's heaven-blessed queen."

"Happiness to you also, stranger," she returned. "What brings you here?"

"Good tidings, my lady," he said with a bow of the head, "for your royal house and for your husband."

"From whom have you come?"

"From Corinth. And on hearing the message I carry, you will both rejoice and grieve."

She frowned. "How so?"

"The people of Corinth will make Oedipus king of the isthmus."

"How can that be? Is the elderly Polybius no longer in power?"

"No, he is dead and in his tomb."

"King Polybius is dead?" she asked with disbelief.

"May I be struck down dead if I lie."

Jocasta became suddenly excited. Turning to the most senior of her handmaids, she commanded, "Go quickly, and tell this to your master:

'Where are your oracles of the gods now? The man you long shunned lest you slay him has died, in the course of destiny, not by your hand.' Hurry, girl!"

The maid scurried away, and the Corinthian messenger was made to stand and wait. All the while, Jocasta paced back and forth, wringing her hands. After a time, Oedipus appeared, wearing his nightgown and slippers, his hair tousled and with sleep in his eyes.

"Who may he be?" Oedipus asked grumpily as he approached, indicating the messenger.

"He is from Corinth," Jocasta advised, "to tell you that your father has perished."

"Ah. How did he die, stranger?" Oedipus inquired, seemingly unmoved. In truth, Oedipus was distracted by a fear of what might emerge from the forthcoming meeting with the shepherd. "By treachery or by disease?"

"Time brings the aged to their rest, Majesty," the messenger replied.

"By sickness, then?"

The messenger nodded. "Yes, and his advanced years."

Oedipus nodded, taking it in. "He is dead, and here am I, not having put hand to spear, having played no part in it." He looked at Jocasta. "Unless he died of longing for me, in which case I was the cause of his death."

"Not so," Jocasta returned, shaking her head.

"You are right." Oedipus smiled with obvious relief. "The oracles have all been swept to Hades with Polybius. They are worth nothing!"

"Did I not say so?" Jocasta said with a smile.

"You did. But I allowed my fear to mislead me." Suddenly, his smiled faded. "But must I still fear lying in my mother's bed, as was prophesied?"

"No. Many men have dreamed of such a thing before now. Put it from your mind. We should take great comfort from the fact that your father is dead."

"Yes, great comfort . . ." Even as he spoke, doubts quickly filled his mind. "Yet my mother is still living."

"Forgive me, Majesty," said the messenger, who had taken all this in, "but who is this woman you fear?"

"Merope, old man," Oedipus absently returned. "Polybius's queen."

"And what is it that you fear?"

"A heaven-sent prophecy of great importance."

"Is it lawful for me to know the content?" the man asked.

"Quite lawful. Loxias said that I would one day bed my mother and shed my father's blood."

"Was it through fear of this that you exiled yourself from Corinth?"

Sadly, Oedipus nodded. "I didn't wish, old man, to be the murderer of my own father."

"But, you didn't know? They didn't tell you? Polybius was not your father. You are not related by blood. He begat you no more than I did."

Jocasta looked at the old man in amazement.

"Why then did he call me his son?" Oedipus demanded, becoming angry now, as the accusation of the drunk in Corinth that he was adopted resonated in his memory, and he fought to suppress it.

"He received you from me, as a gift, long ago," the old man revealed. "My reward was the post in his household I have held all these years."

"What? He received me from you? Yet he loved me so dearly?" Oedipus protested, unwilling to believe that he was not of royal blood and merely adopted.

"His former childlessness bound him to you."

"And you—how did you come by me? Did you buy me? Or you just happened to find me?" He was scoffing at the old man now.

The messenger sighed. "I found you in the winding valleys of Mount Cithaeron."

"Cithaeron?" Oedipus looked at Jocasta, who had paled. "And why were you roaming around there?"

"I was in charge of mountain flocks."

"A shepherd? A vagrant employee?" Oedipus attempted to maintain his scoffing attitude, but his previous assuredness was fading. Too much of the old man's story was beginning to sink in.

"Yes, I was a shepherd—and your savior. I freed you when your ankles were bound together to prevent your crawling away. It was because of that that they gave you your name, Oedipus."

Jocasta gasped.

Bells were ringing in Oedipus's mind too. Now Oedipus believed the man. Pale-faced, looking at Jocasta, he asked the messenger, "For the love of the gods, who cast me out? My mother, or my father?"

"I have no idea. The man who gave you to me would know. Another shepherd gave you to me."

"Another shepherd? Who was he?" Oedipus demanded. "Are you in a position to know?"

"Oh, yes. He worked for King Laius."

"Is he still alive?"

"Your people should know that better than I."

Wild-eyed, Oedipus looked around the forecourt. Several servants had overheard all this—the doorman, Jocasta's two handmaids, the guards. "Do any of you know the shepherd that this man speaks of? Answer me!"

"Majesty," said the doorman hesitantly, "I think he speaks of none other than the peasant you sent for earlier. But our Lady Jocasta might know more about that than I do."

Oedipus swung on Jocasta. "Lady, what do you know of the man we have summoned? Is he the one this fellow speaks of?"

Jocasta, shaking her head, put up her hands as if to ward off an evil spell. "Disregard it. Don't waste a thought on what he says. It's idle gossip . . ."

"It can't be! With such clues within my grasp, I can bring the facts of my birth to light."

Tears began to form in Jocasta's eyes, as denial finally gave way to a realization of the truth. "For the gods' sake, if you have any care for your own life, give up this quest. My pain is enough!"

"Be brave. Even if I'm found to have a mother who was a slave, that has no impact on you. You are still a queen twice over."

She grasped his arm. "Listen to me! I implore you—don't do this!"

"I couldn't even contemplate not discovering the truth," he said with growing irritation. "Not now."

For a moment, Jocasta looked at the messenger from Corinth, seeing in his aged eyes that what he had said was true. She guessed that the man had volunteered to deliver the message of Polybius's passing because of his past connection with Oedipus, and he was driven by a curiosity to see the grown man he had saved as a babe in arms. How many others in Corinth had known that truth about Oedipus's origins only the gods could know. "Then," she said with a resigned sigh, letting go her grasp on Oedipus's arm, "I wish you well, Oedipus. The gods know, I've counseled you with the best intentions."

"Well, your counsels try my patience, Lady," he said, with rising anger.

"Oh, ill-fated man!" Turning, she began to walk away, back to her quarters, with her fretful handmaids bustling after her. "May you never learn who you really are," she added.

"Go!" he snapped, knowing that the truth, for her, was too hard to bear. It was as if she were now running from it. Looking around at the servants, he commanded, "Someone fetch the shepherd to me, at once!" Then, as several guards hurried out the door to do his bidding, he called after Jocasta, "As for you, woman, you can glory in your royal blood. You have nothing to fear."

"Do I not?" she called back. "I'm in misery! That word alone can I utter to you now. And no other word can I speak to you, forever more." She ran from his presence, sobbing.

"Even if my origins are lowly, I crave to learn the truth," said Oedipus, half to himself. He called after Jocasta, "You, woman . . ." But she was no longer there. "She is too proud," he said, looking at the messenger from Corinth. Now, with his pride stinging, he sought to excuse himself in the eyes of the messenger with a concocted explanation of

Jocasta's departure. "She is ashamed of my common background. Well, I am a son of fortune, and refuse to be ashamed!"

———————

A full day was to pass as the guards rode to Mount Cithaeron and returned with Menoetes, the elderly shepherd. All the while, Oedipus kept the Corinthian messenger under guard. When the king was informed that Menoetes had arrived at the palace, he had the shepherd and the messenger brought to him in his audience hall, where he was conferring with several elders, including Astacus and Oenops.

As the shepherd was brought in by the guards and was made to stand beside the Corinthian messenger, Oedipus studied the man from his throne, resting an elbow on the wooden arm and thoughtfully fingering his beard. "He is the right age," he said to his elders. "The same age as the stranger from Corinth. Have any of you seen the herdsman before?"

"Yes, I know him," said Oenops. "He was in Laius's service."

"As trustworthy as any man, considering he was a shepherd," Astacus added.

"I'll question you first, Corinthian," said Oedipus. "Is this the man you referred to?"

"This is the man," said the messenger from Corinth, smiling at the shepherd beside him, who looked back at the messenger worriedly. Ever since he had been brought in, Menoetes had deliberately failed to make eye contact with the king.

"Shepherd, look at me," said Oedipus, "and answer all that I ask you. Were you once in the service of King Laius?"

"I was," he responded with an anxious nod, eyes flashing around the faces that were all directed his way, but still not looking Oedipus in the eye. "Not purchased, but born and reared a slave under Laius's roof."

"Employed in what line of work? Speak up, man."

"For the best part of my life, I tended flocks," he replied, with his eyes to the floor.

"And in what regions did you chiefly work?"

"Sometimes it was Cithaeron," Menoetes said; "sometimes it was neighboring land."

"And what do you know of the man beside you?"

"Know of him . . .?"

"Have you ever met him before?"

The shepherd, looking the messenger up and down, frowned. "Not that I could speak of at once, from memory."

"I will help him remember, master," said the Corinthian. "I'm sure he well knows the time we both lived in the Cithaeron region, he with two flocks, me with one. Three full half years it was, from spring to autumn, and then for the winter I drove my flock to my sheepfold and he took his to Laius's fold." He turned to the shepherd. "Did any of this happen as I've said, or did it not?"

Menoetes nodded. "You speak the truth, although it was a long time ago."

"Come, tell me now," the messenger continued, "do you remember giving me a boy in those days, to be reared as my foster-son?"

"Why do you ask?" the shepherd replied anxiously.

"Yonder man, my friend, is he." Smiling, the Corinthian nodded toward Oedipus.

"A pox on you!" the other exclaimed. "Keep your mouth shut!"

"Don't admonish him, old man," Oedipus intervened. "It's my words you should be worried about."

"And how, noble master, do I offend you?" Menoetes asked nervously.

"In not telling of the boy the Corinthian refers to."

"Pah!" Menoetes came back dismissively, defensively. "He doesn't know what he's talking about. It's a fuss about nothing."

Oedipus's eyes narrowed. "If you don't speak freely now, you will speak through pain." He nodded to the two guards standing directly behind Menoetes. "Pinion him this instant!"

The guards stepped forward and clasped the shepherd firmly by each arm.

"No!" wailed Menoetes. For the first time, he locked eyes with the king. "For the gods' love, don't harm an old man. What more do you wish to know?"

"Did you give to this man the child of whom he speaks?"

Menoetes momentarily closed his eyes, then, with a sigh, replied: "I did—and I wish that I had perished that same day!"

"It'll come to that if you don't tell the honest truth," Oedipus warned.

"No, no, I said before that I gave the boy to him."

"Where did you get the child?" Oedipus pressed. "In your own home, or another?"

"Not from my own home," Menoetes admitted. "He was born of another man."

"From among the citizens here?" Oedipus sat forward. "From which home?"

"For the gods' love, master, ask no more!"

Oedipus glared at him. "You are a dead man if I have to ask again. From which home?"

The terrified shepherd burst out: "It was a child of the house of Laius!"

Oedipus's eyes narrowed. "Born of a slave, or of Laius' own family?"

"I dare not say!"

"And I dare not hear, but I must. Speak!" Oedipus insisted.

"Then know that it was said to be Laius's own child." Menoetes covered his eyes in terror.

"Laius's own child?" Oedipus couldn't believe it. "His own son?"

"Your lady knows best how these things were," the shepherd protested.

"Jocasta knows?" Only now did the awful truth, that had clearly already become plain to Jocasta, begin to dawn on the king. "She gave the child to you?"

"Yes, Majesty."

"For what purpose?"

"So that I might do away with it. The child's feet were bound together on King Laius's order—a cruel and pointless thing to do to one so young, who was months away from being able to crawl. This, I felt, was Laius's way of punishing the child, and its mother, for its very existence. I was instructed to abandon the baby to die, in the wilds of Caetheron where I lived and worked."

Oedipus's jaw dropped. "She wanted you to kill her own child? The monster!?"

"Because of fear of evil prophecies. The tale ran that the child must slay his own father."

In a daze of full realization, Oedipus asked, "Then why did you give the child to this Corinthian, rather than killing it?"

Menoetes squirmed where he stood. "Through pity, master. I could not bring myself to do it. I believed that the Corinthian would bear the boy away to the faraway land from whence he'd come." He began to weep. "If you are who this man says you are, then you were born into misery."

The room was hushed. Slowly, Oedipus came to his feet, unable now to look anyone in the eye. "It has all been brought to pass," he mumbled. His suspicions all these years, long forced to the back of his mind because they were just too horrible to contemplate, had come to face him via the agency of the now trembling shepherd. "It's all true!"

As Oedipus had wished, the light had been shed on his past, and it was not a pretty picture that was revealed. Oedipus had been born to Laius and Jocasta, who had given him to Menoetes when he was just three days old. Instead of killing the child, Menoetes had given him to the Corinthian, who had sold him to King Polybius and Queen Merope, who had raised him as their own son. Years later, after Oedipus had received the warning about killing his father, he had blundered into Laius at the crossroads in Phocis, where he had unwittingly killed his own father, thus fulfilling the first part of the prophecy.

The servant of Laius, whom Oedipus had unsuccessfully pursued for days after the killings at the crossroads, had fled back to Thebes, taking care to pass the sleeping Sphinx in the night to reach the city. Fearing capital punishment from Creon if he admitted that he had permitted a single man to kill the king he had sworn to defend, that he had failed to put up a fight and fled the scene, the servant had claimed that a large band of robbers had been responsible for the slaying at the crossroads. There had been too many of them, he claimed, for him to fight them off and save King Laius's life.

To ensure that his lie, and his cowardice, were never discovered, the servant had requested a rural posting from Queen Jocasta, far away from the city. It is likely that, on a later visit to Thebes's markets, this man had seen his new king, none other than Oedipus, passing in the street, and recognized him as Laius's killer. But, to publicly identify Oedipus as the murderer, the man would have had to admit to his previous lie, and his cowardice. So it was that, to save himself, the servant never again ventured into Thebes, an act of self-preservation that also ensured that no one would link Oedipus with the slaying of Laius . . . until now.

At what point Oedipus himself came to realize the identity of his chief victim at the crossroads, that he had killed the king of Thebes and not a prosperous farmer, only Oedipus knew. For a long time, he would not even admit it to himself.

In marrying Laius's widow Jocasta, Oedipus had fulfilled the second part of the prophecy given to Laius, for Oedipus had married and bedded his own natural mother and fathered children with her. His wife was also his mother, his sons his half brothers, his daughters his half sisters. In trying so valiantly to avoid his prophesied future, Oedipus had fulfilled it.

"May I never look upon the light again!" he moaned. "I, who have now been proven to be cursed in birth, cursed in marriage, and cursed to shed my own father's blood!" Pushing away his gathered courtiers as they attempted to console him and with his head down, he rushed from the audience hall.

Not knowing what he would do or say, Oedipus strode to Jocasta's bedchamber, only to find that the double doors had been barred from within. Jocasta's handmaids clustered in the doorway, all in tears.

"Where is the woman who is my wife but is not my wife?" he demanded. "The woman who is the mother of me and my children?"

"Majesty," said the chief handmaid, "my mistress bade me listen at the door when you questioned the shepherd, then run to tell her if you discovered the truth about her, which I did. Once I passed on what I'd heard, she made me leave and barred the doors behind me. I fear she may have done herself an injury."

"A sword!" Oedipus cried. "Someone give me a sword!"

The nearest guard hurried up and unsheathed his sword, which he handed to his king.

"Stand aside!" the king commanded all present, as the handmaids fearfully scattered.

Using both hands, Oedipus swung the sword down, again and again, chopping at the narrow gap between the doors, trying to slice through the wooden bar on the far side. All he achieved was to hack wood from the edge of the doors. So he ran at the doors with such violence that they were knocked from their bolts. The bar shattered and the doors fell back, revealing Jocasta within, hanging from a rafter by a length of bedding tied around her neck.

With the bellow of a wounded beast, Oedipus dashed into the room. Again he swung the sword, slashing at the cloth above Jocasta's head. Several blows it took before the cloth separated. Jocasta dropped into his arms as he cast away the sword. He eased her to the stone floor, where she lay, crumpled, like a sleeping child.

"Stay back!" he called to those who gathered in the doorway, as tears flowed from his eyes. "Don't look at her, any of you." Dropping to his knees beside her, he cradled Jocasta's head in his lap. Then, with a growl, he ripped a golden brooch from her garment. "No more, eyes of mine, will you see such horrors as I have suffered and wreaked. Long enough have you looked at those you should never have seen. From now on, you shall be dark!" With that, he used the pointed end of the brooch's clasp to stab himself first in one eye, then the other, blinding himself.[16]

Maids screamed with horror. Servants began to run in panic around the palace, crying that the queen was dead and the king had taken out his own eyes. Elders rushed to the bedchamber. Carefully helping Oedipus to his feet, they led him to his own bedroom. Blood and gore streamed down his cheeks from his now-empty eye sockets, and he mumbled incoherently. Physicians were sent for. A semblance of calm returned to the palace.

In the queen's bedchamber, Jocasta's chief handmaid knelt beside her still mistress. First wiping tears from her own eyes, she held Jocasta's limp hand. And then she saw her mistress's chest move. "She breathes!" exclaimed the maid. Rising to her feet, she cried, for all the world to hear, "Jocasta lives! The queen is alive!"

POLYNICES AND ETEOCLES:
BROTHERS AT WAR

In the Audience Hall of the Cadmea, the children of Oedipus and Jocasta came together for a meeting with their uncle Creon and the Governors, the most senior members of the Spartoi of Thebes. Tall, dark Polynices was there, with his shorter, younger brother Eteocles and their sisters Antigone and Ismene. Looking glum, Polynices sat on the steps to the throne, his chin on his hand. Unconsciously, he was replicating the thoughtful pose of his father. Polynices's elder sister Antigone stood with her arm around little sister Ismene, who sobbed uncontrollably. Younger brother Eteocles paced back and forth.

"A decision must be made," said Eteocles, "to either slay or banish Oedipus. The decree came from his own lips. And once he is dealt with, the oracle from Delphi will be fulfilled. The blight to our lands will end, the plague will be lifted from our city."

"Yes, but we cannot allow them to kill our father," Antigone countered.

"Our father, or our brother?" Eteocles contemptuously returned. "Which is he?"

"Both, or so it seems from yesterday's shocking revelations," said Polynices with a sigh. "But this is no time to be particular. Father or brother, it must be banishment he suffers."

"To where?" asked Antigone.

"Wherever he chooses," said Eteocles, "just so long as the pollution is removed to well beyond the borders of Thebes. The sooner Oedipus goes, the sooner we will all benefit."

"Yet, he is still our king," said Antigone.

"In name only," Eteocles countered. "No man will bow to him now, let alone obey his commands."

"Oedipus is no longer sovereign of this land," came a new voice—that of Creon, as he strode into the hall followed by the senior Governors Astacus and Oenops. "He has laid down his crown." Creon held aloft the simple golden crown in his right hand.

"Then who should rightfully succeed him?" asked Polynices.

"And decide his fate?" Eteocles added.

"That is what we must discuss and agree upon," said Creon, walking to the throne, where he reverently placed the crown.

"You should all know," said Astacus, "that the feeling among the Spartoi is that Oedipus's royal successor should be Creon."

"No!" Eteocles quickly cried. "Polynices and myself, we are the man's heirs."

"How is our father?" Antigone inquired. "His wounds . . ."

"The wounds to his eyes will heal, although he will never again see," Creon replied. "The wounds to his heart, his pride, his self-belief, they are another matter. Never will he recover from those."

"And our mother?" asked Polynices. "Is Jocasta recovering?"

Creon nodded. "Indeed. My sister will recover. And she has promised me that never again will she attempt to do herself ill."

"Can we see her?" asked Antigone. "Her children need her."

Creon shook his head. "She will see no one at present. Her shame overwhelms her. Give Jocasta time. She will need many months to reconcile past deeds with present needs."

"She is much loved in Thebes," said Oenops the elder.

"Jocasta has the sympathy of the people," added Astacus. "The incest, they say, was Oedipus's doing, not hers."

"As to the crown," said Creon, "I have no desire for it. I have never lusted for power. If I were to rule, it would be much against my own pleasure. I told this to Oedipus. In his tormented state of mind, he wouldn't believe me. How could I now accept the crown after so vehemently rejecting it before the citizens of Thebes?"

"Then who shall rule us?" asked Oenops concernedly.

"His offspring are legitimate, whatever name we give to them," Creon answered. "Would the Governors support Polynices or Eteocles as our king?"

Oenops looked at Astacus, who nodded, then said carefully to Oedipus's sons, "Both of you two young men have your rough edges, but both of you are well enough liked by the people and, to my mind, stand untarnished by your parents' wrongdoing. Which son of Oedipus do you propose, Creon?"

"Yes, Creon, your recommendation will carry much weight," said Astacus, "especially if you were to continue to serve as counsel to the king—enough weight to carry the boy over the threshold. Is it to be the eldest?"

"Barely a year separates Eteocles and myself," Polynices remarked. "We have always done everything together. Could we not rule Thebes together, as Amphion and Zethus did in days gone by?"

"But look how they ended up," said Eteocles unhappily. "Both took their own lives. That will not work, brother. However, if one of us took the throne, the other could take Oedipus's fortune."

"No, no, no," said Creon. "A king without a fortune would soon lose his throne. Gold is power. One of you must have both the crown and the fortune that pays for it."

"Could we not take turns?" Polynices suggested. "One year, one of us rules, then the other takes a turn for a year, then the other, and so it would go, year in, year out."

"Eteocles?" Creon asked. "How does that sit with you?"

"That could work, uncle," Eteocles agreed.

Polynices nodded. "Who should take the first turn?"

"Draw lots," Creon suggested.

"Or," said Eteocles, "we could throw spears to determine the order. Whoever throws the farthest, rules first."

"You realize, Eteocles," said Polynices, "that I outdistanced you the last time we threw?"

"I've been practicing since," said Eteocles with an impish grin.

"So be it," Polynices responded. "The throw of a spear will determine it."

"Then," said Astacus, "once that is settled, the fate of Oedipus must be determined."

"Oedipus has asked that he be permitted to remain here in Thebes, as a private citizen," said Creon, "and I have promised him I would support that."

"Impossible!" exclaimed Eteocles. "By his own decree, issued while he was still king, the murderer of Laius must either be killed or banished to satisfy the oracle. That decree is lawful and must be obeyed. Else why obey any decree of our kings?"

"Killed or banished?" Creon responded with a grimace. "I gave him my word it would be neither."

"You had no right to make such a commitment, uncle," said Eteocles.

"We have agreed among us, Creon, before you came," said Polynices, "that it must be banishment for Oedipus, not execution."

"That is something, I suppose," said Creon.

"In the meantime," said Eteocles, "no one must have anything to do with the wretched man. By his own decree, no grace can be shown to Oedipus, no assistance rendered. He should be denied everything, even bread from the palace kitchens."

"No, that is much too harsh, much too cruel," their sister Antigone protested. "Even prisoners under sentence of death are permitted to eat bread."

"But he has shamed us all," Eteocles retorted.

"Through no fault of his own," Antigone replied. "The Fates conspired against him, Eteocles."

"Sister, it was entirely his own fault that he ruthlessly murdered Laius and his companions. We have all known his temper—have all suffered for it. Had he controlled that temper . . ."

"Had he controlled that temper and not killed Laius," said Astacus with a wry smile, "and subsequently not come to Thebes and made the widowed Jocasta his wife, you children would not exist."

"Still, my niece is right," said Creon. "We cannot punish a broken man with cruelty. He will have to be fed until he leaves the city."

"You think him broken?" asked Oenops.

"At the very least, in mental turmoil. He accused his brother-in-law of a crime which it eventuated that he himself had committed—and then demanded that brother-in-law's death without evidence," Creon said bitterly.

"And his mental instability is proven all the more by his blinding himself," Eteocles added.

"Which leads us to another dilemma," said Astacus. "How does a blind man find his way into exile? Do we give him a boy to lead him, like the boy who leads Teiresias the prophet?"

"I will accompany my father," Antigone quickly and firmly declared.

"What?" said Creon with surprise.

"You can't be serious, Antigone!" exclaimed Eteocles. "Sister, no one will help you, or even speak to you, along the way. Once this is known, Oedipus will be odious to all mankind!"

"Yet he is my father, and I his eldest daughter, bound to him by nature, tradition, duty," she said. "I will guide him wherever the gods determine. That is my decision. It is done, and I will speak on it no more."

They were all silent for a time, until Creon said, "Nobly do you cast your lot with your father, niece. Unlike Oedipus, you will always be welcome back here in your home city, should you ever choose to return."

"Yes, it is a brave thing you do, Antigone," said Polynices.

"No, it's foolish," said Eteocles dismissively. "But our sister has always been led by her heart, not her head. Let her pay the price." Smiling now, he put his arm around Polynices's shoulders. "As for us, let's not tarry, brother. The fate of our country rests with us and our spears. Let us settle the matter of where first sits the crown, at once."

Polynices nodded. "Go, all of you, and arrange the contest. I will join you presently."

Eteocles enthusiastically led the way, hurrying from the hall with Creon and the elders and leaving Polynices with his two sisters. By this stage, Ismene had cried her reddened eyes dry.

"Antigone," said Polynices, "are you sure you want to do this thing? You will have to live in exile with Oedipus, without a single hand to help you."

"My mind is made up," she said determinedly. "Could you perhaps help me now, with a withdrawal from the city treasury, so that we might buy food and lodging on our way?"

"From the treasury? No, that would not be approved by the elders."

"No matter. I can sell my jewelry along the way."

"And I will give you a little gold I had put away."

She smiled, and gripped his arm. "Thank you. And our father will thank you also."

"Polynices! Hurry along, brother!" It was Eteocles, calling from the distance.

Polynices sighed. "I must go. Is this all just a terrible dream, Antigone?"

"It is real enough, and we must do what we must do for those we love. Go and throw well, Polynices."

She didn't have to say aloud that Polynices was her favorite brother, that she wished him to win the contest. He knew that well enough as he went away to join the others.

"Sister," said Ismene, speaking for the first time, as Polynices departed, "what will become of me, when you leave Thebes with our father?"

"Ismene, dearest sister Ismene, you must remain here and care for our poor mother. And you must keep your ears and eyes open and send messages to me so that our father and I will know what is happening here at home."

"But I am only a girl . . ." Ismene protested.

"Do you remember our father once telling us of a legend about the people of Egypt—that there the men sit weaving in the house while the wives go forth to win the daily bread? We must be like the women of Egypt, you and I. Before now, you ran errands for our father. You listened at doors and asked questions of servants so that Oedipus might know the secrets of oracles of other men coming from the mouth of the Pythia and gauge how they might affect him."

"Yes, but that was like a game to me."

"And you played the game well, little sister. Continue to play the game, for all our sakes. Now come, and we will watch our brothers decide the fate of Thebes."[17]

The sisters were escorted down from the Cadmea to the nearby Hypsistan Gate, which opened onto the road to Leuctra. The Hypsistan's towers were the tallest of all the towers in Thebes's city walls, and Antigone and Ismene climbed the steps to the summit of one. From there, they were able to look down on a gathering swelling in a field beside the Leuctra road, outside the city walls. All the Spartoi who were well enough were there, accompanied by their sons, along with most of the healthy male commoners of Thebes, who had lain down their tools so they could witness the contest that would place the abdicated crown of Thebes on the head of one of the sons of the now-disgraced Oedipus.

Polynices chose Creon to be judge of the mark. With his staff, Creon drew a short, straight line in the earth. Eteocles chose Astacus to be judge of the throw. The two brothers selected bronze-tipped wooden spears of equal length and weight from a collection brought to them by Oenops. Astacus tied a white ribbon to Polynices's spear and a red ribbon to that of Eteocles, then walked with a white flag and a red flag to where he estimated the javelins of the pair would land. Excited spectators quickly lined the route the two missiles would follow.

Creon called on Polynices, the eldest, to throw first. The spectators fell silent as Polynices walked up to the throwing line, spear in hand. He looked over to his younger brother, who smiled confidently back at him.

"Just to be sure, you are content to accept the outcome of only one throw?" Polynices asked. "I am older, taller, more powerful. You have never beaten me before, Eteocles."

"Just throw, brother," Eteocles returned. "Let the most skilled take the crown."

"So be it." With a swivel of the hips and grunt of exertion, Polynices launched his missile, as if throwing it at advancing enemy soldiers.

Creon was watching to ensure that Polynices didn't overstep the mark. "Fair throw!" he called, as the spear left Polynices's hand and flew through the air.

The weapon lanced into the ground at an angle, burying its head. There it sat, quivering for several moments. The crowd cheered and applauded.

"A mighty throw," someone said.

"Can the boy beat that?" asked another. "I doubt it."

"Now, Eteocles will throw," said Creon.

Flexing his throwing arm, Eteocles stepped up. Starting a little farther back than his brother, he ran at the mark, then released with a yell.

"Did he not overstep?" someone nearby queried.

"No," Creon replied. "Fair throw!"

Eteocles's spear flew high and far, then fell to earth very close to that of his elder brother. Again, the spectators cheered and applauded. Astacus walked to where the two spears jutted from the ground, then knelt on one knee and studied their relative positions as members of the crowd gathered expectantly around.

"Astacus," called Creon, "the two spears fell mightily close to each other. Is it a draw? Or is there a winning throw?"

Nodding, Astacus came to his feet. "There is a winner, by the breadth of a hand," he announced, before raising a flag. It was a red flag. Eteocles had won. Eteocles was the successor of Oedipus and new king of Thebes.[18]

4.

TYDEUS AND POLYNICES: THE BOAR AND THE LION

In the early evening, a two-horse chariot surged in through the gate to the citadel of the city of Argos in the Greek Peloponnese. That citadel sat on the Aspis, a hill more than three hundred feet high in the north of the roughly circular city, overlooking the fertile plain of Argolis. Aspis means "shield" in Greek, and that was what this hill did; it shielded the rulers of Greece's second-oldest city from attack.

Followed by mounted bodyguards—heavily armed grim-faced men from Mycenae and Sicyon—the chariot came to a halt in front of the citadel steps, with its tawny horses rearing up on their hind legs as the charioteer drew back hard on the reins. A passenger, a tall, golden-haired and -bearded man of close to forty years of age, grimy from days of travel, stepped down from the vehicle with a regal air. The richly embroidered black-and-white cape draped from his shoulders was fixed in place by a golden clasp. The sword on his left hip had a golden hilt and was encased in a scabbard decorated with gold and silver. And on his left arm he wore a golden amulet, its design that of the nine-headed Hydra, emblem of Argos.

At the foot of the citadel steps, in twilit shadows of statues of the gods gracing the entrance, a chamberlain bowed low and welcomed back his master.

"What news?" demanded King Adrastus, ruler of Argos and Sicyon, washing his dusty hands and face in a bowl of perfumed water proffered by a slave.

"Your arrival was preceded by a pair of royal visitors, Majesty. Kings without thrones. Your brother gave them permission to use the royal guest chamber."

"Did he indeed?" King Adrastus's brow furrowed. "Has my citadel been turned into a wayside inn during my absence?"

First gulping down a cup of water offered by another slave, Adrastus stormed up the steps and into the palace. Striding toward the guest quarters, he heard his new guests before he saw them. With their voices echoing around the stone walls, they were arguing about which of them should occupy the guest quarters. Servants swiftly stood aside and bowed as the king arrived on the scene.

"Raised voices in the corridors of my house?" Adrastus growled.

The pair ceased their brawl and turned to face their royal host. Both were aged around twenty. One was impressively tall, with dark hair. The other, who was fair-headed, was shorter, but broader at the shoulders. Both young men were well built, with facial features that were not unattractive, although the fairer one's head seemed just a little too small for his muscular body. Both men showed signs of a fistfight; the nose of the taller one was bloodied, while the left eye of the shorter fellow sported a bruise. And both men still had their shields strapped on their backs, suggesting they had arrived within a short time of each other and had almost at once come to blows.[19]

"My lord," said the dark-haired youth, reverently bowing his head, "I am Polynices, legitimate king of Thebes."

"A king no more, if what I heard on my travels is true," said Adrastus. "Deposed by your own brother Eteocles, were you not?"

"It's true," Polynices glumly replied. "We had a sacred agreement to share the throne of Thebes, with each of us to rule for a year and then give up power to the other, year upon year. But after Eteocles ruled for a year and came the day I was to ascend the throne, my younger brother chose to break his oath and keep the throne for himself, banishing me."

"Your agreement was naïve," Adrastus declared. "Rare is the man who will surrender power once he has had a taste of it. Would you have surrendered the throne to your brother, every second year?"

"Of course. That was our agreement, before the gods. But Eteocles used our father's fortune to win the favor of the city elders. I discovered that he had even bribed my own servants to report everything I said and did. And of course, with the famine and plague lifting from Thebes during his year on the throne, Eteocles took credit for that also, claiming the favor of the gods."

"As one would," said Adrastus, nodding.

"But Eteocles wasn't alone in his chicanery," Polynices bitterly went on. "His chief accomplice, our uncle Creon, had my cousins Megareus and Haemon come to me on the day I was to begin my year's reign, to escort me, not to my throne, but to the Asopus River, Thebes's southern border with Plataea, where they banished me from my homeland! I could not believe that my own brother, my uncle, and my boyhood friends would betray me like that! My own family!"

"Then you have much to learn, boy," the king said with a knowing smile, "if you think that members of our own families are beyond betraying us."

Polynices sighed and nodded. "I did, however, win one small victory. My cousins would not let me go armed—in case I attempted to resist them. But I managed to trick them into allowing me to take some valuables with me, in a casket made from boar tusks." He broke into a grin. "I told them that it contained religious artifacts. Which, in a way, it did."

The king, more concerned with arms than artifacts, said, with a questioning frown, "You were exiled without arms?" He had already noted the sword at the young man's side, the helmet sitting on a table, and the shield still hanging on his back.

"At Plataea I purchased a sword, at Corinth a helmet, at Nemea a shield," Polynices explained. "A man cannot go unarmed in foreign lands."

"Indeed." Adrastus turned to the fair-haired youth. "And what is your story, young man?"

"My lord, I am Tydeus, king of Calydon—until my uncle Agrius concocted a charge of murder against me." He broke into a grin. "But, of course, I am innocent of the charge."

"Who are you supposed to have murdered?" Adrastus demanded.

"My uncle's brother-in-law, eight cousins, and my own brother!"

"What, only ten victims?" There was a hint of mockery in the king's voice.

"No man can employ spear and sword better than myself," Tydeus remarked with a sigh, "but it was my uncle's men who were the guilty parties. The murders conveniently left the throne of rocky Calydon with just two claimants: my uncle, and myself. My uncle bought the loyalty of the household guard, and I escaped. So, here am I, my lord, granted sanctuary by your generous royal brother Mecisteus."[20]

"As was I, my lord," Polynices quickly said.

"But he granted sanctuary to me first," Tydeus countered.

"Yes, but I have first call on these royal quarters," said Polynices. "My kingdom is larger and richer than yours. Go find a bed in the stables of Argos, Calydonian."

"But my father was an ally of the city of Argos," Tydeus countered, "while Thebes has snubbed its nose at Argos and Athens for generations."

"Enough!" King Adrastus snapped, raising a hand to silence the pair. "Why should I tolerate either of you squabbling cubs in my city?"

"Once I regain my throne, King Adrastus," said Polynices, "I will be your ally for life."

"As will I," said Tydeus, "once I regain my throne."

"In the meantime, you are nothing but a pair of wastrels who wish to share my roof, eat my food, and drink my wine."

"But we are of royal blood, sire," Tydeus replied, smiling still, exuding self-confidence—and cheek. "And in the eyes of the gods, we are kings."

"You *were* kings," said Adrastus severely. "And what is a king when he is not a king? He is nothing! In the eyes of this king, you two are nothing but a potential drain on my purse. Lay aside your shields and your animosity, while I decide what to do with you both."

As the young men removed the shields from their backs and propped them against the wall, the king's eyes were drawn to the designs painted on each. Polynices's shield was of the Boeotian type, oval, with a half-moon gap removed from each side, as if a toothless giant had bitten the sides away with his gums. On the face of the shield was painted an image of the forepart of a lion, emblem of the city of Nemea. Tydeus's shield was circular, and on its boar skin covering was painted the image of the forepart of a boar, symbol of Calydon.[21]

"Majesty?" said Polynices, seeing the strange look now on King Adrastus's face. "What is it? Is anything wrong?"

Adrastus did not reply. The king had just returned from a visit to the Oracle of Delphi, where he'd sought the guidance of the god Apollo. Two years before this, he had married off his eldest daughter Eurydice to Ilus, king of Troy, cementing a valuable alliance. Ever since, Adrastus had been seeking potential royal marriage partners for his two remaining daughters, but not one suitor had matched up to his high expectations. In desperation, Adrastus had gone to Delphi to ask who his daughters would marry.

The Pythia had answered King Adrastus's question by saying that one of his daughters would marry a boar, the other a lion. And here now were the boar, and the lion—Tydeus and Polynices, a pair of kings without thrones. But as wise Adrastus well knew, thrones, like reputations, can sometimes be regained. He had done it himself.

"King Adrastus," said Tydeus, "you look like you have seen a ghost."

"No, my boy, not a ghost," said the king, suddenly sounding much more friendly than before. "I have seen the future." Now, he clapped both young men on the back. Smiling, he said, "You are both welcome to stay here as my guests, for as long as you choose."

Polynices and Tydeus looked at each other with surprise, unable to make sense of the king's cryptic comment or to comprehend why he had so suddenly changed his attitude to them.

"And, which of us is to occupy the royal guest quarters, Majesty?" Tydeus asked.

"You both shall."

"Both of us?" said Polynices with distaste. He had attempted to share the throne of Thebes with another king, his brother, and look how that had turned out. Now Adrastus expected him to live in the same quarters as another king, a total stranger. "Together?"

"Both of you, together," said Adrastus, nodding and smiling. "Now, join your right hands in friendship. Become acquainted with each other, my boys. Become acquainted with me and my family. We may be spending a lot of time together in the future."

And so, begrudgingly, Polynices and Tydeus shook hands.

5.

THE KING'S PROMISE

There came a day when the deposed young Calydonian king Tydeus was among the courtiers who watched as two princesses danced before the royal court of Argos. With their father King Adrastus proudly watching from his cushioned ivory throne, the pair joined other unwed maidens dancing to the music of pipes and hand-drums in honor of Hera, patron goddess of Argos and Greek deity of marriage and the family, on the day of her annual festival at Argos.

Adrastus's unmarried daughters Argia and Deipyle had been likened to the goddess Diana for their beauty. Their jet-black hair shone with vitality. Their eyes were large, their cheekbones high. Argia, the elder, was fifteen years of age. Bold and spirited, Argia laughed as she danced and smiled at the clapping bystanders as she pounded her little hand-drum and her white dress swirled to the music. Deipyle, a year younger and a little shorter than her sister, coyly dipped her eyes as she danced so that they might not fall on any male bystander and be taken as suggestive. That very act was as seductive as a wink or a smile, and Deipyle knew it.

The solid, blond Mecisteus, younger brother of King Adrastus, smiled as he stood beside Tydeus, who was clapping to the music and taking in the two princesses. Leaning close to the young exile, Mecisteus said, in a low voice, "Many a man has aspired to these maidens' hands, my young friend, but none has met with their father's approval."

Tydeus looked around at Mecisteus and smirked. "I don't know what you are talking about, Your Highness," he lied.

This was an era when girls were considered marriageable at thirteen, making both these royal teens eligible as wives. The ambitious Tydeus appreciated that marriage to one of these young beauties would do no harm to his royal aspirations. Marriage to the daughter of the king of Argos and Sicyon would give his family name added luster, and would cement an alliance with the powerful King Adrastus.

"But," Tydeus continued with a wink, "whatever Tydeus of Calydon sets his mind to, Tydeus of Calydon gets."

Mecisteus moved to stand beside Polynices, deposed young king of Thebes, who was also clapping but without a smile on his face. "Beauties, are they not, Polynices?" said Adrastus's brother.

"The king's daughters, your nieces?" said Polynices. "Oh, yes, beauties indeed, Highness."

"If you had a choice, which one would you make your wife?"

"My wife?" Polynices responded with a look of surprise. "I am a man without a kingdom. Not an ideal suitor for a daughter of the king of Argos and Sicyon, my lord."

"Ah, but you have prospects, Polynices."

"Prospects? I need an army to turn those prospects into reality, not to mention the favor of the gods."

Mecisteus shrugged. "Treat the gods well and they will treat you well, so my late father Talaus used to say."

"A wise man, your father," Polynices responded.[22]

At the other end of the room, the enthroned King Adrastus pulled his eight-year-old son Aegialeus up onto his knee so that the boy could better see the dancing. The king's wife, Queen Amphithea, sat on a smaller throne a step below her husband on the royal dais. The king had been carefully watching the faces of his two new guests as his brother spoke with them. He knew his brother was putting thoughts of marriage in their heads at his own behest. Now, leaning to his wife's ear, Adrastus said, discreetly, "What do you think of our houseguests, my dear—the pair of handsome young princes from Thebes and Calydon?"

Aged in her thirties, Queen Amphithea was an exceedingly attractive woman. Her name literally meant "On Both Sides, a Gift of the Gods," the two sides being her handsome father and mother. "What do I think of this pair?" the queen responded. "Handsome, as you say, husband."

"Matches for our daughters, perhaps?"

The queen frowned. "But they are penniless exiles!"

"As I was, when you first met me."

"Yes, but you were the victim of injustice, husband."

"As are they."

"Yes, but in exile you found the favor of a powerful king."

"As they have."

The queen turned to him with a scolding expression. "I don't want you squandering money on that pair, husband. Neither of them is an Adrastus. They may have your past, but I doubt they have your future."

"Yes, my sweet," said the king, smiling, before easing back in his chair. He had shared with no one the words of the Oracle of Delphi about the boar and the lion. To do so, Adrastus felt, would only tempt Apollo's disfavor. Only Adrastus knew that Apollo pictured his two daughters married to the boar and the lion. Despite being king of two cities and many towns and villages, like many a husband Adrastus was not the ruler in his own house. To have his way in this affair, Adrastus realized, he would have to steer a careful course with his queen. But have his way he must, for Apollo had spoken.

Which of his daughters would marry the boar, and which the lion? Adrastus pondered on this question. The oracle had not said which would marry which, and Adrastus was prepared to see hearts entwine of their own accord, once he had put the four young people together. Argia was, like Tydeus, outgoing, and confident to the point of rashness. Deipyle was, like Polynices, less outgoing, and more thoughtful. Would like attract like? Or would opposites attract?

A year passed at Argos—a year in which Polynices and Tydeus lived in the palace of the king, trained together daily to maintain their skill with spear, sword, and shield, and became as close as loving brothers despite their very different characters and initial antagonism. The confidence of Tydeus and quiet purpose of Polynices brought the pair together, like sea and sky.

Polynices and Tydeus began to spend time with the king's daughters, having no idea that King Adrastus had set his mind on making them his sons-in-law. The king frequently put them together with his daughters, for meals, for outings, always with chaperones present. At the same time, when other potential suitors for the hands of Argia and Deipyle dared show their face at Argos, they were given short shrift by the king.

Fortunately, the members of this exclusive royal quartet enjoyed each other's company. Tydeus would tell jokes and show off his physical prowess. Argia, though quick to anger if offended, would make them all laugh with her quick wit and love of riddles. Polynices would recite poetry and devise word games for them all, and, with a peerless knowledge of the gods and their offspring and their works, would quiz the others on the deeds of Greek heroes. Deipyle would sit quietly with her needlework and enjoy the frivolity going on around her, but then would surprise everyone by piping up with the answer to a question about the Argonauts or the labors of Heracles.

The king was not surprised the day that Polynices and Tydeus came to him together and nervously announced that they wished to pose him a question; the same question.

"What question is that?" said Adrastus teasingly. He knew all too well what was on the young men's minds.

"It concerns your daughters, Majesty," said Polynices seriously, as he and Tydeus stood before the seated king.

"And their future husbands," said Tydeus, smiling.

"Ah, I would like to make the acquaintance of those gentlemen, one day," said Adrastus, "whoever they might be."

Polynices's face dropped. "But we know who they are," he said.

"Indeed? And who might they be?"

"They stand before you," said Tydeus.

"Where?" Adrastus cast his eyes past the pair, as if looking for someone else in the room.

"They are ourselves, Majesty," said Polynices, sounding frustrated.

"Yourselves?" Adrastus responded, feigning shock.

"My friend Tydeus and I have come to ask for the hands of your daughters in marriage, Majesty," said Polynices.

"We love your daughters, and they love us," said Tydeus.

"Indeed? I see." Adrastus stroked his gray-tinged beard. "And, which of my daughters does each of you seek to marry, may I ask?"

"I seek the hand of Argia," Polynices replied.

"And I seek the hand of Deipyle," said Tydeus.

"Indeed?" Now the king was genuinely surprised. The wife he had chosen for himself was very much like him—strong-minded, arrogant, stubborn. As a consequence, Adrastus and his queen frequently argued. Not that he loved her any less. Now, self-possessed Polynices wished to marry tempestuous Argia, and brash Tydeus sought the hand of quiet but loyal Deipyle.

"We know that we are at present poor exiles, Majesty," said Polynices, seeing the king's hesitation, "but we mean to take back our thrones."

"With the help of our father-in-law," said Tydeus, elbowing Polynices.

"With my help?" said Adrastus. "Indeed?"

"The daughters of mighty King Adrastus must be queens," Tydeus went on.

"You speak the truth. I would want nothing less for them," said Adrastus, nodding. "Their elder sister is Queen of Troy, after all."

"Exactly, Majesty," said Tydeus.

"We would make your youngest daughters queens of Thebes and Calydon, Majesty," said Polynices.

"And ally the thrones of Argos, Troy, Thebes, and Calydon," Tydeus added.

"A powerful alliance," said Polynices. "The most powerful in all of Greece."

Adrastus nodded, feigning thoughtfulness now. "And how would I help you regain your thrones?"

"Put together an army and march with us on Thebes and Calydon," said Tydeus.

"Indeed? Putting together an army is a costly business," the king responded. "A very costly business."

"But your daughters are worth it," said the grinning Tydeus.

"I tell you this," Adrastus announced. "When the time is right, I will indeed put together an army, and I will help you both regain your thrones."

"You will!" Tydeus exclaimed. "Majesty, that is wonderful!" Taking the king's hand, he kissed it.

"But will you permit us to marry your daughters in the meantime?" Polynices asked, looking worried.

Adrastus nodded, producing a smile. "Yes, you may marry the girls. But here is my condition. As I say, an army, a war—these are expensive enterprises. In the marriage of Argia and Deipyle, you will not receive a single gold piece as dowry."

The two suitors looked shocked. This was unheard of.

"No dowry?" said pragmatic Polynices.

"I did not say that," the king continued. "The girls' dowry will take the form of an army, raised by me, to restore you both to your thrones. Not now; when the time is right. Do you agree to that condition?"

Polynices and Tydeus looked at each other and, smiling, nodded. "Yes, Majesty!" both enthusiastically responded, as one.

When King Adrastus a little later informed Queen Amphithea that he had given Polynices and Tydeus permission to marry their daughters, she not unexpectedly exploded.

"I told you not to squander a single gold piece on that pair, and you now want to make them our sons-in-law?" she raged. "And enrich them with my girls' dowries?"

"Calm yourself, my sweet, I won't be parting with a single gold piece," the king smugly returned. "Both girls' dowry is a promise."

"A promise?"

"A promise to help restore Polynices and Tydeus to their thrones. And it will be up to me to decide when the time is right to keep that promise."

"If at all," the queen said, smiling now. "Your legendary wisdom has not deserted you after all, Adrastus."

6.

RECRUITING THE SEVEN

Each year, on the anniversary of their marriages to Deipyle and Argia, Tydeus would haul his brother-in-law Polynices before the king at the court of Argos and, in front of all the nobles of the realm, ask when the king planned to keep his promise to them. Each year, for nine years, King Adrastus would reply that the time was not yet right and change the subject. During this time, too, the royal wives of the two deposed kings gave them children—first, boys each, followed by a gaggle of girls.

Come the ninth anniversary of his marriage, Tydeus lost what little restraint he had left. This year, in front of the entire court, he asked, after another negative reply, "Your Majesty, did you lie to Polynices and myself?"

A cloud came over King Adrastus's face. "Lie? I do not make a habit of lying, son-in-law."

"Then when do you propose to deliver our wedding dowries?" Tydeus demanded with Polynices, his face displaying embarrassment, at his side.

The king now angrily ordered the court cleared until just Tydeus and Polynices stood before him.

"You test my patience, young Tydeus," the king said, seething, once they were alone.

"As you have tested ours, Majesty," Tydeus retorted. He began to pace back and forth. "In good faith we entered into the bonds of marriage with your daughters. Have we not been good sons-in-law to you, good husbands to our wives, good fathers to our children? All this time, my uncle has occupied the throne of Calydon, and Polynices's brother has enjoyed the fruits of Thebes. Nine years ago, you made Polynices and myself a promise. When did you say you would keep that promise? 'When the time is right,' you said. Well, father-in-law, after nine long years, *I* say the right time is *now*."

"Indeed?" Adrastus turned to Polynices. "What say you, Theban?"

"Majesty, forgive my brother-in-law his passion and his lack of good manners," Polynices replied, calmly, carefully.

"Lack of good manners?" said the king, raising his eyebrows. "An understatement."

"Nonetheless, Tydeus speaks the truth," Polynices went on. "We are as ready as we will ever be to retake our thrones. And in the name of the gods, we cannot see why you are unable to now deliver on your promise to help us do that!"

"I see." The king stroked his bearded chin and was pensive for a time. He failed to reveal that, behind the scenes, his eldest daughter, Polynices's loyal wife Argia, had for years past been pestering him to go to war on her husband's behalf. Argia had even made Polynices a fine cloak to wear on the campaign. Finally, Adrastus said, "Have you two given thought to which city you would first launch war against? Thebes or Calydon?"[23]

"We thought of drawing lots to decide," Tydeus replied, ceasing his pacing now that the king was finally entering into a dialogue about his promise.

"Draw lots, would you?" Adrastus shook his head. "Fine generals you two make! It must be Thebes first. Why? Because we could not bypass Thebes and have the enemy at our back, between us and our source of supplies here in the Peloponnese, while we assaulted Calydon. It would have to be Thebes first."

"The king is right," said Polynices. "Do you not agree, Tydeus?"

Begrudgingly, Tydeus nodded. "Yes, I suppose so."

"And once you helped me make Thebes mine, brother-in-law, I would support your campaign against your uncle," Polynices added. "You have my word on it, Tydeus. I will help you regain your throne, if you help me regain mine."

"Naturally, I will be at your side when you go against Thebes," Tydeus came back.

"Well, now, we have some progress," said Adrastus. "Next, let us consider the tactics for an assault on Thebes. You have considered what tactics you would employ, Polynices?"

"Well, Majesty, we would storm the gates of Thebes."

"Storm the gates? And tell me, Polynices, how many gates are there in the city walls of Thebes?"

"Seven, Majesty."

Adrastus nodded. "Thebes has seven gates, created by Amphion while he played his lyre—seven being Apollo's holy number." He came to his feet. "Here is what you must do: find me seven champions who will lead the assault on each of those gates. I am prepared to lead the overall army in such a venture, but I need worthy commanders for each of its seven divisions."[24]

Tydeus found a smile. "Polynices and I will lead the assaults on two of those gates."

"Which leaves another five gates," said Polynices, "requiring five more champions."

"Then bring me five champions apart from yourselves," said Adrastus. "First and foremost, like yourselves, they must be of royal blood. They do not need to be men of wealth, but they must be experienced fighters, men of great deeds—men of legendary deeds, even. These must be men who meet with my approval, champions alongside whom I would be proud to fight." The king now took each of them by the shoulder and turned them toward the door. "Go, find those champions."

"We will ask your brother, Mecisteus, to be one of the five," Tydeus said over his shoulder.

Adrastus shook his head. "No. I will require Mecisteus to rule here at home while I am away fighting your wars. Think again."

"Your cousin and brother-in-law Amphiaraus, sire, the one they call the Prophet," Polynices quickly suggested. "He was one of the heroes of the Hunt of the Calydonian Boar. Surely he would be acceptable to you as one of the five?"

"Yes, of course he would be acceptable to me—if you are acceptable to him. Go now, find your champions. Say nothing more to me about this matter until you can bring all five before me. Then, and only then, will the time be right to pursue this matter further. Then, and only then, will I keep my promise to you. Now, go!" Putting a hand in the middle of the back of each of them, he propelled them, like children, toward the door.

Outside the king's chamber, Tydeus's excitement rose. "At last, brother-in-law!" he exclaimed, putting an arm around Polynices's shoulders. "At last we shall regain our thrones."

"Yes, but first the wily Adrastus has set us a difficult task," the pragmatic Polynices returned. "Five champions acceptable to the king will not be easy to find."

"How difficult could it be?" said Tydeus confidently. "We shall find our men in no time."

Polynices and Tydeus began by seeking out Amphiaraus, the king's brother-in-law. A servant at his quarters in the citadel of Argos informed the pair that they could find him in the Sanctuary of Apollo and Athena that sat at the bottom of the Aspis Hill, below the citadel.

It had been no surprise to King Adrastus that his sons-in-law would seek to recruit Amphiaraus to their cause. Amphiaraus was famous throughout the Greek world. In his youth, he had been one of the forty warrior heroes from throughout Greece who had gone against the Calydonian Boar, a massive beast the size of an elephant said to be released against the people of Calydon by the hunting goddess Artemis. The goddess had supposedly been offended by the then-king of Calydon, Oeneus, father of Tydeus, and, until the heroes killed it, the boar had terrorized the entire region. Amphiaraus, a Calydonian himself, was a son of King Oeneus and his first wife, which made Tydeus his half-brother: Tydeus's mother was the king's second wife. This blood connection, the two aspiring kings hoped, would make Amphiaraus open to their proposal that he join them for the war on Thebes.

Through his mother's line, Amphiaraus was descended from Melampus, a man who could famously see into the future. Amphiaraus, too, had developed a reputation as a man who could foretell future events, so much so that he was widely known as the Prophet. Not long after participating in the Hunt of the Calydonian Boar, Amphiaraus had married Eriphyle, sister of Adrastus, and had come to live at Argos with his bride. Following a quarrel with Adrastus's father King Talaus, Amphiaraus had killed the king and taken the Argive throne, and this had sent Adrastus and his brother Mecisteus fleeing to exile in the city of Sicyon.

Yet, once Adrastus had succeeded his foster father Phobus as king of Sicyon, Amphiaraus had handed the throne of Argos over to him. Some said this was because he had seen a vision of Adrastus on the Argive throne, others that Apollo had come to him in his sleep and commanded him to give his crown to Adrastus. Adrastus and Amphiaraus the Prophet had settled their differences, and as part of their agreement Adrastus had set aside any desire to avenge his father and had returned to Argos to take its throne. From there he ruled his joint kingdoms of Argos and Sicyon, while Amphiaraus retired, to lead a quiet but comfortable life at Argos with his wife, often spending contemplative time in the Sanctuary of Apollo and Athena, the gods to whom he felt closest.

It was a hot summer's day when Polynices and Tydeus found Amphiaraus the Prophet in the Sanctuary. From a gateway, they saw him at the far end of a courtyard, sitting on a stone bench, a broad-brimmed hat on his head, and staring into a pool. Like King Adrastus and Mecisteus, Amphiaraus was golden-haired and fair of beard.

"If he truly has the powers of a prophet," said a grinning Tydeus, nudging Polynices in the ribs, "Amphiaraus will be expecting us."

The pair walked the full length of the courtyard with their steps falling loudly on the paving stones, but the Prophet did not look up.

"My lord Amphiaraus," Polynices said as he and his brother-in-law stood before the seated man, "may we intrude on your time? May we pose you a question? We are—"

"I know who you are, and I know what you want," said Amphiaraus, without raising his eyes.

An impressed Tydeus looked at Polynices. "What did I tell you?"

Now Amphiaraus raised his eyes. His beard was beginning to gray, his face was strong. His neck, on the left side, was marked by a long sword scar. "The king told me to expect a visit from you, and told me your purpose," he revealed. No powers of prognostication had been involved after all.

"Then, would you consider marching with us against Thebes, my lord?" Polynices asked.

"Why would I want to do that?" Amphiaraus returned, looking the pair up and down with a disdainful eye.

"To help put right a wrong," said Polynices.

"The world is full of wrongs. If I were to attempt to put every one of them right, I would not have the time to eat or drink or sleep."

"Then, for reward," Tydeus suggested.

"What reward do I need?" Amphiaraus came back.

Tydeus smiled. "The glint of plunder." He mimicked struggling under the weight of bags of gold. "The thrill of conquest." He mimicked making a sword thrust. "The grateful thanks of my colleague here, once he is crowned King of Thebes." He bowed extravagantly before Polynices, then looked at Amphiaraus. "Name your reward, my lord."

Amphiaraus shook his head. "I have had my fill of plunder, conquest, and gratitude."

"But Thebes holds great treasures," said Polynices. "In Thebes's Temple of Pallas there is a shield of solid gold, dedicated by the people to Pallas. Who would not want to carry that off?"

"And think of all the gold of the votive offerings at the various temples of Thebes," said Tydeus. "Gold that increases year by year. Piles and piles of it!"

"And my wife Argia has reminded me of the necklace of Harmonia, daughter of Aphrodite and Ares," Polynices went on. Aphrodite was the goddess of love and beauty, while Ares was the god of courage and war. Ares, who was part of the foundation myth of Thebes, was so linked with the city in the minds of Greeks that the plains around the city were commonly known as the Dancing Floor of Ares.

"What of it?" Amphiaraus snapped.

"The necklace was given as dowry to King Cadmus, founder of Thebes, when he married Harmonia. That necklace once resided in the Cadmea, the citadel of Thebes. But I brought it with me out of Thebes, in a casket made from boar tusks. It's beyond price, but I would be prepared to part with it, if—"[25]

Amphiaraus held up a hand. "I told both of you, I have no interest in riches," he growled impatiently. "What else can you offer?"

Polynices, forced to think fast, replied, "The opportunity to once again number among heroes."

"It is said," Tydeus quickly added, "that Amphiaraus no longer has the skill or the courage that once had his name spoken throughout Greece in the same breath as Heracles."

Amphiaraus scowled at him. "Who says that?"

"Oh, many people." Tydeus was being inventive. He had not heard anyone say any such thing. "But of course they are idle gossipers, and we take no notice of them."

"My lord, we seek seven champions of royal blood to assault the gates of Thebes," said Polynices. "Tydeus here and myself will each take a gate. King Adrastus has said he will lead the Argive army to Thebes."

"He has?" said Amphiaraus with surprise. "He said nothing of this to me."

"He gave us his word," said Tydeus.

"Seven heroes, whose names will be spoken of for all time," said Polynices. "We would be honored, my lord, if you would agree to join us and be one of the Seven."

Amphiaraus did not reply.

"What would the gossipers say if you remained behind when the king and the other champions marched on Thebes?" Tydeus asked.

"I have no interest in gossip." Now Amphiaraus was lying. Proud of the heroic reputation that he had gained in his youth, he was tempted to march with these youngsters and show the world that he was still no less a champion. But, ever since this pair had been at the court of Adrastus, there had been talk of marching on Thebes and on Calydon—talk that had made Amphiaraus uneasy, for reasons that not even he could explain.

"My lord, will you not at least consider joining us?" Polynices pleaded. "Once others know that the famed Amphiaraus is one of the seven champions going against Thebes, our friends will take heart and our enemies will quake with fear."

"Adrastus has agreed to lead your enterprise, you say?" said Amphiaraus.

"Yes, my lord," Polynices and Tydeus chorused in reply.

Amphiaraus was torn. Much respect had come his way for giving up the throne of Argos to Adrastus. Where would that respect go should Adrastus march on Thebes and Amphiaraus remained timidly at home with the women? But an anonymous dread nagged away at him every time he thought of Thebes. Amphiaraus decided that he needed guidance; the guidance of the gods.

"Well, my lord?" Polynices asked. "What is your answer?"

Now Amphiaraus pointed to a cone-shaped hill rising up on the western side of the city, the Larissa Hill. Standing nine hundred feet high, the Larissa was three times the height of the Aspis. "Go to the top of the Larissa Hill," Amphiaraus said. "There, you will see the answer to your question."

Although bemused by this instruction, Polynices and Tydeus took their leaves of the Prophet and departed the sanctuary. Impatiently crossing the Deiras, the ravine that separated the Aspis and Larissa hills, they set about climbing the Larissa in the noonday heat. The steep sides of the hill were clothed with olive trees, and every now and then the pair would halt beneath a tree to catch their breaths and wipe their perspiring brows with the back of the hand. It took some time to climb the nine-hundred-foot slope, but in the early afternoon they finally reached the summit. From there, they could see across the Plain of Argolis in all directions. Away to the north spread the waters of the Gulf of Corinth. To the immediate south, they could see the Sanctuary of Aphrodite, hugging the city wall. And just across the street from the sanctuary was the Agora of Argos, the public square and marketplace of the city, quiet now after teeming with people since before dawn when the farmers of the district streamed through the city gates to sell their produce.

Scouring the hilltop by looking on rocks and under them, Polynices and Tydeus sought to find the answer that Amphiaraus had assured them they would find.

"Are we meant to find a written message?" Tydeus pondered, scratching his head. "A sign, perhaps? Something requiring interpretation as a yes or a no? Could it be the flight of birds?" The direction that birds flew or where they landed or the number of their flock—every number from one to nine was sacred to a particular god—these were often taken as a sign from the gods. Tydeus turned his eyes to the sky, but not a single bird could be seen flying.

"There is nothing," said Polynices, disappointed, after a long search. "We have been sent on a fool's errand." He turned to look out over the city to the east and the north. Then movement on the almost-deserted street leading to the Aspis Gate in the northeast wall of the city caught his eye. A man in a broad-brimmed hat rode an ass toward the gate, escorted by a small bevy of attendants on foot. Polynices narrowed his eyes as he focused on the distant figure. "Look, Tydeus," he said, pointing. "Is that the Prophet on that ass, heading for the Aspis Gate?"

Tydeus followed his colleague's gaze. "It is! That is Amphiaraus. And he's leaving the city."

"Is that what he sent us up here to see? Is that his answer?"

Disappointed, they watched Amphiaraus pass out through the Aspis Gate with his servants and head northeast on the Corinth Road until he was out of sight. Uncertain what they should make of this, the pair clambered back down the hill. Once they had reached the Deiras, Polynices came to the conclusion that perhaps the Prophet's wife could make sense of his strange behavior.

So they walked back up the road that circled the Aspis to the citadel. Calling at the quarters of Amphiaraus, they asked for an interview with the Prophet's wife, Eriphyle. After a long wait, the chamberlain of Amphiaraus ushered the pair into a small, sunlit courtyard. Here, on the shady side of the courtyard, Eriphyle was weaving with her female attendants. Because etiquette required that a man could not visit a lady without a male member of the household being present, the chamberlain remained as the conversation unfolded.

"My lady," Polynices began, after bowing to the lady of the house, "thank you for seeing us. We have hopes that you will clarify a matter for us."

"A matter relating to your husband," Tydeus added.

Eriphyle, like her husband, was now in her forties. Once she had been attractive, but now frown lines made her long face haggard. Her hair was graying in streaks. Large brown circles hung beneath her eyes. Yet her dress was of expensive Eastern silk, and around her neck hung an exquisite necklace of gold supporting a single large pearl. "Go on," she said to Polynices in a rasping voice, her face expressionless.

Polynices went on to explain the request that he and Tydeus had put to Amphiaraus that morning and the Prophet's odd response.

Eriphyle nodded. "My husband has departed for Delphi," she advised, "to consult the oracle about your quest."

"Delphi?" Polynices returned, surprised and disappointed—a journey to Delphi and back again would keep Amphiaraus away for many days.

"That was his way of giving us his answer?" asked Tydeus. "Sending us to the top of the hill to witness his departure for Delphi? Does your husband always answer requests in such a cryptic way?"

"That is his habit," said Eriphyle with a sniff. "It allows him to avoid giving a direct answer, you see. My husband fancies himself a seer. He claims that Zeus himself bestowed the power of foreknowledge on him. Unfortunately, a great many simpleminded people have also come to believe it, and honor him as a result."

"Your husband is indeed very highly respected," Polynices responded, surprised by the cynicism of the Prophet's wife.

"Respect is all well and good, when it is honestly earned," Eriphyle replied. "Personally, I have never found Amphiaraus even able to predict the next day's weather, let alone forecast the future of kings and cities. Once, he gave up his throne, our throne, on the strength of a dream. Now we are next to poor. And when great decisions are forced upon him, what does he do? He scurries off to Delphi to seek the help of a genuine oracle."

"We hope that he decides to join us on our quest, my lady," said Tydeus. "Do you think he might?"

Eriphyle shrugged. "Who knows? What does he have to gain by doing so?"

"Great wealth resides in Thebes, just waiting for us to take it," said Tydeus. "The gold shield of Pallas, for example."

"And then there is the fabulous gold necklace of Harmonia," Polynices added, "which I currently possess."

"The necklace of Harmonia?" Eriphyle was suddenly interested—very interested indeed. "It's said to be priceless."

"Who can put a price on the gift of a goddess?" said Polynices. "My wife Argia says that the woman who wears that necklace—"

"You say you have the necklace of Harmonia, Polynices?" Eriphyle interrupted. "Does it look magnificent?"

"Indeed it does, my lady. I brought it with me out of Thebes. The mouths of two golden serpents meet to form its clasp."

"Does the necklace include precious stones?"

"It is indeed inlaid with precious stones. They sparkle like the stars. The necklace would look spectacular around your neck, my lady."

The Prophet's wife began to smile dreamily, then drew herself back. "All well and good, but you will have to await my husband's return from Delphi to receive an answer to your proposition."

Rather than wait for the return of the Prophet, Polynices and Tydeus decided to continue their quest for champions. To find men of warrior strength, skill, and reputation was one thing, but to find men of royal blood with those credentials was even more difficult. Then, one day, a chance conversation with the king's brother Mecisteus reminded Polynices that a noted warrior named Capaneus lived in Argos, and that he had royal blood. Polynices and Tydeus tracked down Capaneus at his house in the city.

The thirty-year-old Capaneus, son of Hipponous, was a massive man. Tall and barrel-chested, he possessed biceps the size of an ordinary man's thighs. He wore the simple clothes of a rustic countryman, without adornment of any kind. His house, too, was without luxuries. Yet Capaneus, through his own acts and inheritance, was a wealthy man, although he had no pride in that wealth. In fact, Capaneus would have been ashamed if anyone thought he spent more on himself than did the poorest citizen.

Capaneus welcomed the two royal visitors and introduced them to his comely wife Evadne, who, like himself, was a descendant of the past Argive king Iphis. He then listened in silence to the pair's proposition, as did Capaneus's seven-year-old son Sthenelus, while Evadne busied herself outside.

When Capaneus would not commit himself to their cause, Tydeus attempted to flatter him by remarking on the helmets, armor, spears, and swords that decorated the stone walls of Capaneus's house—obviously trophies taken from defeated opponents over the years since Capaneus had first gone to war at the age of sixteen. Noticing that some of those trophies were blackened by fire, Tydeus asked why.

"The flame is a mighty weapon," said Capaneus, smiling. "Did not Heracles use fire to prevent the Hydra's heads from growing again?" He thought for a moment, then said, "Were I to join your venture, I can promise you, I would burn mighty Thebes to the ground."

"So, you will join our expedition?" asked Polynices hopefully.

"Who else is with you?"

"King Adrastus is with us," said Polynices, "if we can recruit another five apart from ourselves."

"Who else have you approached?"

"Amphiaraus," Tydeus replied.

"The Prophet," said Capaneus, nodding approvingly. "If Amphiaraus believes the venture will end in success, then so it shall. What was his answer?"

"He has reserved his answer," Polynices advised, "until he returns from consulting Apollo's oracle at Delphi."

"Delphi?" Capaneus was impressed. "Well, then, gentlemen, if the Prophet returns with an affirmative answer, then you can count Capaneus to be among the Seven. But if Amphiaraus turns you down, don't bother coming to see me again, for your venture will surely end in failure."

A few days later, along a dusty road toward swampy Lake Lerna, which sat less than a mile south of Argos, rode Polynices and Tydeus on the king's horses. This lake was famous as the place where Heracles had killed the nine-headed Hydra as one of the legendary twelve labors set for him by the god Apollo as penance for killing his own wife and children in a fit of madness. Lake Lerna was also known for its tasty crabs.

After their meeting with Capaneus, Mecisteus had suggested another potential recruit to the pair's exclusive little band. His name was Hippomedon. The son of Talaus and the second sister of King Adrastus, he lived near Lake Lerna and reputedly enjoyed comforts and adventure in equal measure and trained for war every day.

When the riders arrived at the lake, a small boat was gliding over the silken water toward the reedy shore. One of the men in the boat was immensely tall. This fellow, the pair of travelers knew from descriptions of him they had received back in Argos, was the object of their journey. Dismounting, Polynices and Tydeus waited for the boat to slide onto the lake's bank. The tall man, in his late thirties, stepped out into the shallows barefoot, then lifted a small boy, his son Polydorus, from boat to shore.

"Hippomedon of Mycenae?" Polynices called to the tall man.

"Yes. Who calls my name?" Holding the child by the hand, Hippomedon walked toward the pair.

"I am Polynices of Thebes, and this is my brother-in-law Tydeus of Calydon. We two married the younger daughters of King Adrastus, making us your cousins by marriage."

Hippomedon nodded. "I've heard of you," he said, coming to a halt in front of the pair and towering over them. "One of you is the eldest son of the man who mastered the riddling Sphinx. The other is accused of killing most of his own family, or so the story goes." He scowled down at Tydeus. "Did you really kill ten male relatives in a fit of rage, as they say?"

Tydeus smiled. "If I didn't kill them, then I am the victim of an outrageous lie, and I am to be pitied by my friends," he said. "On the other hand, if I did kill them, then I am a fighter beyond peer and to be feared by my enemies."

Hippomedon produced a deep-throated chuckle. "I had heard that you were a master of weapons, but not of words," he remarked.

"To be honest," said Tydeus with a guiltless shrug, "Polynices came up with that riposte for me. He is much better with words than I."

"So, does that make you the better warrior?" Hippomedon asked.

Polynices laughed at this.

"We're equally skilled," Tydeus assured the big man. "Tell me, why do you never come to the court of Adrastus, cousin? We would have welcomed you into our family. Even giants are welcome at our table."

This remark brought a giggle from Hippomedon's son.

Hippomedon shrugged. "I'm happy enough here at Lake Lerna with my little family and my friends. Court life is not for me."

"Yet, not that long ago, you led a warrior life," said Polynices.

"Your skill with spear and sword are renowned far and wide," said Tydeus.

"That was before I married and settled down."

"Settled down?" asked Tydeus, with a scoffing laugh. "Why, yes, I can see the marks the chains of matrimony have left on your ankles and wrists. Does your wife forbid you to come out to play with your fellow warriors?"

Instead of being insulted by this, Hippomedon threw back his head and roared with laughter. Then his smile faded, and earnestly he said, "Horse is his own man."

"Horse?" Polynices responded.

"The name I call myself," said Hippomedon. It was a play on his actual name, which literally meant Horse Ruler but was more accurately Horse Tamer, given to him by his parents after he had shown a natural affinity with horses as a young child. "My sword and shield may be hung up, cousins," he went on, "but that is only to keep them out of the reach of children, not to gather dust."

"So, if you are your own man," said Tydeus, "you will be amenable to a proposition. Will you join a band of seven heroes to go against Thebes, and restore your cousin Polynices to his rightful throne?"

"Against Thebes?" Hippomedon responded, pursing his lips. "A tall order."

"Not for the band of champions we are assembling," said Polynices.

Hippomedon nodded pensively. "Mecisteus said that you might come calling on me."

"Word of great deeds soon spreads," said Tydeus.

Behind them, a fisherman called for Hippomedon's help.

In response, Hippomedon waved and nodded. Turning to his new-found cousins, he said, "Come, make yourselves useful."

Polynices and Tydeus joined Hippomedon and the other men unloading wicker baskets filled with crabs. Hippomedon, toting one basket under his arm and holding his son by the hand, then invited the pair to be his guests for a meal. Together, they walked up a gentle slope to a comfortable house on nearby Mount Pontinus, which had a commanding view of the lake. Hippomedon's wife cooked a meal of crabs from the morning's catch, then left the men to talk. And as they ate, with Hippomedon's silent son watching them intently, Polynices and Tydeus spoke about going against Thebes.

In response, Hippomedon quizzed them about the city, its defensive walls and towers, its people, its wealth. Finally, he asked, "Who else is with you, cousins?"

"King Adrastus will lead us if we can recruit five more champions like yourself," Polynices answered.

"Good, good. Who else have you approached?"

"Capaneus, son of Hipponous and grandson of Iphis," Tydeus replied.

"Capaneus?" Hippomedon burst out laughing.

"What is so funny?" Polynices asked.

"I call Capaneus the Torch. The man is a pyromaniac! He would blacken all of Greece if given the chance."

"Really?" said Polynices, surprised. "I thought it an idle boast."

"There you have it—the fellow is such a boaster!" Hippomedon rolled his eyes. "The gods give me strength, he can be a tiresome fellow."

"But he is a powerful fighter," said Tydeus. "His strength would be of great value to us when we go against Thebes. Would you not agree?"

Hippomedon nodded. "Oh, yes, I agree that he is strong and feared by his enemies. And the common people like him for his disdain of luxury—they would follow him over any city wall if he led the way."

"Then you would be prepared to fight with Capaneus at your side?" Polynices hopefully asked.

The big man scratched his neat black beard. "I would rather that the Torch were with me than against me, that is for sure. I agree that he could be a worthy addition to your Seven. What was his answer to your proposition?"

"He said that he would join the Seven if Amphiaraus does," said Polynices.

"Amphiaraus?" Hippomedon's eyebrows raised. "You have approached the Prophet?"

"Indeed we have," Polynices acknowledged.

"What was his response?"

"It wasn't a 'no,'" said Tydeus. "Amphiaraus has set off for Delphi, to seek higher guidance in the matter."

"Has he, indeed?"

"He'll give us his reply on his return," said Polynices.

"Then so shall I," said Hippomedon. "If Amphiaraus agrees to join your band of heroes, that will be good enough recommendation for me."

"You will join us if Amphiaraus does?" said Polynices, trying to hide his pleasure.

"That is correct," said Hippomedon. "Where goes the Prophet, so too will Hippomedon."

With the fate of their venture hanging on the decision of the absent Prophet, Polynices and Tydeus returned to Argos not knowing whether to feel elated or depressed. In Capaneus and Hippomedon they would have two excellent champions, men sure to win King Adrastus's approval. The pair was so close, yet so far from forming their band of champions. There was, of course, still the matter of sixth and seventh champions, two more warriors to add to the list should Amphiaraus and the other two join the band as they hoped.

One early morning a little later, as Polynices and Tydeus wandered absently past the market stalls of the bird and animal sellers in the crowded Agora, with Greek commerce going on noisily all around, a youth appeared in front of them. His fair hair was long. His eyes were a sparkling blue, his face almost as pretty as that of a girl. For a beard, all he could manage was a few tufts of ginger hair. Over his shoulder hung a quiver containing the small bow and arrows of a huntsman.

"I hear that you are looking for champions, good sirs," said the youth, folding his arms and standing in their way.

"Is that so?" said Polynices, annoyed that word of their recruiting drive had reached the common marketplace.

"Choose me," said the youth.

"You!" Polynices and Tydeus exclaimed together. Tydeus began to laugh.

"How old are you, boy?" Polynices demanded. "You look no more than twelve."

"Don't be fooled by my long locks!" the youth retorted, running his fingers through his long, flowing hair. "Apart from the fact that my father was no longer alive to cut my hair when I came of age, the ladies prefer a longhaired lover," he declared, pushing out his chest. "But I am of age. I'm sixteen. Almost seventeen, in fact."

As they all knew, a boy achieved manhood status once he turned sixteen years of age. At that time his father cut the boy's hair and offered it to the gods in a coming-of-age ceremony.

Tydeus screwed up his face. "Perhaps you are sixteen, but you still look no more than a child. Which are you, a man-boy, or a boy-man?" he teased. Reaching out, he ran two fingers over the young man's jaw.

"Look, what's this duck's down growing where a man's beard should be?"[26]

The youngster pulled away. "This 'child,' I will have you know," he declared with annoyance, "only recently fought along-side his boyhood friend Telephus to repel an invasion of Teuthrania. This 'boy' stripped many a fallen opponent of his armor and weapons."

"Robbing the dead is no great deed," Tydeus scoffed.

"But killing the foe is," the youth retorted.

"So, what is your name, boy?" Polynices asked.

"I am Parthenopaeus of Arcadia."

Polynices shook his head. "Not a name familiar to me."

"Nor to me," Tydeus agreed.

"Perhaps my mother's name would be more familiar."

"And what name is that?" queried Tydeus disdainfully.

"Atalanta."

"Atalanta, the female warrior?" Tydeus was incredulous. "You are the child of Atalanta?"

All Greeks had heard of the huntress Atalanta. She had been the only female member of Jason's band of fifty Argonauts in their famed quest for the Golden Fleece, an exciting adventure that was equal to the labors of Heracles in the minds of Greek youth. What was more, Atalanta had participated in the Hunt of the Calydonian Boar, with Amphiaraus of Calydon and Theseus of Athens, among others. Her involvement in that hunt had created much disharmony among her male companions, not because she had been the first to wound the boar using a well-aimed arrow but because she was awarded the boar's head and hide by the male warrior who finally felled the massive animal. She had defeated a male warrior in a wrestling contest to secure the prize, but even that had not satisfied some of her male companions.

"I had heard that Atalanta discarded a son at birth and that he was raised by shepherds," said Polynices. "Are you that child?"

"One and the same," the youth proudly confirmed. "You see before you the lioness's cub. I inherited my mother's good looks, her fleet-footedness, and her skill with the bow."

"Good looks? Ha!" Tydeus scoffed. "Skill with the bow? Ha! It seems to me, cub, that you also inherited Atalanta's lack of modesty."

"My good looks you can see for yourselves," said young Parthenopaeus, with a grin that produced dimples in his cheeks. "As for my skill with the bow, watch this."

He went to a nearby market stall where live birds were displayed in a wicker cage. After purchasing a single small bird, the youth had the stallholder bring it out into the marketplace. The conversation between the king's sons-in-law and the country boy had already attracted attention, and now a crowd gathered, joining Polynices and Tydeus to watch what would follow.

Parthenopaeus took the bow and an arrow from his quiver, then instructed the stallholder to stand with the bird twenty feet from him. Threading the arrow and bringing the bowstring back to his chest, as was the fashion in those times, the young man commanded the stallholder to throw the bird as far as he could into the air.

Up went the bird, which, once released, began to flap its wings to escape. Up came Parthenopaeus's bow. With a thwack, the arrow left the bow, even as the bird seemed to be flying away. The eyes of the crowd followed the arrow's flight. There was a collective gasp as arrow and bird connected. The bird plummeted to earth, landing in the middle of the marketplace. A youngster of seven or so picked up the bird and brought it at the run through the crowd to Parthenopaeus, who, smiling, held it up, for the crowd to see that his arrow had neatly skewered the bird. The crowd applauded. Smiling, Polynices also applauded, but Tydeus folded his arms.

"Was that not impressive?" Parthenopaeus inquired. "Would I not be a valuable addition to your band of champions?"

"A very valuable addition," said Tydeus, adding, with a smirk, "if we were going against an army of starlings."

The crowd laughed, bringing an embarrassed flush to the boy's cheeks.

"I'm sorry, Parthenopaeus," said Polynices, feeling genuinely sorry for the youth, "but you don't meet our requirements."

Anger flooded over the young man's face. "What do I have to do to prove myself?" he demanded. "Kill a man before your very eyes? I am as skillful with the spear as I am with the arrow. In fact, my spear is sacred to me."

"Don't be foolish, boy," said Polynices, beginning to lose patience with the youngster. "You are too young for our enterprise. Much too young—and inexperienced."

"We seek lions, boy, not cubs!" Tydeus declared. "Come, Polynices, we have wasted too much time on him as it is." Taking Polynices's arm, he steered his friend away, back toward the Aspis, leaving Parthenopaeus to watch them go.

"You have heard the legend," Polynices said as the pair walked on, "that Atalanta was cast out by her own father as a child and was suckled by a lion?"

"A myth created and circulated by her boastful son, no doubt," Tydeus replied.

As Tydeus and Polynices strode away, the young man, fuming, replaced his bow in its quiver and glared at their receding backs. But Parthenopaeus had not finished with Polynices and Tydeus. His day in the sun would come.

———————

It was autumn by the time Amphiaraus the Prophet returned to Argos. As he had intended, he had visited the Sanctuary of Apollo at Delphi. Amphiaraus's question to the Pythia had been this: "Would I find success were I to number in a band of champions who went against Thebes?"

This was the oracle's reply:

Beneath seven gates in curved walls,
There the hope of victory falls,
And he who sought the sacred boar
Would go a-hunting never more.

Interpretation was the key to understanding the predictions of the oracle. Amphiaraus had returned to Argos convinced that the prediction meant that a war against Thebes would end in disaster and would result in his own death, should he, the one who had "sought the sacred boar" during the Hunt of the Calydonian Boar, participate.

Amphiaraus did not send a message to Polynices and Tydeus advertising his return to Argos, but they heard of it soon enough and immediately came to his door.

"Well, my lord Amphiaraus?" said Polynices expectantly, once the pair was shown into his presence. "Have you made a decision concerning our proposal?"

"I have," said the Prophet, without looking at them.

"And that decision is . . .?" Tydeus prompted.

"I will not be participating in your venture."

"You won't?!" Polynices exclaimed, unable to hide his disappointment. "But, why not? Mine is a just cause—as just a cause as any king of Greece could possibly pursue."

"I will not reveal my reasons," said Amphiaraus, looking at his guests at last. "But they are compelling." He spread his hands and shrugged. "I'm sorry, Polynices, but I cannot be dissuaded."

After coming away from their brief and unhappy meeting with the Prophet, Polynices and Tydeus did what many young men do when trying to deal with bitter disappointment: they drowned their sorrows, becoming thoroughly drunk. In fact, that night they drank themselves insensible on Corinthian wine.

The following morning, to find solitude and to contemplate their future, they climbed the Larissa with throbbing heads. Their climb, in their weakened state, took them somewhat longer than the last time they had ascended the hill. Sitting just below the summit beneath an olive tree, the pair looked out over the city, as a haze of smoke from cooking, kiln, and workshop fires hung over Argos.

"You realize that we are sitting beneath olive branches, symbols of peace?" said Tydeus with a chuckle. "How ironic is that? We, who want to make war?"

With his finger, Polynices traced the shape of the city of Thebes in the dirt in front of him—the shape of a spearhead. "Thebes is there for the taking," he said, only half listening to his brother-in-law. "And Amphiaraus is central to our success. What can we do to persuade him to change his mind? What is the secret to winning him, Tydeus?"

"The Prophet is an odd one, if you ask me. All fortune-tellers are the same. They live in a world of their own. What is the secret to winning him, you ask? I wish I knew what he was thinking."

"My wife Argia told me recently of a saying attributed to Iphis, late king of Argos—that the route to a man's innermost thoughts is through his wife."

Tydeus's ears pricked up. "His wife, you say?" He prodded Polynices's arm. "Now there, brother-in-law, you may have found the chink in Amphiaraus's armor. Remember the day we paid a visit to Eriphyle, the Prophet's wife, and she told us that he had set off for Delphi?"

Polynices nodded. "I remember the day vividly."

"Do you also remember the glint in Eriphyle's eyes when you mentioned the necklace of Harmonia?"

"Eriphyle has long had a reputation for liking the good things in life."

Tydeus was smiling, exuding his customary confidence now. "I suggest we pay her a visit, and make the Prophet's wife an offer."

So the two picked themselves up, climbed back down the Larissa, crossed the Deiras, and returned to the Aspis. A servant was sent to keep watch on Amphiaraus's door, and to report as the Prophet ventured out—what Polynices and Tydeus had to say to Eriphyle they could not say in front of her husband. A day passed. Then, early the next morning, the servant came running to report that Amphiaraus had left his quarters and gone down to the Sanctuary of Apollo and Athena. Seizing their opportunity for a private interview with the Prophet's wife, Polynices and Tydeus hurried to Amphiaraus's quarters.

Eriphyle again kept them waiting—so long, in fact, that the pair began to worry that the Prophet would return before they'd had a chance to talk with her alone. To be on the safe side, Tydeus volunteered to keep watch for Amphiaraus, and, should he return before Polynices had transacted his business with Eriphyle, Tydeus would delay him in conversation. Sitting on a low stone wall a little time later, Tydeus looked up and, with surprise, saw Polynices enter the Prophet's quarters, guided by a maidservant. Not much later, Polynices reemerged into the light of day.

Jumping up, Tydeus hurried to join his colleague. "Did you see Eriphyle?" he asked, as they walked away together.

"I did."

"And you put the proposition to her?"

"I did. I promised her that, if her husband joins the Seven, the necklace of Harmonia will be hers."

"Good, good, good." Tydeus rubbed his hands together with glee. "So, what was her response?"

"What woman could resist the offer of the rarest, most famous, most beautiful necklace in all the world?" said Polynices, grinning.

"She will persuade Amphiaraus to change his mind and join us?"

"She will have to, if she expects to take possession of the necklace. And she wants that necklace, Tydeus. She wants it more than anything in the world."

Once Amphiaraus returned, word began to spread, via the wagging tongues of their servants, that he and his wife were arguing, loudly and angrily. Those arguments became frequent events and lasted for weeks. Their affray, although not its subject (which remained between the pair), became the talk of Argos.

"Why won't you agree to join Polynices and Tydeus in their venture against Thebes?" Eriphyle would demand.

"I choose not to," Amphiaraus would irritably retort. "Leave the matter there."

It was always the same question and always the same response. Never once did Eriphyle reveal why she was so keen for her husband to go against Thebes with the others. Never did she let on that Polynices had offered her a bribe to sway her husband. At the same time, never did Amphiaraus reveal the content of the prediction he had brought back from Delphi, the prediction that he interpreted to mean that the venture would be a failure and would result in his own death. As far as Amphiaraus was concerned, the prediction was between Apollo and himself.

Then Eriphyle began to add insult to her harping question. "You won't tell me why you won't join the young men on their venture against Thebes? Could it be, husband, that the great warrior hero Amphiaraus has lost his courage? That years of retirement have made him fearful of battle?"

This accusation enraged Amphiaraus, but for several more days he resisted his wife. Finally, when she threatened to broadcast that accusation to all of Argos, he could take no more. "Very well! Enough! I will go against Thebes with Polynices and Tydeus. As long as you never again accuse me of cowardice, woman. Amphiaraus is no coward!"

Here was Amphiaraus's dilemma: As a result of the oracle's prediction, he was convinced that, if he did join a war against Thebes, he would die in a failed assault on the city walls. Yet, if he did not take part, he would be labeled a coward. After giving in to his wife, he sent a messenger to Polynices and Tydeus, summoning them to a meeting. He would indeed march with the others against Thebes. But, shrewdly, he knew that, even if the pair could assemble their Seven, their march would take months to prepare and weeks to complete—plenty of time for Amphiaraus to talk the others out of making war on Thebes before they even set eyes on the city's walls.

When Polynices and Tydeus arrived at Amphiaraus's quarters, he advised them, simply and without emotion, "I have changed my mind. I will go against Thebes with you. Now, go find your other champions, if you can."

Joyfully, the brothers-in-law embraced each other, and then embraced a far more sober Amphiaraus. As they took their leave, Polynices and Tydeus caught a glimpse of Eriphyle, lingering in a doorway and watching them depart. She, too, was smiling with delight.

Publicly, Amphiaraus would admit that he agreed to go to war on his wife's say-so. But the reason he gave differed substantially from the truth. Because he and his cousin King Adrastus had rarely seen eye to eye when they were younger, when Amphiaraus married Adrastus's sister both had publicly sworn to abide by Eriphyle's arbitration whenever their disputes became insoluble. Now Amphiaraus would claim that, as Adrastus wished him to join the venture against Thebes and he preferred not to do so, Eriphyle had chosen to support her brother, not her husband, in the matter, and Amphiaraus had been forced by his old oath to respect her decision and become one of the Seven.

In high spirits, Polynices and Tydeus hurried to inform the king that Amphiaraus had consented to be one of the Seven. As the pair arrived back at the palace, they were met by the king's brother.

"Mecisteus, uncle by marriage," said Tydeus excitedly, "Amphiaraus has agreed. He will be one of our champions. He will go against Thebes with us."

"We're going to tell your brother the king," Polynices added.

"Rein in there, young colts," said Mecisteus. "Don't bother Adrastus until you can name all seven members of your warrior band. How many champions have signified their willingness to join you, apart from Amphiaraus?"

"If you agreed to be one of us," said Tydeus with a grin, "we would need just one more to complete the Seven."

Mecisteus shook his head. "You know I cannot join you. The king forbids it." In truth, Mecisteus would have given anything to be one of the Seven, but he knew he would be required to stay at home to govern the kingdom in the king's absence. "Who else have you recruited?"

"Now that Amphiaraus has agreed," Polynices replied, "Capaneus and Hippomedon will follow."

Mecisteus nodded approvingly. "Worthy champions both. So just two places remain to be filled? For one of those places, I suggest you seek out Eteoclus."

Tydeus frowned. "Eteoclus? Who is Eteoclus?"

"A young man, modest, and poor to be sure—living in a stable, the last I heard. But he is a descendant of King Iphis, and his sister Evadne is married to Capaneus. Eteoclus is a dignified man, who, although he has no wealth of his own, refuses gifts from his wealthy friends and relatives."

"But this exploit would make him rich," said Tydeus. "Riches make a man independent. Who does not wish to be rich?"

Mecisteus shook his head. "Not Eteoclus. For that very reason, he is respected by all Argives who know him. In point of fact, I would say that no man is more morally upright than Eteoclus. A just cause will always find a friend in him. He is also a fine physical specimen. Seek him out."[27]

"That we shall, Mecisteus. Thank you," said Polynices.

That same day, Polynices and Tydeus found Eteoclus in a stable by the city's eastern wall, working before a fire and pounding an anvil as he made horse fittings. In his early twenties and of average height, stripped to the waist and with his rippling muscles bathed in perspiration, he was, as Mecisteus had told them, a fine physical specimen. As soon as Polynices and Tydeus walked into the stable and saw the man, they nodded to each other in silent agreement—Mecisteus had been right: Eteoclus was indeed Seven material.

"How would you like to become rich, Eteoclus?" Tydeus asked as he and Polynices approached. Despite the warning from Mecisteus that

Eteoclus had no interest in wealth, Tydeus could not believe that a poor man would not be tempted by the sort of riches he was offering.

First pausing his labors and studying them, Eteoclus then replied: "I am already rich. Rich in the blessings of the gods, rich in worthy ancestors, rich in health, rich in friends . . ."

"But not rich in gold," said Tydeus, dropping a purse of gold at his feet. "There are riches beyond description awaiting those who sack Thebes with Polynices and myself. Consider this an advance payment."

Eteoclus looked at the purse, then disdainfully pushed it back across the dirt floor toward Tydeus with his foot as if it contained excrement. Laying down his hammer, he folded his arms. "Who sent you to me?" he demanded.

"Mecisteus," Polynices replied. "He said you would—"

"Then Mecisteus should have told you that I have no interest in wealth. Not of the kind you are talking of. Luxury is abhorrent to me."

"But—" Tydeus persisted.

Seeing the foolishness of pursuing the subject of gold, Polynices took Tydeus's arm and pulled him back, saying to Eteoclus: "Mecisteus did say that you were a good friend to just causes like ours."

"And what just causes are you two peddling?"

"Our thrones were stolen from us," Tydeus declared. "We are the rightful kings of Calydon and Thebes."

"Ah, you are the princely sons-in-law of Adrastus," said Eteoclus. "I've heard your story in the marketplace. You are seeking five champions to join you in going against Thebes."

"And once we place the Theban crown on the head of Polynices, we will go against Calydon, and secure my throne," Tydeus quickly added.

Eteoclus nodded thoughtfully. "Well, you were both betrayed in your homelands, that much is clear. Tell me, will it be a valorous and glorious adventure, this Seven against Thebes?"

Polynices, noting a change in the man's tone, smiled. "Mightily glorious, and all the more valorous if you join us," he said.

Eteoclus nodded. "Very well, for valor and glory, but not for gold, count me as one of your Seven."

Tydeus looked at him with surprise. "Don't you want to know who else will be participating?"

Eteoclus shrugged. "It is of no interest to me. I will play my role, the others will play theirs. I am sure you have chosen well." He grinned. "You were wise enough to choose me, after all!"

"Then give us your hand in comradeship," said Polynices, and each of them gripped him by the right wrist in turn.

Tydeus scooped up his gold-filled purse and stuffed it into his belt, and, as they walked away and Eteoclus resumed working, Tydeus said to Polynices in a hushed voice, "That seemed almost too easy, brother-in-law."

"Don't question the turning of the tide of fortune," Polynices returned. "It would appear, brother-in-law, that the gods have at last decided to favor us."

Eteoclus had been honest when he said he had no interest in wealth. He knew he could not take wealth to the grave with him. It was fame that Eteoclus craved, for he knew that the famous man lives on long after the flames of his funeral pyre die.

Excited now, Polynices and Tydeus went immediately to find Capaneus at his house, and when they located him the pair passed on their news that the Prophet had agreed to be a part of the mission and was now one of them, and that Eteoclus had also just joined the quest.

Capaneus nodded, and said, "We shall make a formidable band. May the gods go with us. And may the people of Thebes enjoy their last days of peace, for I will soon be razing their city to the ground!"

Next, Polynices and Tydeus rode out to Lake Lerna and shared their news with Hippomedon.

"So the Prophet and the Torch will be marching with you, together with the blacksmith with royal blood," said Hippomedon. "Then count the Horse among your seven champions. Fishing can wait a while."

The happy pair of princes had only just ridden back into Argos side by side when a long-haired youth with a quiver on his back stepped into their path, took the bridles of their horses, and waylaid them.

"It's Atalanta's cub," said Tydeus derisively. "Step aside, man-boy! We have men's business to attend to."

"I hear that Capaneus and the Prophet have agreed to join your band of adventurers," said Parthenopaeus. "Has Hippomedon also agreed to become one of your champions?"

"You are well informed, boy," said Polynices. "Where do you come by your information?"

"Servants have ears," said the young man, "and mouths—mouths that pass on secrets when trinkets change hands."

"You bribed our servants?" said Polynices with a disapproving scowl.

"You see, I'm also resourceful," said Parthenopaeus. "Resourcefulness is a quality that every champion should possess. Don't you agree, my lords? So here I am, offering myself as one of your Seven."

It just so happened that, ever since his meeting with Polynices and Tydeus in the marketplace some months earlier, Parthenopaeus had been boasting to the common people that the princes had accepted him into the Seven. This, as he had hoped, had attracted many admirers among the young women of Argos. He had bumped into one beautiful girl in particular, Clymene by name, as she carried water from one of the fountains outside the city. Of course, she had recognized him as the handsome young warrior that everyone in the marketplace was talking about, and she became smitten with him. The upshot was that Parthenopaeus had fallen instantly in love with Clymene and had married the girl. At this very moment, Clymene was pregnant with his child. So, Parthenopaeus's reputation was riding on achieving his boast of inclusion in the Seven.

"I told you before, boy," Polynices responded dismissively, "you are too young."

"Too young? I'm very close to seventeen years of age. Capaneus was sixteen years of age when he fought his first war."

"You are inexperienced," Polynices countered.

"The blood is still warm on my spearhead from the Teuthranian War. I have proven myself in combat."

"Listen, cub," said Tydeus with exasperation, "even if we accept all that you say, there is one credential that all seven of our champions require and which you do not possess."

"And what is that, may I ask?"

"Royal blood, son of a huntress," Tydeus replied, sitting back in his saddle and folding his arms.

"Oh," Parthenopaeus responded. "Why didn't you tell me this before?"

"You were in such a hurry to impress us," said Polynices, "that you failed to ask what qualifications were required. And I'm afraid that royal blood is a prime and necessary qualification—a requirement set by King Adrastus himself."

Parthenopaeus burst into a smile. "Well, then, it just so happens that I can meet that requirement, my lords."

"Not as the son of Atalanta," Tydeus scoffed. "She had no royal blood. From what I have heard, her father was merely a clan chieftain in Arcadia. He was no king."

"That is true," Parthenopaeus agreed. "But, what if I were also the son of a king?"

"A king?" Tydeus exclaimed. "What king?"

"King Talaus, father of Adrastus."[28]

"You are joking!" said Polynices, shaking his head in disbelief. "I had heard your father was Hippomenes—a fine warrior to be sure and one who claimed royal blood. But not a proven prince . . ."

Parthenopaeus was shaking his head. "My mother married Hippomenes, but after my birth. Seventeen years ago, not long before he died, old Talaus had a dalliance with my mother in Arcadia, when she was at the height of her fame and her sensuality. I was the result. Take me before King Adrastus. I am his half brother, I am of royal blood, and qualified to join your band of champions."

In the audience chamber of the citadel of Argos, King Adrastus and his younger brother Mecisteus surveyed the seven men arrayed before them—Polynices, Tydeus, Amphiaraus, Capaneus, Hippomedon, Eteoclus, and young Parthenopaeus. Together, the king and his brother walked along the line, studying each of the seven in turn from close quarters, with Adrastus pausing in front of them and looking deep into their eyes to assess their inner strength.

To Polynices, Adrastus said, "You have the heart of your father Oedipus, who, in his saner days, faced the Sphinx, solved her riddle, and did away with her."

To Tydeus, he said, "You have the fortitude of your father Oeneus."

To Amphiaraus, he said, "You, brother, have the guidance of the gods."

To Capaneus, he said, "You have the strength of ten ordinary men."

To Hippomedon, he said, "You have the wit of the Muses."

To Eteoclus, he said, "You, my cousin tells me, have the determination of a bull."

Mecisteus nodded. "Heart, fortitude, strength, determination, wit, and the guidance of the gods," he said. "They bring all the qualities that a band of champions would need to guarantee success in a dangerous undertaking."

Finally, the king came to stand in front of Parthenopaeus. "So, stripling, what do you bring to the enterprise?"

"If I may answer by way of a rhetorical question, Majesty," Parthenopaeus boldly replied, "what do *you* bring to the enterprise?"

This caught Adrastus by surprise. But then a smile creased his face, before quickly fading. "I, my boy, bring wisdom, and an army. While you, if I am not mistaken, bring lack of respect."

"Not at all, Majesty. Should we not all be equals in this affair? We will all take equal risk, therefore we should know our fellows' strengths. As for myself, I bring youthful vigor to the enterprise."

"Equals, you say? That remains to be seen. I'm informed that you claim to have the blood of my father running through your veins, young man. Is that so?"

"Yes, Majesty. King Talaus was my father."

"Indeed? What proof do you offer?"

"You have my word on it, my lord, as I had the word of my mother. She told my stepfather Hippomenes, who told me."

"Indeed?" Adrastus turned to Mecisteus, who raised his eyebrows. But then a warm smile appeared on the king's face, and he pulled Parthenopaeus into an embrace. "Welcome, little brother. You may be the illegitimate son of King Talaus, but you are of my royal blood nonetheless. I can see Talaus in your face—and in your boldness." Then, standing back, he looked Parthenopaeus up and down, and said, "So, you wish to march with us against Thebes."

Now, Mecisteus ventured a cautioning comment. "You don't think the boy a little young for the venture? He must command a division of the army and must storm one of the seven gates of Thebes. Is he up to it, brother?"

"As he says, he brings youthful vigor to the enterprise. And both his parents were Argonauts with Jason. Were I to reject him, do you think Polynices and Tydeus could easily find another champion of royal blood to replace him?" Adrastus walked to Polynices, and stood in front of him, arms akimbo, locking eyes with him. "It's your throne that we are talking about here. So what is it to be, Polynices? Do I accept the boy into the Seven, or do we delay the enterprise, perhaps indefinitely? The final decision is yours, son-in-law."

All in the room had their eyes on Polynices as he weighed the options. In truth, he had his doubts about the reliability of the son of Atalanta when battle was opened. The boy seemed much too overconfident for his liking. Yet Adrastus was right—delay now, and Polynices might lose his opportunity to lead an army against Thebes and regain his throne, forever. It even occurred to him that perhaps King Adrastus expected him to reject Parthenopaeus, so that the mission would never take place and Adrastus would not have to part with the money for an army and a war. "Very well, Majesty," Polynices said after thinking it over, "Parthenopaeus is acceptable to me. Let us proceed. Lead us against Thebes."

Adrastus nodded. "Very good. So it shall be."

There were smiles of relief along the line of the Seven, from all but Amphiaraus.

"Thank you, Majesty," said Polynices.

Turning to the door, Adrastus called, "Bring the shield."

Attendants now brought in an Argive shield—round and concave, it was covered with the thick hide of a black bull. From clay jugs, blood so dark it was almost black was poured into the shield as it was held horizontally in front of the Seven. That blood had been taken from a bull sacrificed by Adrastus immediately prior to this meeting. Silver cups were handed to each of the seven warriors, and Adrastus led them in dipping their cups into the blood.

"Repeat after me," said Adrastus, holding his filled cup high. "By the blood of the sacred bull and in the sight of the gods . . ."

"By the blood of the sacred bull and in the sight of the gods," chorused the Seven.

"Ever faithful to my fellow champions, the men who follow me, and the gods . . ."

"Ever faithful to my fellow champions, the men who follow me, and the gods."

"I vow to destroy Thebes to the last stone or to spill my life's blood in the attempt, the gods willing!"

"I vow to destroy Thebes to the last stone or to spill my life's blood in the attempt, the gods willing!"

Adrastus gulped down the contents of his cup, and the others followed suit, drinking the still-warm blood of the bull, which had been raised by Argive priests with just one purpose in life—sacrifice to the gods.[29]

Wiping his bloody lips with the back of his hand and handing his cup to a servant, the king looked around the faces of his companions. "Now," said Adrastus, "you are the Seven, bonded in blood. Go forth, make your preparations. The army will assemble at Argos next spring. We will arrive outside the curved walls of Thebes before summer bakes the fields."

7.

ON THE MARCH: TRAGEDY AND
DISCOVERY AT NEMEA

Over the winter, preparations for war were made at Argos and in all the communities of Greece that were subject to or allied to King Adrastus. In cities and villages, men worked to manufacture the weapons and ammunition; fashion the shields, helmets, and armor that thousands of soldiers would bear into battle; and craft the horse-fittings and chariots to be used by the nobles and their sons. In the autumn, Adrastus had sent out orders for each community to supply a number of handpicked men for the campaign, and by the following spring thousands of men had assembled at Argos in readiness for the march north. Additional contingents would join the army en route to Thebes. Of course, word of martial preparations in Argos spread, but at this point King Adrastus had not announced where or when his army would be marching.

One of the cities subject to the Argive king was Mycenae, seven miles north of Argos. For hundreds of years, Mycenae had ruled much of Greece, leading the way in the development of weapons and creating the distinctive figure-of-eight shield, known as the Mycenaean shield. But unwise kings had led to the city's downfall. Now only a shadow of its former self with much of its population dispersed, Mycenae did King Adrastus's bidding. And like the other cities and towns subject to Argos, Mycenae had agreed to Adrastus's request for a body of hundreds of handpicked warriors for the Thebes campaign. Yet, on the day in late May when the contingent from the four main tribes of Mycenae was due to arrive at Argos, by sunset not a single man had appeared.

The following day, Adrastus sent Polynices and Tydeus riding to Mycenae to personally collect the Mycenaean troops. On their arrival, they were informed by the Mycenaeans that the omens from a sacrifice to their patron deity Hera, conducted on the day their men were to set out, had not been propitious. Hera, the wife of Zeus, was the queen of heaven. In addition, at Mycenae, as at Argos, she was considered the "shield of the city," and to Mycenaeans the safety of their city depended on her goodwill. Because Hera had not blessed their participation in the Theban campaign, Mycenae had withdrawn from it.[30]

Even though Polynices and Tydeus returned from Mycenae with pack animals loaded with weapons and ammunition collected by the Mycenaeans for the campaign, Adrastus was infuriated by the Mycenaean withdrawal. But, never one to argue with the will of Hera, he masked his disappointment with activity as he made the last preparations for the campaign and gave final instructions to his brother Mecisteus, who would be in charge at Argos in the king's absence.

The night before the army was due to march, the Argive men going to war ate with their families for the last time. Before dawn, one day in the first half of June, commoners, nobles, and the members of the Seven bade farewell to their wives and children. Young Parthenopaeus had recently joined his fellow champions in fatherhood—his wife Clymene had given birth to a healthy baby boy. The proud father had named the child Promachus, meaning Battle Leader—as Parthenopaeus hoped the boy would one day become. He hoped to embrace his second child on his return from the Theban war, because Clymene was again pregnant—while Parthenopaeus was away, she would give birth to a daughter.

Come the day the army was to march, on the king's orders women were sent indoors as their husbands, brothers, and fathers departed so their tears would not weaken the resolve of their men. King Adrastus himself was composed and dignified as he kissed his infant son

Aegialeus on both cheeks. A sad Polynices bade farewell to his sons Thersander, Timeus, and the newborn Adrastus, a boy named by the prince in honor of his royal father-in-law. On the other hand, Tydeus parted from his boy Diomedes with a confident grin and predicting he would be back by the autumn to collect him after having helped Polynices gain his crown and with his own crown of Calydon firmly on his head. Capaneus was equally upbeat when he said farewell to his son Sthenelus, laughing as he went. Hippomedon set off from Lake Lerna waving to his young sons Polydorus and Demophon, while, in contrast, in the city Eteoclus walked purposefully away from his infant son Medon without a backward glance.

Of all the farewells, that between Amphiaraus the Prophet and his two sons Alcmaeon and Amphilocus was the most dramatic. Before dawn, accompanied by eldest son Alcmaeon, the Prophet offered Apollo a libation at the family altar, with father and son naked as the rite required. With the offering complete and prayers offered for the family's safety, Amphiaraus then called for youngest son Amphilocus. Kneeling between the two prepubescent boys, putting an arm around each, he lowered his voice.

"You must both make me a solemn vow," he began. "If I should fail to return alive from this expedition to Thebes, you must kill your mother."

"Kill our mother!" Alcmaeon exclaimed with horror.

"Why?" his little brother asked.

"Your mother has betrayed me," Amphiaraus bitterly declared. "She has been seduced by a bribe to send me to my death."

"How do you know that, father?" Alcmaeon asked.

"How does your father, the most noted seer in all Argos, know anything, boy?" Amphiaraus angrily retorted. "Through the favor of the gods! Your mother would prefer to hang the necklace of Harmonia around her neck than have her husband by her side."

Amphiaraus had learned that his wife Eriphyle had succumbed to the bribe of Polynices after she chose to send him to war—and, if the oracle was correct, send him to his death. How he had learned of the offer of the necklace of Harmonia, he never revealed. It may have come from a servant of Tydeus, for Amphiaraus seemed to think that using the necklace to tempt Eriphyle had been Tydeus's idea.

"The necklace of Harmonia?" asked the confused little Amphilocus. "What is that, father?"

"You will learn all in time. Just listen, the pair of you. I will do all in my power to prevent a war from taking place outside the walls of Thebes. If I am successful, the Pythia's oracle will be thwarted, and I will return to you. If I fail and I fall, you must avenge my death with the death of your betraying mother. Therefore, I require you to swear this oath before me and the gods."

So the young sons of Amphiaraus, stunned, frightened, and holding each other by the hand, swore a sacred oath of revenge that their father dictated to them. Amphiaraus then kissed them both before walking out to the garden where his wife Eriphyle and daughters Eurydice and Demonissa waited. He kissed each daughter on the forehead. Then, without a word to Eriphyle, he strode out the house's door and joined his waiting armor-bearer.[31]

As the sun rose, amid a buzz of a thousand conversations, an army of three thousand men assembled for several miles along the Nemean Road north from Argos. This road, the main route from Argos to Corinth, passed through valley farmland before running through hills, more than forty miles to the Corinthian isthmus.

The army's vanguard was made up of a troop of cavalry, which would move ahead of the main column, clearing the road and locating and preparing overnight campsites. For now, the horsemen had yet to mount up. Behind the cavalry, divisions of spearmen (common foot soldiers) had formed up. The torso of each spearman was covered by chainmail fish-scale bronze armor sewn to a linen corselet. His helmet hung around his neck. On his back was slung a large convex shield, while on his right shoulder he would carry a baggage pole to which several spears and two bronze shin-guards were tied and from which hung cooking utensils and a bag containing personal possessions.

Following the spearmen came scores of two-man war chariots, loaded with the equipment of their noble owners. Each chariot was made from a wooden base on two wooden wheels with four spokes. Atop the base, a wicker frame three feet high ran along the sides and the curved front, and stretched over this frame were sheets of thick hardened leather. The aim of the Greek chariot-maker was a vehicle that was very light so that, matched with a fine pair of young horses, it was fast and maneuverable in battle. On the march, their drivers would lead each team of two spirited horses while their owners walked elsewhere in the column. At the moment, the drivers stood, soothing their steeds, amid the mass of men and animals.

Most of these chariots had been paid for by their owners. In the cases of four of the champions, Polynices, Tydeus, Parthenopaeus, and Eteoclus, none of whom were wealthy men, King Adrastus had provided their vehicles. Adrastus had also gifted these men with squires— experienced horsemen who would drive their chariots and tend their horses—as well as an armor-bearer each—commoners who could carry their master's shields, helmets, and spears on the march and would help them strap on their armor.

Following the chariots came a long line of bullock-carts and baggage animals carrying the folded leather tents, equipment, and rations of the army. Next, herds of sheep, goats, and cattle that would feed the army filled the road. There was also a small herd of massive black bulls, chained to each other, chosen, for their magnificence, to be sacrificial animals in the days and weeks ahead. Hundreds of noncombatant boy shepherds brought in from their farms by their spearman fathers would herd the animals on the march. One more division of spearmen followed, with another troop of cavalry making up the army's rearguard.

Most of these men were Argives, from the city of Argos and the villages and farmlands of the surrounding district of Argolis. Others had come from neighboring towns such as Nauplia, a port nine miles southeast of Argos on the Argolic Gulf. On the march, more contingents would join the king's army, bolstering this already-impressive initial force.[32]

The army's second-largest contingent would come from Sicyon, the city due north of Argos and overlooking the Gulf of Corinth west of the city of Corinth, which had been ruled by Adrastus since before he assumed the Argive throne. While the people in the lands east of the Nemean River owed their loyalty to Corinth, the territory immediately west of the river fell into Sicyon's sway and provided part of the city's military recruiting grounds. This meant that a solid swathe of territory from the Argolic Gulf to the Gulf of Corinth, west of the Nemean River, was controlled by Adrastus.

The Sicyonians, bringing more than a thousand spearmen and slingers, plus more chariots, would join the main force outside Megara, on the isthmus east of Corinth. There, too, a contingent of Megarian levies and nobles with chariots would also be added to the army—for while Megara was an independent city-state, Megarians honored Adrastus as a wise king and heroic warrior who had the favor of the gods.

The army's line of march would bypass Corinth and take it to Megara, but Corinthian troops would also join its ranks at Megara. Adrastus had formal alliances with both Corinth and Megara. In addition, volunteers joining the army for this as-yet-unannounced Theban War came from as far afield as the Greek islands of the Aegean, from Tydeus's home city of Calydon, even from Thebes itself. These men were soldiers of fortune, intent on enriching themselves from the spoils of a ransacked Thebes. Meanwhile, another organized body of troops joining the army at Megara would come from Colonos, a town just to the north of Athens, in Attica to the southeast. The Colonosians, like the Megarians, held Adrastus in high esteem.

King Adrastus now emerged from a northern Argos city gate, clad in his armor and accompanied by the Seven and members of the Argive nobility. From a gate tower, Adrastus's brother Mecisteus, who was staying behind to govern the city, observed the king's departure together with older nobles. Apart from these men and a few guards to watch over slaves, only old men and boys would remain with the women and girls in Argos and her fields, keeping agriculture and city life operating until the soldiers' return.

Argos was famous throughout Greece for breeding fine horses. When the king reached the head of the line of chariots, he went to his own steeds and patted them. One horse was as black as night. The other was a magnificent, spirited pearly-white stallion with a black mane and tail, a horse that won the admiration of all who laid eyes on him.[33]

"Majesty," said Polynices, "that is the finest horse I have ever seen."

"His name is Arion," Adrastus replied, stroking the animal's muzzle. "Sired by Poseidon with the goddess Demeter, and a gift from Heracles," he added. "I have reserved him for an exploit such as this."

The story that Arion was a gift of Heracles emboldened the entire column. Young boys and old men would boast that, with Heracles on the Argive side, their opponents surely stood no chance! Heracles, later called Hercules by the Romans, had reputedly been born to Zeus, king of the gods, and Alcmene, a human mother. To all Greeks, he was part god, part superhuman warrior hero. Any king who could claim a connection with Heracles stood above mere mortals, or so the Greeks believed. Heracles had in fact been born at Thebes; so being able to boast that Adrastus of Argos possessed Arion, Heracles's horse, gave Adrastus an edge in the propaganda war that would precede the actual Theban War.

Adrastus and the Seven now walked to their appointed positions in the column. The king went to the front, stationing himself behind the cavalry vanguard and ahead of the first division of spearmen. Immediately behind him stood his armor-bearer, a powerful man who carried Adrastus's helmet and a round kingly shield. The shield's leather face, painted a gleaming white, was emblazoned with a stylized Gorgon's face, emblem of Argive royalty, painted in black with its tongue audaciously poking out.

On a signal from Adrastus, the trumpeter of the first division raised his long, narrow instrument and blew a short signal. The trumpets of the following divisions followed suit. The king stepped forward, and the army moved off. The column's progress would be dictated by the speed of the slowest stock, which meant it proceeded at a trundling sheep's pace. Marching each morning and making camp each afternoon, the army would cover some ten miles a day. On the often-winding and sometimes-elevated roads to Thebes, the army could theoretically reach its destination in some twelve days. But there would be stops along the way to gather water, supplies, and troops, which would slow progress.

On its first night on the road, the force camped in open fields. On the second night, it camped near the Nemea River in the Asopia district. As a contingent of armed spearmen and slingers from the chief town of Asopia, Nemea, joined the force and set about raising their tents, Amphiaraus and his charioteer Baton drove the short distance to Nemea in the Prophet's chariot, taking water jars with them.[34]

As Amphiaraus knew, there was a well sacred to Zeus on the town's outskirts. Even in the worst droughts, the people were forbidden to drink from holy wells such as this. Its water could only be used for libations to Zeus; this was why Amphiaraus had come, to stock up on holy water for the rites that would have to be performed during the army's march. Nemea was a town without walls, and Amphiaraus had his charioteer drive until they came to a large house near a grove of trees. A nursemaid, a mature woman, sat in the afternoon shade on the steps that led up to the house's door, cradling a baby.

"Woman," called Amphiaraus, "whose house is this?"

"These are known as the wealthy halls of Lycurgus, who was chosen from all of Asopia to be keeper of our local Temple of Zeus," came the reply from the nursemaid. A slave, her name was Hypsipyle, and she was a native of the island of Lemnos.[35]

"Ah, Lycurgus, son of Pheres, the very man I was seeking," said the Prophet. "I need him to lead me to Zeus's well. The army of King Adrastus is in need of holy water." Amphiaraus knew that Lycurgus had recently been elected by his fellow citizens to the important post of priest of Apollo in Nemea. That appointment had saved Lycurgus from joining the king's army for the Theban campaign, because never could an altar to Zeus be left unattended if the community it served wished to remain in the god's favor.

Hypsipyle advised that Lycurgus was absent, but she could guide Amphiaraus to the well. Eagerly, she came to her feet, still clutching the baby in her charge. The child's name was Ophelles, and he was the son of Lycurgus and his wife, another Eurydice. With Amphiaraus and charioteer Baton following, each carrying a water jar, Hypsipyle, toting baby Ophelles, led the way. It now became clear why Hypsipyle had been so keen to guide Amphiaraus, the cousin and brother-in-law of the all-powerful King Adrastus. As the trio walked, Hypsipyle revealed that she was no common slave.

Hoping to win the sympathy of Amphiaraus and perhaps her freedom, she told of how she had become enslaved. Hypsipyle was in fact of royal blood, being the daughter of the former King Thoas of Lemnos. Several years back, the men of Lemnos had turned their backs on their wives to bed Thracian women they had brought back to the island as prisoners after a raid in Thrace. The wives of Lemnos had become so angry that they formed a murder pact, and on the same night all murdered their husbands in their beds.

As part of this pact, Hypsipyle, who was herself the mother of twin teenage boys to Jason—of Jason-and-the-Argonauts fame—was supposed to behead her father King Thoas as he slept. But she couldn't bring herself to do it. Instead, she had smuggled her gray-haired parent out of the city and put him in an old boat, which she pushed out to sea. Old Thoas would be found and saved by fishermen from Taurinas. Meanwhile, back in Lemnos, when the women discovered that Hypsipyle had broken the pact and helped her father escape, they put her in chains and sold her to pirates. Those pirates had brought her to the Greek mainland, where they'd sold her to Lycurgus of Nemea.

What Hypsipyle didn't reveal to Amphiaraus as they walked was that Lycurgus and his wife had struggled to conceive. Once Ophelles was born, they were overjoyed, and as a precaution Lycurgus had gone to Delphi and asked the Pythia what he should do to ensure long life for his son. The oracle had told him that the child's feet must not be allowed to touch the ground until he was old enough to walk, and Lycurgus had passed this instruction on to nursemaid Hypsipyle.

Once they reached the well, to impress Amphiaraus, the nurse laid the baby in a soft patch of celery, then, taking the jar from Amphiaraus, tied a rope around the jar's handle and lowered it into the well to draw water for the royal from Argos. All the while, she continued to tell her story, which culminated in servitude under the roof of a stern master and cruel mistress here at Nemea. Amphiaraus and Baton, their attention fully on the nursemaid and her story, failed to notice a venomous snake emerge from the undergrowth. A cry from the baby had them turning to see the viper slither away after biting the child on the chest.[36]

Drawing his sword, Amphiaraus strode after the serpent and dispatched it. Letting out a scream, Hypsipyle ran to baby Ophelles and picked him up. But the child was dead. The venom had gone straight to his small heart. Amphiaraus immediately sent Baton driving back to the army with all speed to inform King Adrastus of the calamity, knowing that it could have political ramifications with the only child of the chief man of Nemea killed right under Amphiaraus's nose.

In the meantime, Amphiaraus carried the dead child back to Nemea with the distraught Hypsipyle trailing along behind, dripping tears of guilt. At the house of Lycurgus, Amphiaraus presented the dead child to his mother Eurydice and told of how Ophelles had died. Eurydice flew into a rage and demanded the immediate death of nursemaid Hypsipyle.

When King Adrastus arrived on the scene soon after this, driving himself to Nemea accompanied by son-in-law Tydeus, he found that

Lycurgus, the dead child's father, had returned home by that point and was locked in a physical struggle with Amphiaraus. Urged on by his almost-demented wife, Lycurgus was intent on putting the child's nurse to death, while Amphiaraus was striving to protect Hypsipyle, whom he now knew to be of royal blood. After Adrastus ordered the fight to cease, Tydeus physically stepped in and pushed Lycurgus back with his shield. Calming down, the nonetheless distraught Lycurgus demanded to know how the king proposed to set things right.

Amphiaraus, thinking fast, said to his brother the king, "This child must have enduring honors. The truth is, he merits them." Amphiaraus knew that when Adrastus had first ruled in Sicyon, he had initiated a semi-annual sporting contest to honor the gods, and this seems to have prompted what he now proposed. "You should host funerary games here at Nemea in honor of the son of Lycurgus and Eurydice."[37]

Adrastus thought this an admirable solution and commanded that these games go ahead at once. This enabled Lycurgus to persuade his wife to forget about punishing the nursemaid and focus on honoring their dead child. So Adrastus and all the members of the Seven presided over Ophelles's funeral—the child's father Lycurgus, as a priest, was not permitted by Greek religious law to have anything to do with the dead—and added offerings to the boy's funeral pyre. The child's ashes were subsequently interred in a tomb that could still be seen at Nemea many hundreds of years later.

It took several days to prepare the games' courses and equipment and to select the judges. Then, commencing on the twelfth day of June, the funerary games of Ophelles were held in a rectangular area called a stadion, or stadium, some 350 yards in length, which was cleared by the army in a grove midway between the nearby villages of Cleonae and Philus.

These Nemean Games, as they became known, lasted three days, and in their original iteration involved seven events: a chariot race using chariots drawn by four horses, a discus throw, a javelin throw, a wrestling contest, a boxing match, and two running races—one a sprint covering one length of the stadium, the other a much more demanding event over two lengths of the stadium. Known as the Hoplitodromos, this grueling second running race required all competitors to run wearing helmet, body armor, and leg greaves and carrying a heavy round bronze shield.

The judges for the games' events wore black mourning robes in honor of Ophelles, while every free man in Adrastus's army was entitled to enter the contests. The entire army was permitted to line the course to watch each event play out and encourage and applaud the contestants. With all but the chariot race requiring the athletes to compete naked, in the interests of decorum, women were prevented from attending those six events.

As the games were contested, many a spectator would have remarked to colleagues on how the death by snakebite of baby Ophelles contrasted with a legend about Heracles. In the story, known to all Greeks, the goddess Hera had been furious with her husband Zeus because of all the children he had fathered with mortal women. Once she learned that Heracles had been fathered by Zeus, when the golden-haired Heracles and his dark-haired mortal twin Iphicles were eight months old, Hera waited for the children's nurse to leave their nursery, then slipped two venomous snakes into the room. On seeing the reptiles slithering toward them, Heracles's brother began to cry with fear, but Heracles simply picked up a snake in each hand and strangled both. When the nurse returned, she found Heracles happily playing with the dead snakes in his cot. Sadly, many a man at the Nemean games would have remarked, little Ophelles was no Heracles.

In memory of Ophelles, winners of the games' seven events were awarded victors' crowns made from fresh celery, and this custom would be observed when the Nemean Games were regularly celebrated centuries later. As with all later pan-Hellenic games such as the Olympic Games, there were no prizes for second- or third-place finishers.

Members of the Seven, who stayed at the house of Lycurgus during the games, participated in these initial games' events.[38] King Adrastus

won the chariot race, driving a four-horse team that included his famous Arion. It was Eteoclus who won the sprint. Polynices won the
games' wrestling contest and Amphiaraus the discus throw. An otherwise unknown competitor, Laodocus, won the javelin throw. Tydeus
won the boxing—an event called the Pyx, which involved naked, oiled
contestants binding their hands and wrists with strips of leather before
standing toe-to-toe to slug it out. The first man to be knocked out or
yield was the loser.[39]

Tydeus, who'd earlier interceded on Hypsipyle's behalf, was back
at the house of Lycurgus after winning his event, and was still feeling
pleased with himself, when he was approached by the nursemaid Hypsipyle.

"Gracious lord," said she, "I had heard it said that two brothers,
twins from Lemnos, had won the Hoplitodromos running race. Is it
true?"

"Why, yes," the champion replied. "The race was won by Thoas
and Euneus of Lemnos, grandsons of King Thoas. The judges couldn't
separate them at the finish—they crossed the line together. So both
youngsters were awarded the winner's crown."[40]

Tears began to stream from Hypsipyle's eyes. "My lord," she said,
"I think those two young men are my sons."

Adrastus was immediately informed, and he commanded that
there be a meeting in his presence between the two young men and the
maidservant. Thoas and Euneus, who had joined Adrastus's army at
Nemea as volunteers, were brought to the house of Lycurgus. The pair
had not been told the reason behind the king's summons and stood
nervously before Adrastus with questions in their eyes.

The king waved for Hypsipyle to be brought in, then asked her,
"Do you recognize these two young men?"

Thoas and Euneus immediately looked fearful.

"They were only babies when last I saw them," Hypsipyle replied,
looking at the faces of the young men intently, as, already, both began
to see much that was familiar about this drably dressed woman. "Their

father, Jason, took them away with him when the *Argo* sailed from Lemnos to continue the quest for the Golden Fleece," she went on. "Out of my sight, they have gone from children to men."

This Jason that Hypsipyle spoke of was none other than the heroic leader of the legendary Jason and the Argonauts. Setting off aboard the ship *Argo* to seek the famous Golden Fleece, which they would eventually secure at Colchis in the Black Sea, the Argonauts were a band of fifty adventurers led by Jason. Their number had included the hero-god Heracles, the famous poet and musician Orpheus—of *Orpheus in the Underworld* fame—and Atalanta, the Argonauts' only female member and mother of Parthenopaeus of the Seven.

The island of Lemnos had been an early, and lengthy, stopping place for the Argonauts. By some accounts, the women of Lemnos had willingly become the adventurers' lovers, but according to others some members of the band had forced themselves on the women, which had disgusted Heracles. Jason had taken Hypsipyle, daughter of Thoas, then the king of Lemnos, to his bed, and the twins Euneus and Thoas had been the result. When the Argonauts had eventually sailed on, Jason had taken the baby boys with him, leaving them at Colchis. Following Jason's death in Corinth, his fellow Argonaut Orpheus had taken them to his native Thrace, where he had raised them. Later, their elderly grandfather Thoas had found them and taken them back to Lemnos. The boys had been looking for their mother ever since growing to manhood.[41]

"Is there one single feature that would identify them with any certainty?" Adrastus asked Hypsipyle.

"Yes, there is one thing," she replied, nodding. "Before Jason took them away, I hung a medallion around the neck of each infant. It's called the Golden Vine."

"What?" cried Euneus with amazement.

"Why, here it is!" exclaimed Thoas, as, reaching beneath their tunics, he and his brother both pulled out a golden medallion that depicted a grapevine.

"Then," said Hypsipyle, bursting into tears and rushing to embrace the pair, "you are my sons, and I am your mother!"[42]

The upshot of this reunion was that Adrastus gave Thoas and Euneus money and excused them from service with his army. They in turn purchased their mother's freedom from Lycurgus and returned with their mother to Lemnos, where the women of the island would elect her to the island's vacant throne. Queen Hypsipyle would reign there for many years, always grateful to Amphiaraus for her life and to Adrastus for her freedom, for reunion with her sons, and for her reign. One of her boys, Euneus, would rule Lemnos after her.

Twelve days behind schedule, the Argive army struck camp and marched away from Nemea, heading for the isthmus. Once it reached Megara and its ranks grew to more than five thousand fighting men in seven divisions with the addition of men from Sicyon, Megara, Corinth, and Colonos, the army would take the road northwest to Mount Cithaeron. The mountain range, which rose to 4,800 feet and ran almost due east from the Gulf of Corinth, served as the physical boundary between the Attica region to the south and the region of Boeotia north of the mountain. Once having crossed the mountain using the Dryoscephalae Pass—called Oak Heads Pass by the Attics but Three Heads Pass by the Boeotians—Thebes, in Boeotia, would be another two days' march away.

By the time the army resumed its progress, Amphiaraus the Prophet had lapsed into deep depression. The death of the boy Ophelles right in front of him, when he might have saved the child's life by being more attentive, was playing on his mind. The prediction of the Delphic oracle that Amphiaraus himself would perish outside the walls of Thebes should he attack the city, a prophecy which he had managed to dismiss for a time with the hopes of finding a way to avoid war with Thebes, was once again dominating his thoughts.

As the army set off from its Nemean campsite, Amphiaraus was heard by those around him to say, "In my mind, the name of the dead child has changed, to Archemorus."[43]

The soldiers who heard this couldn't fathom why the Prophet would call the dead boy Fate Beginner, which was what Archemorus meant. It wasn't that these men were unintelligent. They, like everyone else in the army, were merely blissfully ignorant of the fact that Amphiaraus truly believed he was going to die outside the walls of Thebes. Neither were these men aware that Amphiaraus was now convinced that the death of Ophelles represented the first step toward his own fated demise, which, he now dreaded, was drawing closer with each passing day.

Nine days of marching brought the army east, past Corinth and Megara, then north over Mount Cithaeron through the Dryoscephalae Pass. This mountain route was steep and narrow, with the slopes on either side lined with fir trees. At one point, as men, animals, and vehicles slowly made their way up the mountain trail, the troops, many of whom had never gone far from their hometowns before, were able to see Cithaeron's highest point, towering thousands of feet above them away to their left.

When the army descended the mountain's northern slopes, it came upon the village of Erythrae, which sat to the right of the road, in Cithaeron's foothills, a little south of the Asopus River. This river, reputedly possessing the tallest reeds in all of Greece, formed the border between the lands of Thebes and those of the city of Plataea. Once the road leveled out on the flat below Erythrae, there was a junction. Here, one road branched sharply left, leading to Plataea, several miles west of Erythrae, immediately below the mountain. This road, the main western highway, continued on to Delphi and all places west, including Calydon. A second road continued on from the junction almost due north across the plain. This was the road to Thebes.

Neither Adrastus, Polynices, nor Tydeus had any quarrel with Erythrae or the city that controlled it, Plataea; but just days before the arrival of the largest army Greece had ever witnessed, the people of Erythrae abandoned the village and fled to Plataea, herding their stock with them. Adrastus left the village unmolested; but, to make use of its wells, he halted the army outside Erythrae and ordered camp made.

So strung out was the army that, as the advance guard dismounted at Erythrae, the rearguard was just commencing the climb up the Dryoscephalae Pass miles to the south.

Once the baggage train arrived, tents sprang up on the mountain's lower slope, beginning with the pavilion of Adrastus. The troops would prop their spears outside their tents, use their shields as their pillows, and eat with their tent-mates at campfires that sparked into life outside each tent. That evening, as the Seven dined with Adrastus at his pavilion, Amphiaraus made an attempt to prevent any conflict erupting at Thebes (and thus save his own life) by making an announcement as they ate and drank.

"I am troubled," he began. "More than once, as I listen to the birds, the gods have told me that victory in the quest for the Theban throne will only go to those who have the support of Oedipus."

"Indeed?" said Adrastus, nodding slowly. Looking the way of Polynices, who had paled, he asked, "Would your father have sympathy for your cause, Polynices?"

"I, er, I don't know," Polynices replied. "Perhaps. I have no idea of his state of mind."

"Could not Polynices go to his father and bring him over to his side?" Amphiaraus suggested. "That way, once the people of Thebes were made aware of that support, they would be likely to abandon Eteocles. This would make the war unnecessary and give Thebes to Polynices intact—all without a drop of blood being spilled."

"An excellent idea," Adrastus agreed. "Polynices, are you prepared to go to your father at Colonos with just such a proposition?"

It was common knowledge that as soon as Eteocles had taken the crown of Thebes, Antigone, sister of Eteocles and Polynices, had taken their blinded father Oedipus to Colonos, just a mile north of Athens. There, the Athenian king Theseus had given them refuge. Theseus was respectful of Oedipus's legendary defeat of the Sphinx. He also sympathized with the banished former king, as he himself had been an exile in his younger days.[44]

It didn't take long for Polynices to embrace the idea of approaching his father. "Of course I am prepared to go to Oedipus, Majesty," Polynices responded. He would much prefer to take the Theban throne through diplomacy, which would leave Thebes intact, than to see the city destroyed brick by brick, as the Seven had vowed to do in the case of war. "I would even be prepared to share my throne with my father, if he would agree."

Adrastus nodded with satisfaction. "Then, Polynices, tomorrow to Colonos you will go." He looked over at Tydeus. "And if Polynices succeeds in securing Thebes by peaceful means, the army will march on west to Calydon, Tydeus, to secure your throne."

This brought a broad smile to Tydeus's face. "A bright prospect indeed, Majesty," he responded.

Not long after dawn the next morning, following an offering to Zeus conducted by Amphiaraus, Polynices set off on horseback to travel back through the Dryoscephalae Pass, retracing his steps down the road to Megara, where he would turn sharply left to join the Athens road that would take him to Colonos. Meanwhile, the army entered into a daily routine of foraging and training drills as it remained encamped at Erythrae, awaiting the outcome of Polynices's mission to Oedipus at Colonos.

The spirits of Amphiaraus briefly lifted with Polynices's departure, as the Prophet pictured a lifesaving termination of hostilities with Thebes before they even began. But he was soon again overwhelmed by negative thoughts. What if Oedipus refused to support Polynices? And even if Polynices were to win his father's endorsement, what if the people of Thebes ignored it, remained loyal to Eteocles, and chose war with Adrastus and the Seven over a peaceful settlement? Amphiaraus therefore conceived another plan to prevent war with Thebes—an even more practical plan, in his view.

Taking Tydeus aside, Amphiaraus told him that he sympathized with the Calydonian prince's desire to have the matter of the Theban throne swiftly and bloodlessly dealt with. This would enable the army to go immediately against Calydon to restore Tydeus's throne to him. To speed this process, Amphiaraus urged Tydeus to offer to go to Thebes and act as an impartial intermediary. There, he said, Tydeus could negotiate a solution that suited both Eteocles and Polynices, such as sharing the throne as Polynices had originally suggested. After all, with an army of five thousand men encamped just two days' march from Thebes, as the Thebans would be well aware by this time, Tydeus would be negotiating from a position of strength.

The vain Tydeus, who had a high opinion of his own skills in both war and peace and whose eyes were fixed firmly on the Calydonian prize, quickly agreed to this idea. He went with Amphiaraus to put the proposal to Adrastus. At first, the king was in favor of waiting for the outcome of Polynices's visit to Oedipus. But, when Amphiaraus pointed out that, even should Oedipus agree to back Polynices, Eteocles and his Thebans might well remain firm in their opposition to him, Adrastus agreed that a peace mission by Tydeus could do no harm and indeed could bring a simple and bloodless solution.

As a result, Tydeus immediately left the camp at Erythrae, mounted on one of his chariot horses. He went fully armed but taking an olive branch as a symbol of his peaceful intent. Away the young warrior galloped on his mission, up the dusty Plataea Road toward Thebes. Amphiaraus watched him go with high hopes of a negotiated peace, even though he knew in his heart that Tydeus was much more expert with blade and shield than he was with discourse and reason. Tydeus's preferred method of persuading people to his way of thinking was the point of his spear, not pointed words. But Amphiaraus desperately hoped that the threat of the Argive army camped on Thebes's border would give Tydeus the power of persuasion that his words might lack.[45]

8.

CREON'S KIDNAP ATTEMPT

As mentioned, when Eteocles took the throne of Thebes, Antigone had helped her banished, blinded father Oedipus leave the city. For many days they had walked, all the way south to Colonos, just a mile or so to the northwest of Athens. At Colonos, the forgiving Furies were worshipped as the Kindly Powers, and by that stage forgiveness was one of just two things that Oedipus wanted from life. The other was revenge against the two sons who had sent him into exile, even though they had been following his own decree.

Out of respect for the onetime monarch who had famously outwitted the Sphinx, the aged King Theseus of Athens had offered Oedipus sanctuary, providing the former king of Thebes and his daughter with a house at Colonos. When Oedipus told Theseus he was convinced that assassins would be sent from Thebes to take him away and eliminate him, the famous Athenian king, who'd been an associate of Heracles in his younger days, assured Oedipus that the wise elders of Colonos would ensure that that didn't happen and that he was safe within the bosom of Athens.

Antigone's younger sister Ismene, left behind to care for their mother Jocasta, had been instructed by Antigone to keep her eyes and ears open for information that would be of value to Antigone and their father. But all through the following year, the teenage Ismene found herself being watched by her own servants in the Cadmea. Every move she made, every word she uttered in public, was reported to her brother Eteocles. Only one single mature male servant refused to be bribed to betray her, remaining loyal to the girl.

One night a year later, when Eteocles refused to give up the Theban throne and banished Polynices, young Ismene, fearing for her life,
slipped from the Cadmea and from Thebes, accompanied by her loyal
slave. The pair subsequently walked for days to reach Colonos, where
Ismene reported Eteocles's coup to Antigone and joined her sister and
their father. Ismene had been living with them at Colonos ever since.

Like the rest of the residents of the Attica region, Ismene and Antigone heard that their brother Polynices had passed through Megara
and crossed Mount Cithaeron with Adrastus's Argive army, bound for
Thebes. They also knew that a contingent of volunteers had gone from
Colonos to join the force. They had no idea, though, that Polynices
was on his way to Colonos, intent on winning the support of his father.

In the first days of the new summer, a surprise visitor reached the
house of Oedipus from the north—but it wasn't Polynices. Creon,
uncle of the girls, arrived at Colonos, accompanied by his adult sons
Haemon and Megareus and a party of mounted Theban troops of the
Cadmean Guard.

Creon was now gray-headed and in his sixties, and, stiff after the
long ride from Thebes, he was feeling his age as he and his sons walked
up the steps to the door of the house being used by Oedipus. Several
elders of Colonos stepped into their path.

"What is your business here, stranger?" asked one of the elders.
"You, and your men?"

"Fear not," said Creon to the Colonosians, "I come with no thoughts of
force. I'm old, and I know what a powerful city I've come to." He raised his
arms to highlight the fact that he carried no weapons. "I wish to speak with
Oedipus, my brother-in-law, as the envoy of Thebes."

Deciding to permit him entry, the elders ushered Creon and his
sons into the house, but one of the Colonosians hurried away with a
purposeful stride, toward the nearby hilltop altar of Poseidon. Once inside the door, Creon could see, across the open forecourt of the house,
Antigone sitting in discussion with her blind father, whose thinning,
unkempt white hair wafted in the breeze.[46]

"What is happening, my daughter?" Oedipus asked, having heard voices at the door.

"My uncle Creon has come, father, and he is not alone," Antigone replied with a worried scowl.

"Gentlemen," said Creon with a weary smile to the elders of Colonos who gathered around him, "I've been sent, in my advanced years, to plead with the man yonder to return with me to the land of Cadmus. I come not as one man's envoy but sent by all our people because, as his close relative, no Theban better knows the woes he has suffered."

This explanation was enough for the elders to part, and Creon and his sons approached Oedipus as his eldest daughter eyed him with suspicion.

"Unhappy Oedipus," Creon said as he drew near, "hear us, and come home. Rightfully you are called home by all the people of Thebes and chiefly by me. Come home with me, and help prevent a war. Unless I am the lowest of all men who has ever been born, I cannot help but sympathize with your plight, old man—a stranger and a wanderer, a beggar in a foreign land, with just a single handmaid, your daughter, to help you. I never imagined she could fall to such depths of misery." Looking at Antigone now, he said, "Unlucky girl! While you tend your penniless father, you, who are still in your youthful prime, remain unwed and a prize for the first poor man who comes along."

Antigone said nothing. Marriage was the last thing on her mind.

Creon, returning his attention to the girl's father, said, "Oedipus, Polynices camps on Mount Cithaeron with a mighty Argive army. In the name of the gods of your fathers, forget your shame and consent to return to your city and your home. It is right that you thank Athens for her welcome; but your own city, the city of your father and grandfathers, has first claim on you since it was she that made you her king. It is right that you return to her and persuade your sons to settle their old dispute peacefully, before it comes to war. And if it does come to war, it is right that you side with your city."

"What a daring rascal you are!" Oedipus exploded. "Using a plea of what is right as a crafty device! Why do you strive to take me back to where I would be nothing but a sorry captive? In the old days, when, deranged by my self-inflicted woes, I yearned to be cast out of the land, you chose not to allow me to do so. Then, once my fierce grief had spent its force and the seclusion of the palace was sweet to me, you were for thrusting me from my home and country. Our kinship meant nothing to you!"

"All untrue—" Creon protested.

But Oedipus shouted him down. "Now that you see I have a kindly welcome from this city and her sons, you seek to pluck me away, wrapping dark intentions in soft words. That is what is true, Creon! What joy is there in kindness we don't seek? It's as if, after a man had everything his heart could desire, only then you offered the gift of aid. Wouldn't you find that a vain and empty pleasure? Yet such is your offer to me—good in name but evil in its substance."

"Oedipus, old man—" Creon began again, sounding exasperated.

"Let these others hear what I believe you have in mind for me." Blindly, Oedipus waved a hand in the general direction of the cluster of Colonosian elders and raised his voice for all to hear. "You, Creon, have come here to fetch me, not to take me home, but so that you can bury me within Thebes's borders. That way, the city can escape any troubles connected with me."

"Not so," Creon responded. "I have only the best of intentions for you."

"Indeed? Well, this is what I have for you—an everlasting curse on Thebes. And for my sons, this wish—just enough space in the lands of Thebes in which to die!" He laughed, sounding quite mad, then said, "Am I not wiser in the fortunes of Thebes than you, Creon? You come here with fraud on your lips. Yes, and with a tongue sharper than the edge of a sword. Go! Let us live here in peace. For even though we live with many torments, evil is not one of them. Here we are content."

Creon was shaking his head. "Who do you think has come off worst from this exchange?" he asked. "Me, from your words, or yourself? Unhappy man, have these years taught you nothing?"

"Depart! I say it in the name of these Colonosians, as well. We have all had enough of you." Oedipus turned away and faced the wall.

"I call on these men," Creon said, "not you, to witness your tone toward your own kin. If I ever take you from here—"

"Who could take me from among these men, my allies?"

Creon's anger was rising. "I have come to prevent war between your sons. Mark my words, these men can't save you from the pain you are about to endure if you ignore me."

Oedipus, turning back in Creon's direction, demanded, contemptuously, "Where is the action to back such bluster?"

"One of your two daughters has already been seized by me and sent on her way back to Thebes. The other I will remove at once."

Oedipus visibly paled. "You have my child Ismene?" he said, aghast.

"And will also have this one on her way before long." He indicated Antigone.

"Friends, will you help me?" Oedipus called despairingly to the Colonosian elders. "Don't forsake me! Drive this godless man from your land."

The Colonosians looked at each other in consternation.

"Depart, stranger, depart!" said Xenon, the most senior of their number. "What you have done and what you threaten to do are offenses against all that is right."[47]

Creon shook his head and motioned to his sons. "It's time you led off this girl. By force, if she won't go of her free will."

The pair stepped forward. Haemon, Creon's eldest son, was a man of around forty. A widower, he himself had a son, a teenager named Maeon who had recently entered manhood. Haemon had grown up with Antigone, his cousin. With a compassionate look in his eyes, he held out his hand to her.

"Helpless that I am, where shall I fly?" cried Antigone with alarm, pulling back from her cousin. She looked to the Colonosians. "Where will I find help from gods or men?"

"What's your intention, stranger?" Xenon the elder demanded of Creon.

"I won't touch the old man," Creon replied, "but I will take my niece. Her father is clearly out of his mind. I claim her guardianship. She is mine to take." With that, he stepped forward and, brushing aside his hesitant sons, he took a firm hold of Antigone's arm.

"Release her!" growled Xenon, as he and his colleagues advanced threateningly on Creon and his sons.

"Stand back!" Creon cautioned. "It'll be war with Thebes if you harm me, her duly appointed envoy."

"Did I not say that would be the case?" said Oedipus with a knowing voice.

"Let her go!" ordered Xenon.

"Gladly," said Creon with a smile, manhandling Antigone toward his eldest son, who took hold of her. "Go!" Creon commanded. "Take her away."

Haemon hustled Antigone toward the door, with his brother walking ahead of the pair, pushing aside startled elders to clear a path. This action was against all the accepted rules of diplomacy. Creon had come as the peaceful envoy of Thebes, but now under cover of this role he was attempting to kidnap guests of the king of Athens. It was bold, it was desperate, and it was diabolical.

"Friends! Friends! Help me!" Antigone called to the shocked elders, who hesitated to intervene against young, armed men.

"Where are you, my child?" called Oedipus, sightlessly reaching out. "Take my hands."

"I'm taken by force, father. I'm helpless!"

"Away with you!" said Creon to his sons, before addressing Oedipus. "Your daughters will no longer be your crutches, will never again prop you up. As in the past, Oedipus, you have done yourself no good.

Instead of listening to good sense, you've indulged your anger, which has always brought you down." As Creon turned to follow his sons, who passed out the door, Oedipus burst into tears.

Xenon the elder put his hand on Creon's chest, stopping him in his tracks. "Hold, stranger!"

"Hands off!" Creon retorted, pushing away his restraining hand.

Xenon shook his head. "I won't let you leave unless you return the maidens."

Now Creon's eyes flashed with anger. "If you aren't careful, I'll take the old man as well!"

"Don't you dare touch me!" Oedipus cried.

"Be quiet, old fool!" Creon returned.

"I will not be quiet," Oedipus replied. "May the heavenly powers that govern this place hear my curse—for wresting from me those who were my eyes, I bid you and all Thebans an old age as dark as mine!"

"See what he is like?" said Creon to the elders with exasperation. "Hear his words? Nothing but venom and curses. I've had enough. You are coming with me, old man." He advanced back toward Oedipus.

"What is this all about?" came a new, powerful voice.

Creon turned to see Theseus, the Athenian king, enter accompanied by armed Athenian soldiers. Like Oedipus, the king was white-haired, but despite his advanced years he was a much healthier and more athletic-looking man than the former ruler of Thebes.

"What is so important that it interrupts my sacrifice to the sea god, patron of Colonos?" demanded the crusty sovereign of Athens. It just so happened that Creon had unknowingly timed his arrival at Colonos with the day that Theseus made his regular offering at the town's altar of Poseidon, which sat on one of two small hills that rose from the plain a mile north of Athens's Dipylum Gate.

"Ah, friend, I know your voice," cried Oedipus. "But you have failed me. The man you see before you has taken away my two children. They are all I have in the world!"

"What are you saying?" demanded the king.

"His daughters, Majesty," said Xenon. "This Theban has taken away Oedipus's two daughters, to return them to his city—the elder girl just now, the younger a little while before."

Theseus's expression darkened. Turning to one of his companions, he said, "Quickly, send footmen and horsemen at once, at full speed, to the place where the two highways meet, to cut off these wrongdoers while they're still on our soil." The junction he was referring to was where the road from Athens branched west to Eleusis and Megara and northwest to Mount Cithaeron and Thebes beyond. As the man hurried away to fulfill the king's order, Theseus turned to Creon. "You will not be leaving this land until those maidens are presented to me. Your actions are a disgrace to yourself and your city. You come here, to a city that observes justice and observes laws, and take captives as if the city were manned by slaves and I didn't exist. If I were in your land, I would never plunder without the permission of its ruler."

"Do as you think best for you," a bristling Creon responded, looking fearlessly at the king's men as they surrounded him. "Though my cause is just, the lack of supporters makes me weak. But, as old as I am, Theseus, I will strive to match deed with deed."

"Shameless soul!" snarled Oedipus.

"I think this stranger a good man, Majesty," interjected Xenon the elder, "but he is fated to be on an accursed mission. We should be lenient with him."

"Enough of the talk," Theseus returned. "The doers of the deed are in flight, while we, the victims, stand still."

"What would you have me do?" Creon asked.

"Lead us on the path your people have taken. Are they fleeing at the gallop? Or are they hiding locally, perhaps? Do you have an accomplice on my soil? I think this exploit was not without planning. If they flee, my men will apprehend them. If they hide, you will lead me to them." He grasped Creon by the arm. "Come!"

"I have no fear of you, Theseus. And when I'm home again, I'll know how to act!"

Theseus was unimpressed. "Threaten as much as you like, but for now lead the way to the maidens. As for you, Oedipus, stay here in peace. I pledge to you that, unless I die beforehand, I will return your children to you."

"Heaven bless you, noble Theseus," Oedipus called.

With that, Theseus escorted Creon from the house, with the elders and soldiers following.[48]

9.

POLYNICES'S MISSION TO OEDIPUS

Before the end of the day that they were kidnapped, both Antigone and Ismene were recovered by King Theseus and his troops and brought back to their father at his house in Colonos.

At the same time, Theseus set Creon, his sons, and their accompanying Theban soldiers on the road back to Thebes with a warning to never again set foot on Athenian soil. Creon and his mounted party took the same road they had used to reach Colonos. This road climbed over Mount Cithaeron via a narrow pass farther east from the main road and the Dryoscephalae Pass, the route used by Adrastus and his army. Little more than a goat track, this eastern pass had allowed Creon and his party to avoid Adrastus's army as it camped at Erythrae in the mountain's northern foothills. On the return, they used the same route, again avoiding the Argive army. After crossing the Alpheus River back into Theban territory, they sped across the plain via the Tanagra Road to Thebes's Fountain Gate.

As Theseus reunited blind father and tearful daughters in the house at Colonos, he was brought a message. "You should know, Oedipus," the king announced, once he had received the message, "that there is a relative of yours—but not a countryman—who only recently arrived to sacrifice at the altar of Poseidon and who is asking to be permitted to briefly speak with you."[49]

"What about?" Oedipus asked suspiciously.

"He won't say. He asks to speak with you, then be allowed to go on his way."

"Then who is he?"

"Do you have any relatives at Argos?" Theseus asked.

Oedipus snorted. "Argos! Say no more. Don't ask me to see him."

"You know him?"

"It must be my son, Majesty—the hated son who would be the last person whose painful words I would want to hear."

Now Theseus realized that the stranger must be Polynices and that a solution to the impending conflict between Argos and Thebes might be at hand. "Can't you at least give him a hearing?" he asked. "What could he say that was painful to you?"

Oedipus shook his head. "No, no, no!"

"Father, listen to him." It was his daughter Antigone. "I may be young to be offering advice, but, please, for your daughters' sake, allow our brother to come. Just hear what he has to say. What harm is there in that?"

Oedipus could not see it, but his younger daughter Ismene was nodding in earnest agreement with her sister. The old man, who could deny his favorite child nothing, groaned, then said, "Daughter, you ask a lot of me. But, very well, as you wish. Theseus, just let no one else threaten my life."

"Rest assured, my friend," Theseus replied, "while any god preserves my life, I will preserve yours. I will send the fellow here."

Theseus departed, and Antigone went to the open door to look out into the gathering twilight. Before long, she saw a tall, fair-haired man of around thirty, dressed in a dusty tunic and expensive cloak trimmed with purple, being escorted by Xenon the elder toward the house.

"Father," called Antigone, "I see him coming, without attendants. There are tears in his eyes." Her voice began to quaver. "Polynices has come to us."

Ismene hurried to join her at the door. When Polynices topped the steps alone, both sisters rushed to him, and he pulled them into an embrace.

"Why do *you* cry, brother?" sobbed Ismene.

"I don't know whether I'm crying for myself or for my old father in there," Polynices replied, snuffling up tears.

The three of them went in the door together, Polynices in the middle, with his arms around his sisters on either side of him. Looking around the interior, he saw not a single decoration—no luxury, no comfort—while his father, clad in the same now-worn, grubby clothes in which he had departed Thebes, sat on a cold stone bench across the forecourt, munching a stale crust of bread in the light of a single lamp.

"I had no idea you were living like this," Polynices exclaimed. Parting from his sisters, he walked toward Oedipus. "My father," he said, "may Zeus and Hera have mercy on you. If we can converse, the faults can be healed. Or, at least, they can never be made worse."

On hearing his eldest son's voice, Oedipus deliberately turned to face the other way.

"Please don't turn away from me, father," Polynices pleaded. "Have you no words for me?" When he received no reply, he looked to his siblings. "Dear sisters, can you persuade our father not to send me away, an ignored and dishonored son, without a single response?"

"Tell him why you are here," Antigone urged. "As your words flow, perhaps they will unlock his heart, and his tongue."

"Then I will speak boldly," said Polynices, turning back to his father. "I have come with my allies, who, with seven divisions behind our seven spears, sit encamped at this very moment on the edge of the Theban plain. You will have heard of many of them. There is Amphiaraus, matchless warrior, matchless auger; Tydeus, son of King Oeneus of Calydon; Eteoclus, of Argive birth; and Hippomedon, son of Talaus the Argonaut. Capaneus, the fifth champion, boasts that he will burn Thebes to the ground. The sixth, Parthenopaeus of Arcadia, trusty son of Atalanta, is impatient for war. As for myself, your son—or, if not yours, then child of a dark fate—I lead the fearless army of Argos against Thebes, as I go forth to overthrow my brother, who has thrust me out and robbed me of my fatherland."

To this Oedipus merely snorted with disgust.

"If ever the truth is told by oracles," Polynices continued, "they say that victory will be with those whom you join. So, as a beggar and an exile like yourself, both of us dependent on others for a home, I beg you to listen to my plea. My brother the king mocks us both. But if you aid my quest with just minimal time and effort, I will scatter his strength to the winds! And I will bring you back to your own palace and share it with you. Are you with me? Can I declare that you support me?" His voice began to shake. "Without you, I can never return alive."

Oedipus remained mute and unmoved.

Xenon the elder had followed Polynices into the room; and on hearing what he had proposed, he spoke up. "Oedipus, for the sake of King Theseus, who sent him here, before sending your son on his way, speak, and say what seems best to you in response."

"Had not Theseus sent him to me," Oedipus gravely replied, "never would this man have heard my voice. But now he will be graced with it and hear words that will not gladden his heart." Slowly, he turned in the direction of Polynices. "Villain! Who, when you had the scepter and the throne, which your brother now has in Thebes—"

"But I never had the throne!" Polynices protested.

Ignoring this, Oedipus continued on, his rage growing as he spoke. "You drove me, your own father, into exile! And now you come to me, in tears, an exile yourself. Well, the time for tears has passed. Had these daughters not been born to be my comfort, I would be dead, without any help from you. These girls, my nurses, are men, not women, but you and your brother are aliens, and no sons of mine."

"Father—"

"Therefore, let the eyes of Fate look upon you, if these troops you speak of are indeed moving against Thebes. Never will you be able to overthrow that city! No, first *you* will fall, stained with bloodshed, and your brother the same. Such are the curses that my soul sent out against you both before, and such are the curses I invoke now so that you will revere your parent as your sisters do, and cease to utterly scorn your sightless father. Now, be gone, abhorred by me, and fatherless! Go, vilest of the vile! And take these curses with you that I call down on you now—that never will you vanquish the land of your birth, nor ever return to Argos; that instead you will die by the hand of your own kin and you will slay the one who has driven you out."

The blood had drained from Polynices's cheeks. Turning to his sad-faced sisters, he sought solace. But, unable to influence the old man's increasingly bitter, vengeful, and tangled thinking, they could offer their brother nothing but silent sympathy.

As for Oedipus, he still had more bile to vent. "This is my prayer. I call on the spirits of the Underworld to take you. I call on Ares, who created that dreadful hatred between you brothers, to destroy you both. Go, with these words in your ears. Go, and publish to the Thebans, and yes, to your own staunch allies, that Oedipus has divided such honors between his sons!" Once again, he turned away.

Xenon the elder now stepped up and took the stunned prince by the arm. "Polynices, in what has just passed between your father and yourself, I take no joy. But now, you must go your way, and quickly. There is no more to be said."

Polynices was shaking his head. "What do I tell my comrades?" he said to Xenon as the Colonosian steered him across the courtyard, toward the door. "We set forth from Argos with such high hopes. Now, this! I can't utter a word of this curse to my friends or turn them back. I must go in silence and meet my doom."

"Brother, wait," said Antigone, as she and Ismene hurried to the door and clutched him close.

Looking back at Oedipus across the forecourt, Polynices said, "My sisters, if our father's curses are fulfilled and you can find some way to return to Thebes, please don't dishonor me. Give me burial and due funeral rites."

"Polynices," said Antigone, "hear me in one thing."

"What is it, dearest Antigone? You have only to speak."

"Turn your army back to Argos, at once, and save yourself and Thebes."

"No, it cannot be. For how could I ever again lead the same army against Thebes, if I flinch now?"

"But why, dear brother, would you march against Thebes a second time? What's to be gained from destroying your native city?"

"I can't bear the shame of being an exile, the eldest son, yet mocked by my own brother."

"But don't you see, you'll only enable the fulfillment of his prophecies?" Antigone nodded in the direction of their father. "It means mutual death for Eteocles and yourself."

Polynices shrugged. "Yes, if he wishes it. But I can't back away."

Ismene now entered the conversation. "But who will dare to follow you, hearing such curses as he has uttered?"

"I won't tell my comrades. It's a good leader's role to pass on good news, not bad."

"Brother!" exclaimed an exasperated Antigone.

"You have made up your mind?" asked Ismene.

"Yes," Polynices said. "May Zeus bless you both, if you do as I wish when I'm dead, even if you can't accomplish my wishes while I'm alive. Now let me go." Gently, he disengaged himself from their embrace. "Farewell. Never again will you see me alive." He walked out the door. When Antigone burst into tears, he turned back to her. "Don't cry for me. I go to meet my fate."

"Who would not cry for you, brother," Antigone returned, trying to wipe her eyes, "when you are hurrying knowingly to your death? I don't want to lose you."

"I'm in the hands of Fortune, good or bad. As for you two, I pray to the gods that you never meet ill fortune. For, in all men's eyes, you don't deserve to suffer."

Polynices tramped down the steps to the street, then hurried toward his tethered horse on the northern outskirts of the town, leaving his weeping sisters behind him.

10.

AMBUSH: TYDEUS'S PEACE EMBASSY TO THEBES

At Thebes, the sun was setting. A sumptuous banquet was being staged in the Cadmea's Audience Hall. Eteocles, brother of Polynices and king of Thebes for the past decade, was defying fears of an impending Argive invasion of Theban territory by lavishly drinking and eating with the Spartoi. Beside him reclined his nine-year-old son Laodamas, whose name meant "Tamer of the People." Eteocles had married shortly after he took the throne of Thebes, and his bride, a daughter of one of the Spartoi, had later given birth to this healthy son and tragically died during childbirth. The young king was so devastated by his wife's death that he forbade any mention of her name thereafter.

With Creon yet to return to Thebes from his mission to secure Oedipus from his sanctuary at Colonos, a mission conceived by Eteocles, the king's other senior advisers, including Astacus and Oenops, were close by him as the banquet raged. Into the night, a procession of servants brought meat on platters from the spits in the kitchens beside the hall, and silver cups overflowed with a seemingly endless supply of wine. Now, a messenger from the Electra Gate came to the king, bending to his ear so that he could be heard amid the chatter and laughter around them. The messenger passed on word that a noble visitor was at the gate, bearing the olive branch of peace and seeking a parley with Eteocles.

Calling Astacus and Oenops to him, Eteocles told them, "Tydeus of Calydon has come, seeking to confer with me."

"What can he have to say to you?" Oenops pondered.

"Perhaps he's come to surrender to us," Astacus joked, and the three of them laughed. It was nervous laughter on the part of the two Governors. Despite knowing that the Argive army was just days' march away, Eteocles had not called the men of Thebes to arms, had not announced any plans to march out of the city and do battle with the enemy before they reached the walls of Thebes. It seemed that he hoped, or even believed, that his elder brother was only bluffing, that he would not dare march on Thebes. Eteocles was also hanging on to the hope that Creon would return with Oedipus, and that this would persuade Polynices to turn the Argive army around and go back where he came from.

"Polynices's brother-in-law has bought himself more trouble than he bargained for," Eteocles then said. "Astacus, arm fifty of our finest young men, sons of the Spartoi. Put them in the charge of Maeon, son of Creon's boy Haemon, and Polyphontes, son of Autophones. Send them discreetly out along the Plataea Road, to the sacred grove at Potniae. There, they are to wait in hiding until Tydeus makes his return journey. They are to then intercept him and send him on his way to meet Persephone."[50] Persephone was goddess of the Underworld.

Astacus frowned at the wisdom of the order, which required the killing of Tydeus. But he didn't question it. He merely nodded.

"To give the young men plenty of time to get into position," Eteocles went on, "I will delay our vain friend Tydeus a while."

"It shall be done," Astacus acknowledged with a sigh before hurrying away.

Eteocles then sent the messenger back to the Electra Gate with an invitation for Tydeus to be brought to him. A little while later, Tydeus appeared in the doorway, unarmed but dressed in expensive tunic and cloak with gold on his wrists and around his neck. The Audience Hall fell silent as all eyes turned his way and he swaggered confidently through the door.

"Welcome, Tydeus of Calydon," called Eteocles with a false smile, still reclining on his dining couch. "Stop right there. What can we do for you?"

"Eteocles, noble king," called Tydeus, with a slight bow of the head, "I have come in hope of finding a way of avoiding war between your brother and yourself."

"Is that so? But why should I entertain any proposal from you, a stranger?"

"I speak for my brother-in-law, and for my father-in-law Adrastus, mighty king of Argos, commander of the Argive army that camps on your border, just two days' march from here."

"Then why didn't Adrastus himself come to me, so that one king dealt with another? Or my brother, for that matter? Where is he? Not that I would deign to see him."

Many a noble grinned and chuckled. Eteocles's young son and heir Laodamas giggled in concert with them, even though he was not entirely sure why the adults were laughing.

"Polynices is otherwise engaged," Tydeus responded. "However, you will find that it is only a matter of time before I gain the throne of Calydon. You see before you a king in waiting."

Eteocles laughed, his nobles laughed with him, and his son with them before the expression of the king of Thebes hardened. "You will need to prove your worthiness before you can speak with me as an equal, Calydonian."

"And what do I have to do to prove myself your equal?"

"We hear tell that you won the Pyx at the funerary games of Ophelles, at Nemea."

Tydeus smiled. "I most certainly did. And I would challenge any man here to test his skill in the ring with me."

"Then, are you prepared to take on Thebes's finest boxer, here, now? Win that contest, and perhaps we two can speak about my brother, as one victor to another."

This brought a frown to Tydeus's face. "One victor to another?"

Eteocles smiled. "Was I not victor over my princely brother in the contest for the Theban throne? In my case, my wits were my weapons. Well, what say you to the contest? Or is it not a warrior I see before me?"

Tydeus was weary from traveling all day, but it was one of his strengths, and one of his weaknesses, that he never shied from a challenge. "Bring on your champion!"

Eteocles motioned to one of his dinner guests. A tall Theban noble rose up, smiling. Both men proceeded to strip naked, and attendants rubbed them with oil as the dining couches were cleared away. Eteocles and his dinner guests then formed a circle around the two contestants as they stood toe to toe.

Tydeus's taller opponent had greater reach than he did. But he was flat-footed, and Tydeus was able to dance around the man, jabbing his bound fist into the face of the Theban, snapping the man's head back time and again. The Theban's patience exploded. With a frustrated roar, he swung wildly at Tydeus, who ducked and weaved away from each flying fist. And then, as the man stood open to him after another wild swing, Tydeus put the full force of his powerful shoulder into a right uppercut. This lifted the Theban off the ground and sent him sprawling onto his back, to lie unconscious at Eteocles' feet. There was a groan of disappointment from the partisan spectators.

Unbinding his right hand and watching the boxer being carried away, Tydeus smiled. "Now, noble king, may we speak about the throne?"

Eteocles shrugged. "Was that skill, or luck, we just witnessed, Calydonian? We have a fine wrestler in our midst. Defeat that Theban champion, and prove to me that you are a true champion."

"Bring on your champion," Tydeus responded with a grin, taking the bait.

So a member of the Spartoi who had yet to reach middle age and had a reputation as a wrestler stepped forward, stripped off, and was oiled. On the command from Eteocles, the pair began to circle each other, hunched over and with hands outstretched to secure a grip. But Tydeus, the shorter man, was able to avoid most of his opponent's attempts to land a grip by pushing his hands away and ducking and weaving, to the Theban's growing frustration.

And then, to more groans from the spectators, Tydeus expertly slipped around behind his opponent, tripped him up, and pressed him to the floor. Twice more in quick succession Tydeus put the man down. That was three falls to none. Tydeus had won the contest, with ease.

"Now, will you speak to me about your brother and the throne of Thebes?" demanded Tydeus as he toweled himself down, his patience growing thin. "War, and the destruction of Thebes, can be averted if you will agree to share your throne with Polynices, as he originally proposed—"

Eteocles interrupted him. "How do I know that he would surrender the throne to me every other year or that my son will be permitted to succeed me? Where is the guarantee?"

Tydeus was tempted to say that Polynices was not like Eteocles and would keep his word once he gave it. But he didn't. Instead, he said, "I will guarantee to you that I will personally ensure that your brother steps down every alternate year, if your uncle Creon guarantees that you will do the same."

Eteocles shook his head. "I do not answer to Creon and never will," he growled. "As for you, Calydonian, you have no standing in this court. I might as well accept the guarantee of a cook or an actor. Or my brother's horse!"

The watching Spartoi erupted in sarcastic laughter.

"He is no better than a horse!" cackled young Laodamas with glee, looking around the nobles for approval.

Tydeus had defied his ill-founded reputation as a man with a temper and remained remarkably calm up to this point. But he still had his pride. Now his pride told him that Eteocles had been toying with him and had set out to humiliate him. How many ambassadors, after all, were required to negotiate in the nude? This convinced him that Eteocles had no intention of giving up his throne—not for a year, nor even for a day. "I have wasted my time," Tydeus declared, commencing to dress. "I will therefore waste no more of yours."

"Yes, go! Go back to your weakling of a brother-in-law," said Eteocles, walking away. "And tell him that Cadmus's people reject him and reject any proposition he has to make. Any man who threatens to destroy Thebes is no son of Thebes and has no right to rule her."

As armed men of the Cadmean Guard appeared beside Tydeus and hustled him toward the door, Tydeus, bitter now, called over his shoulder: "I look forward to reducing your feeble city to rubble, brick by brick, as Adrastus and the Seven have sworn to do, and to seeing Polynices carry your head, Eteocles, on the end of his spear."

Eteocles swung back Tydeus's way. "If you had not come to us under the protection of the olive branch—" he exclaimed.

"You would have ordered me killed—is that it?" Tydeus shot back.

Now Eteocles smiled, knowing what awaited Tydeus on the Plataea Road. "Safe journey, Tydeus of Calydon," he said.

Tydeus was escorted down to the Electra Gate, where a friendly gatekeeper had kept his weapons and watered and fed his horse. Rearming himself outside the gate, Tydeus mounted up. On either side of the Electra Gate, a deep entrenchment line formed part of a dry moat that the Thebans had recently dug with feverish haste around the wall of their city, and Tydeus noted with the interest of a military commander that the only way an attacking army could reach the walls of Thebes was via the thin strip of earth that crossed the trench at each of the seven gates.

Daring not to stay close to the city, let alone think about grabbing some sleep before he undertook his journey, he urged his steed forward, fully resolved to ride through the night, back to the protection of the Argive army's camp at Erythrae. From above, a horned moon would provide enough light for the early part of his journey. When the sun rose on a lengthening early summer's day, he planned to go from walk to canter.

He was just a mile into his journey through the darkness, following the Plataea Road south, when he came upon the village of Potniae, which straddled the River Dirce. There was a temple to Dionysus in

Potniae and a grove of trees on the riverbank sacred to Demeter, goddess of agriculture and fertility, and also to her daughter Persephone, queen of the Underworld. As Tydeus and his horse drew closer to the water crossing, he saw moonlight glint from metal in the trees. He knew then that he was about to have company.

11.

THE DEATH OF OEDIPUS

The day after Polynices departed from Colonos, his father Oedipus awoke feeling very unwell. The twin trials of the confrontations with his brother-in-law and his son had drained Oedipus of energy and sapped his will to live. That morning, he sent a request to King Theseus in nearby Athens.

Oedipus asked the Athenian king to take him, with his daughters Antigone and Ismene, to Thoricos, a small town on the coast southeast of Athens overlooking the Aegean Sea. Thoricos had been one of the twelve settlements around Athens that Theseus, once he became king and quickly expanded the city's power, brought under the immediate control of the Athenian throne. At Thoricos there was a sanctuary sacred to Demeter and Persephone, and it regularly received pilgrims from throughout Greece. Oedipus, you see, was ready to make the acquaintance of Persephone, by entering the Underworld.

Theseus came, bringing a fleet of chariots, and in these Oedipus, his daughters, and the king made the overnight journey to Thoricos accompanied by selected courtiers. Dark clouds were gathering overhead when, late in the afternoon, they arrived outside the town, whose houses sat in unplanned disorder on narrow, winding streets. Oedipus was helped down from his chariot, and, guided by Theseus, who took his arm, he slowly walked toward the sanctuary of Demeter and Persephone.[51]

This sanctuary was in a deep and craggy chasm in the cliffs at the seashore. From the heights, the unseen depths of the sanctuary were reached by a stairway fashioned from bronze, which wound down the cliff face. On one of the many paths on the eastern side of the chasm, midway between it and the massive, flat-topped Thorican Stone (from where the mythical hero Cephalus was said to have been carried off by the gods to join them in the heavens), Theseus described to blind Oedipus a brightly painted rectangular marble tomb and the hollowed-out trunk of a pear tree that they had reached. Here, with the aid of the king, Oedipus decided to halt. Sinking down, he settled on a rock. Then, loosening his clothes, he called for his daughters.

When Antigone and Ismene joined him, with all the members of the king's party gathered in the background, Oedipus said, "Daughters, find a fount. Bring me water so that I might wash myself in preparation and make a drink offering to the gods."

These, his daughters knew, were funeral rites, usually performed by female members of the family of the dead on a corpse after death. The sisters, stunned by their father's determination to die but obedient to his wishes, were guided back to the lower slope of Demeter's Hill, as the acropolis of Thoricos was known, to a spring from which they drew water. Bringing the water to their father, the pair then washed and dressed Oedipus in preparation for making an offering to Demeter and Persephone.

"My children," Oedipus sadly said, "on this day your father's life ends. No more will you have the burden of tending me—no light burden, I know all too well. Yet, one little word voids all those toils: *love*. Love you have had from me—and from no one else. Now, you will have me with you no more, through all your days to come."

As he spoke, thunder rumbled and lightning flashed. The sisters burst into tears and clung to their seated parent's knees. Antigone and Ismene were distraught not because of the electrical storm but because their father had come here to end his life and leave them to the vicissitudes of fortune. As women traditionally did at Greek funerals, they wailed and beat their chests.

Oedipus soothed them with low words, then called Theseus forward. "My friend, please give your right hand to my daughters as a solemn pledge, and you, daughters, give your right hand to the king. Promise, Theseus, never to forsake them of your free will, but to do all things for their good."

The king duly took hold of Antigone by the right hand and made just such a promise, then did the same with Ismene.

Oedipus then reached out to his daughters, saying, weakly, "My children, now you must be brave and take your leave from here, so that you cannot see or hear what must follow. Only Theseus can remain, as is his right, to witness those things that are to be."

Sobbing, Antigone and Ismene reluctantly parted from their father, and, with all the members of Theseus's party formed around them, also in tears, they walked away. After a little distance, they all looked back. Oedipus was no longer visible. He had commenced to slowly wend his way down the stairway into the sanctuary's basin and had disappeared from view. Theseus remained where they had left him, his hand raised to shade his eyes from the setting sun, which poked through an opening in the dark clouds. Then Theseus dropped to his knees, touched the stony ground with his forehead, and began offering a prayer to Demeter and her daughter, as if he had witnessed something devastating.

As Antigone and Ismene gripped each other by the arms and walked back to the waiting chariots, Ismene asked the members of the king's party around them, "Are we to know how our father met his doom?"

"My lady," said Xenon the elder, "by what manner Oedipus perished no man can tell, apart from Theseus. No fiery thunderbolt from Zeus removed him, nor did any storm rise up from the sea to claim him. Perhaps he was taken by a messenger from the gods or from the Underworld. But I can say that it must have been quick, and you can be grateful that he passed without sickness or suffering."

This was some consolation for Antigone and Ismene. They never guessed that Oedipus had deliberately thrown himself from the stairway, to die on the rocks far below. Antigone only spoke of "some swift, strange doom" that had overtaken their father.

As the sisters stood waiting for Theseus to join them, Ismene was distraught. "I wish that Hades would join me in death with my father!" she declared. "I can't live the life that now must be mine."

"Come, now, best of daughters," said Xenon. "Heaven planned it this way. You two loving sisters haven't been put through as much as you have, for you to now fret about your future." As far as Xenon was concerned, the sisters had been set free by the death of their possessive and divisive father.

Ismene, wiping her eyes, looked at her elder sister. "Then, what new fates do you think await us, Antigone, fatherless as we now are?"

"Sister," Antigone replied, "let's hurry back. My soul is filled with a longing to return."

"Return to where?"

"To the dark house of our father."

"Rejoin the royal house of Thebes! But how do you think we could do that? Is it even lawful? Aren't we officially exiled from Thebes?"

Antigone threw her hands in the air. "Then lead me out and kill me too!"

"The gods help me!" Ismene despaired. "Friendless and helpless, where am I to live my unhappy life? Where am I to flee?"

"Fear not, children," said Xenon. "You already have a refuge. No harm can befall you here. You are under the protection of Athens."

"We should go home," said Antigone with determination. "But I can't imagine how."

"Then don't go," Xenon countered.

Antigone looked to the dark sky. "Zeus, which way shall we turn?"

Theseus now came to rejoin them. "Weep no more, girls," he said, trying to cheer them. "For where the kindness of the Dark Powers is an abiding grace to the quick and the dead, there is no room for mourning. Divine anger would follow." Oedipus, he was saying, was in a better place now that he was in the embrace of the spirits of the Underworld, and his children should be happy for him.

Theseus informed Oedipus's daughters that he would have the old man's body recovered, after which he would cremate it in secret, with full rites, interring the remains in an unidentified tomb. When Antigone asked if they would be able to see their father's tomb once he was in it, Theseus said no. He told her that Oedipus had made him swear to always keep its location a secret—from everyone.

"If that pleases the dead," said Antigone with a sad sigh, looking at Ismene, "we must be content. But, we beg you, Majesty, send us back to Thebes. Perhaps we can hinder the bloodshed threatened between our brothers."

Ismene, although unsure about their future there, nodded her silent agreement to this.

Surprised, Theseus said, "I will if it is what you wish, as well as anything else that may be of profit to you. I'm obliged to spare no pains to please the friend who has now gone from us."

So Antigone and Ismene returned to Colonos for the time being, and Theseus sent heralds galloping to find Polynices at Erythrae and Eteocles at Thebes. The heralds were to inform the brothers that their father was dead and that Theseus was sending their sisters back to Thebes, adding that Theseus had sworn to protect Antigone and Ismene and would hold their brothers responsible for their safety. A caravan was then prepared. With chariots, cavalry, and royal Athenian bodyguards, Antigone, Ismene, and Ismene's servant set off to make the return to Thebes.

On the sisters' arrival back in Thebes, their uncle Creon asserted his right under the law to act as their guardian, being their eldest living male relative. He then promptly betrothed his son Haemon to Antigone. She, as Creon's ward, had no say in the matter. But at least Eteocles accepted his sisters' return to Thebes and back into his family, albeit with the servants he assigned to them briefed to report all the sisters saw, did, and said. For the moment, they were safe.

12.

IN THE ARGIVE ARMY'S CAMP

⌐⌐⌐

At the camp at Erythrae, Parthenopaeus was bored. Both Polynices and Tydeus were still away on their peace missions; Amphiaraus had again lapsed into depression and spoke with no one; Eteoclus had nothing in common with Parthenopaeus. And neither Capaneus nor Hippomedon, who appeared less willing than Adrastus to believe that King Talaus had fathered Parthenopaeus, gave him any of their time. Not that Parthenopaeus had come on this expedition to make friends. All he wanted was action—and plenty of it.

By day, the young Arcadian went through drills with his armorbearer. At night, he wandered around the campfires of the men of his division, listening to their conversations. It never ceased to amaze and amuse him that ordinary folk had strong opinions of people they had never met, places they had never been, and events they had never witnessed. But then, campfire storytelling and discourse were the primary sources of entertainment for the people of these times.[52]

"Personally," Parthenopaeus heard one Argive spearman say, as he and his comrades sat around their campfire several nights into the pause in the army's march at Erythrae, "I've never believed that Oedipus killed a Sphinx to gain the crown of Thebes. I think the Sphinx was an invention."

"You don't believe that Hades sent a fiend from hell to plague the men of Thebes?" asked another man, sounding incredulous.[53]

"She may have been a fiend," said the first man, "but I think she was probably a female highway robber who lived in the hills and preyed on the roads to Thebes. And it was she who posed the riddle to humiliate her victims before she killed them."

"You may be right," another foot soldier agreed. "I heard that Theseus of Athens long ago killed a female highway robber called Phaea the Sow, in Crommyonia. In the same way, the Sphinx could have been a woman."

"I heard," a third man piped up, "that Phaea was an old woman who owned a boar called the Crommyonian Sow, and it was Phaea's boar that Theseus killed."

"No, no, no," said another soldier, "that story has been confused by someone with the tale of Theseus capturing the Marathonian Bull on Crete. *That* beast was owned by an old woman. What was her name? It began with H. . . ."

"She was called Hecales," volunteered yet another man.

"That was it—Hecales."[54]

"Both Phaea and the Sphinx were highway robbers, I'm sure of it," said the first man. "But it would be just like the Thebans to invent the story of Oedipus outwitting and slaying a real live Sphinx, just to try to make him appear the equal of the likes of genuine heroes such as Theseus and our own King Adrastus. After all, we have all encountered a boar and a bull or two in our time. But who, apart from the mad king Oedipus, has encountered a Sphinx?"

"You believe the Sphinx was a female highway robber?" scoffed another man. "One with a taste for riddles? A woman holding an entire city in her sway? A woman with the same ability with arms as men? No woman could do that!"

"My mother Atalanta did," said Parthenopaeus from behind them. All in the circle turned his way as he stepped from the darkness into the golden glow of the firelight. "She not only equaled men with her skills with bow and spear, she could outrun any man. After her father instructed her to marry, Atalanta would challenge men to running races wearing armor and helmet and carrying a spear, promising to marry the first competitor to beat her. She would even give them a head start.

But she would always overtake them, and kill them with her spear as she passed."

This brought gasps from around the fire.

"Only one man outran Atalanta," Parthenopaeus continued. "That was my stepfather Hippomenes, one of the warriors involved in the Hunt of the Calydonian Boar. When they raced, he didn't outrun her as much as outwit her. Or, so he thought. As he ran, he dropped three golden apples along the way. My mother stopped to gather up each apple, so of course Hippomenes won the race and won Atalanta's hand in marriage. I have always believed that my mother wanted to lose that race. She ended up with the man she had fallen in love with, and the three golden apples he let fall! But Hippomenes could claim to have outrun her."[55]

"So, she got the man and his gold!" exclaimed one soldier. "A clever woman, your mother, commander."

Again his comrades laughed, and nodded their agreement.

"In the same way, who believes that Oedipus had no idea he had slain his own father?" asked the proponent of the theory that the Sphinx had been a highway robber. "He must have suspected, from the moment he reached Thebes and learned that Laius had been killed on the road, that he had been the man's killer."

"You seem to know a great deal about Oedipus," said his bristling critic. "Do you also dispute that he answered the famous riddle?"

"Oh, I suspect the riddle was real enough," returned the first soldier. "Riddles are the things of women's spinning rooms, the sort of thing women invent among themselves to pass the time. And Oedipus had the wits to work out the female robber's riddle. Having murdered four men on the road from Delphi, he turned the Sphinx into a flying beast to make himself sound heroic to the Thebans. Remember, only her pretty woman's head was later seen in Thebes, not her body, which Oedipus could have disposed of."

"And Creon was happy to embrace the myth of the Spinx and make Oedipus king," another man concurred, "thus wiping the unpleasant and unloved Laius from popular memory."

"What do you think, commander?" asked one young soldier.

"I think," Parthenopaeus answered, "that if you men know as much about fighting as you do about legendary deeds, then before long you will be helping me create new legends at the walls of Thebes!"

The soldiers all cheered loudly.

As Parthenopaeus walked away, he looked to the night sky above and admired its blanket of sparkling stars, the Milky Way. It reminded him of his wife back at home in Argos, who was soon to give birth to their next child. All Greeks knew how the Milky Way had come by its name. According to myth, Zeus, who had fathered the boy Heracles to the mortal woman Alcmene, let the baby suckle at the breast of his wife the goddess Hera while she slept in the heavens so the child could gain some of her godly powers. When Hera awoke and found another woman's child at her breast, she violently pulled it away. As she did so, her breast milk spread across the heavens, creating the Milky Way.

The following afternoon, one of Parthenopaeus's men ran to him with the news that Tydeus had returned to camp. Joining thousands of soldiers, Parthenopaeus hurried to the tent of King Adrastus, where Adrastus and Tydeus stood on a mound of earth, surveying the gathering troops.

"Brother soldiers," Tydeus began, "before you stands a man who went to Thebes bearing the olive branch of an ambassador of peace, and who, on his return, was attacked by fifty Thebans who lay in wait to kill him!"

Shouts of dismay erupted throughout the army, and clenched fists were raised in anger. It took Adrastus to raise his hands to quiet the crowd before Tydeus could go on.

"But they chose the wrong man to ambush," Tydeus resumed, "as these trophies attest." To cheers and applause, he held high an armored cuirass before discarding it with disdain and then raising a large oval shield. The sight of the wolf design on this shield brought a roar from the soldiery—a triumphant roar.

To a Greek warrior, his shield was his most precious possession. It was an extension of himself, a reflection of his identity, and it hung proudly on his wall until he was called to arms by his king. If, in battle, a warrior threw away his shield and ran for his life, he was considered by friend and foe alike to have abandoned all right to mercy. When the warriors of the city of Sparta went to war, they swore an oath that they would return home either with their shield or on it (dead). When a Greek army achieved a victory over its opponents, it ensconced the captured shields of enemy commanders in its shrines and temples. And when it raised a funeral pyre for its own dead warriors, that pyre was built from captured shields of the enemy. The emblem painted with care on a Greek noble's shield was his opportunity to make a statement about his origins, his pride, his lethal intent, and sometimes about past victories.

This particular shield that Tydeus now held aloft had been made, like most Greek shields of war, using a wicker frame reinforced with bronze, over which was stretched a hardened leather facing. It had previously been the property of Maeon, son of Haemon, and its wolf emblem was a symbol of Thebes.

Tydeus told his audience of his meeting with Eteocles in the Cadmea, of the contests required by Eteocles and won by Tydeus before Eteocles sent him away without any attempt to negotiate peace. He told of spotting armed men waiting in the sacred grove at Potniae on the Plataea Road—fifty young men in their late teens who emerged wielding their weapons. He told of riding down the youths in front, killing several with his spear, before jumping off and bounding up a rocky rise from where he threw down rocks on his assailants and speared all who tried to reach him.

Tydeus told of killing one young son of Theban nobility after another, in a flurry of blood, using stone, spear, and sword. Sparks literally flew as metal clashed with metal, starting a fire in the dry undergrowth.

Several terrified young survivors threw down their weapons and attempted to surrender, only for Tydeus to plunge his sword into the throats of all but one. The lone youth permitted to live was Maeon, son of Haemon and grandson of Creon.[56]

"This is what I said to that sole survivor before I sent him home," Tydeus told his troops. "'The dawn will see you spared by my mercy, Theban. Tell your commander to pile earth before your gates, to take up weapons and inspect your walls for signs of aging. Draft your best men and multiply your battle lines. Look how this grove smokes from my sword. See how *we* manage war!'"[57]

The army roared its approval, and Parthenopaeus and the four other members of the Seven who were present roared with them. As Adrastus and Tydeus walked back to the king's tent, Tydeus declared that war with Thebes was now inevitable. But the wise Adrastus counseled awaiting the outcome of Polynices's mission to Oedipus before making any move that they might regret. He needed to know where the old man stood in this conflict before launching the next stage of the campaign.

The following afternoon, Polynices arrived back at the camp. He had left Erythrae before Tydeus had departed for Thebes, and he should have arrived back before Tydeus did. But reluctant to lie to his friends about what his father had said, and hoping not to have to reveal the dark curses that Oedipus had called down on his brother and himself, he had dawdled on his return from Colonos, taking days longer than he needed to.

Polynices went directly to Adrastus and in private dejectedly informed the king that his father Oedipus would support neither himself nor Eteocles, which was no lie. But then Polynices declared that he had decided to go to Thebes and surrender himself to Eteocles, who could thereafter do whatever he chose to do with him. To Polynices's mind, this would thwart his father's curse, leave at least one of the brothers alive, and ensure that their sisters had a brother and protector. This way, too, he reasoned, war with Thebes would be averted, the city would be left standing, and the lives of all his friends of the Seven preserved.

Adrastus immediately balked at this proposition. He had no doubts that Eteocles would promptly put Polynices to death if he handed himself over. And this, the king reminded Polynices, would leave Adrastus's daughter Argia a widow and his grandsons, the sons of Polynices, without a father. Adrastus would not countenance such a wasteful sacrifice by Polynices, no matter how well-intended it might be. The Argive king also had to remind Polynices that he had sworn an oath to his brother-in-law Tydeus that he would help him claim the throne of Calydon, which he couldn't very well do if he voluntarily handed himself over to Eteocles. Polynices had to acknowledge that he had no choice but to go ahead with the campaign against Thebes. Besides, Adrastus doubted that he could restrain his army from attacking Thebes, no matter what Polynices did.

Adrastus now called a meeting of the Seven in his tent, where he had Polynices tell his comrades that his father would not be supporting either Eteocles or Polynices.

"At last!" cried Parthenopaeus on hearing of Oedipus's apparent neutrality. "Now there is nothing to prevent us from attacking Thebes."

The meeting between the king and the Seven was still in progress when the messenger arrived from King Theseus of Athens. Adrastus read the message, then solemnly announced to the Seven that Polynices's father was dead and that King Theseus was sending Polynices's sisters back to Thebes, at their own request.

This changed everything as far as the movement of the Argive army was concerned. Greek religious practice at this time required female members of the family to perform rites for the dead on the third, ninth, thirteenth, and thirtieth days after the death of a loved one. During that period, these family members could not go out and mix with others. Once Antigone and Ismene were back at Thebes, they would undertake these rites. Polynices, realizing this, told Adrastus that he could not in good conscience attack Thebes while his sisters were carrying out those duties. Adrastus decided that the army would have to stay put while the thirty-day mourning period was observed at Thebes.

This dismayed some of his troops and disappointed others, Parthenopaeus among them. A small number of volunteers from distant cities would indeed melt away in the coming days and go home. But the bulk of the army remained in good spirits, with Adrastus promising that the plundering of Theban territory would be his first priority, once the army was again on the move.

Then, within days, a messenger arrived from Eteocles at Thebes. Eteocles let it be known that once the mourning period for Oedipus had ended the following month, he would conduct funerary games for his late father, at Thebes, and he was sending invitations to men with royal blood throughout Greece to participate. But, he said, no man who had sworn to destroy Thebes would be welcome. Of course, he knew that Adrastus and the Seven had all sworn to do just that.

Adrastus realized that Eteocles was trying to gain credit throughout Greece with his Oedipan funerary games while at the same time making Argos look bad through its absence from the games. But Adrastus was much too clever, much too experienced, to be outwitted by Eteocles. He sent a messenger galloping to Argos, instructing his brother Mecisteus to represent Argos at Oedipus's funerary games. Mecisteus had not sworn to destroy Thebes, and as a prince of Argos he was perfectly qualified to compete in the games.

In July, Mecisteus would depart Argos in his chariot to take part in the games. In his absence he would leave one of the remaining Argive nobles in charge of the city. En route to Thebes via Mount Cithaeron, Mecisteus paused at the Erythrae camp to consult with Adrastus. Before Mecisteus continued to Thebes, he discussed with his brother one last attempt to secure a truce between Eteocles and Polynices and a resolution to their dispute over the Theban throne.

13.

JOCASTA'S PEACE CONFERENCE

Oedipus's funerary games were conducted over three days in July on the plain outside the walls of Thebes. Like the games of Ophelles that had been conducted at Nemea, they consisted of seven events. The boxing contest was won by Mecisteus of Argos, and it was with reluctance that King Eteocles of Thebes presented him with the victor's crown.[58]

Once Mecisteus reached Thebes for the games, he had discreetly sent a message to Jocasta, widow of Oedipus and mother of Eteocles and Polynices, asking whether she would be prepared to broker a peace parley between her two sons at Thebes. Pressured by her daughters Antigone and Ismene, who were by this time living in the house of their uncle and now guardian Creon, Jocasta replied to Mecisteus that she was indeed prepared to host talks between her sons. She would persuade Eteocles to recognize the olive branch that Polynices carried to the meeting and declare a temporary truce between the pair.[59]

As a consequence, once Mecisteus left the site of the Games of Oedipus, he took Jocasta's response back to the Argive army camp at Erythrae. When Adrastus was aware of Jocasta's willingness to act as intermediary, he immediately dispatched Polynices to Thebes, unarmed and under the protection of the olive branch as Greek tradition required. Adrastus dictated the terms that Polynices could offer Eteocles once they met: to prevent the destruction of Thebes by the Argive army, the two brothers were to alternate on the Theban throne, with each occupying it for a year at a time. Eteocles would also be required to dig into the rich Theban treasury and pay off every member of the Argive army to ensure that they would march away and leave Thebes unharmed.

So that Polynices would not be ambushed on his return as Tydeus had been, Adrastus sent a large cavalry contingent with his son-in-law. As Polynices approached the city, these cavalrymen waited at the village of Potniae, the very place where Tydeus had been set upon by the fifty youths of Thebes.

On his arrival, Polynices was taken in through the Electra Gate to a house just to the gate's left, close by a sanctuary dedicated to Heracles. This house had reputedly once been occupied by Heracles's mother Alcmenes and stepfather Amphitryon, and was considered holy ground. Here, Polynices found his mother waiting for him. Jocasta had shorn her silvered hair drastically short, and her clothes were black. She was a woman in mourning. But, as much as she mourned her late son/husband, she also mourned the divide that separated her sons and threatened her city.[60]

"Oh, my son, my son," cried Jocasta as the pair was tearfully reunited for the first time in more than ten years. As they embraced and cried tears born of both joy and sadness, Jocasta said, "I hear that you have taken an alien for your wife and are fathering children. They told me you courted a foreign alliance. You must know that this is an endless sorrow for me, your mother, and would have been for your late grandfather Laius as well, to have this marriage foisted on us. It wasn't my hand that lit the marriage torch for you. There was no part for the holy waters of Thebes's Ismenus River to play in your wedding bath. The streets of Thebes were silent when your young bride entered her bridal home for the first time."[61]

Polynices tried to sidestep his mother's disappointment with him by focusing on the reason for this meeting, the rift between his brother and himself. "How terrible, dear mother, is hatred between those once near and dear. How hard it makes all reconciliation."

"Some god with evil intent is plaguing the family of Oedipus," she sadly replied. "But a man's dearest treasure, it seems, is his country. How is it you went to Argos? What was your plan?"

"I don't know. I can only think that some god summoned me there in accordance with my destiny. Besides, poverty is a curse. Noble breeding wouldn't find me food. Now it's against my own city that I'm marching. I call on heaven to witness that it is not willingly that I have raised my arm against the family that I love." He stood back and looked her in the eye. "It's to you, mother, that belongs the task of dissolving this unhappy feud by reconciling brothers who love each other—to end my troubles, and yours, and this city's."

They were interrupted by a servant who announced that Eteocles had arrived. Moments later, the king of Thebes walked in the door behind Polynices, wearing his armor and carrying the golden scepter of the ruler of Thebes. Polynices heard his brother make his entrance but didn't look his way. Instead, Polynices continued to face his mother.

Eteocles likewise failed to acknowledge his brother. Looking exclusively at Jocasta, he said, "Mother, I am here. But it's only to please you that I've come. What do you want me to do? Let someone commence the conference. I've interrupted my work organizing the citizens for the coming fight to hear what you have to say in arbitration between us. It was only because you persuaded me that I let this fellow within our walls."

Jocasta scowled at her youngest son. "Eteocles, do away with that fierce look on your face and that manufactured rage. This isn't the Gorgon's head of Argos you see before you; it's your own brother. And you, Polynices, turn and face your brother. I would give you one piece of advice—when a man who is angry with his friend confronts the friend face to face, he should keep in mind the reason for his coming and forget all other quarrels."

Slowly, Polynices turned to face Eteocles, and the pair stood glaring at each other.

"Now," said Jocasta. "Polynices, my son, speak first, for you've come at the head of a foreign army, alleging wrongful treatment." She raised her eyes. "And may some god serve as judge and resolve the trouble between you."

"The facts are simple," Polynices began, "and they need no subtle interpretation. Years ago, I provided for his interests and for mine in our father's palace. I allowed Eteocles to rule our country for one full year on condition that I would then take the scepter in turn. But he, after consenting to this and calling on the gods to witness his oath, kept none of his promises and kept the sovereignty for himself. Even now I'm prepared to dismiss my army from this land and take my turn in the palace as we originally agreed, instead of ravaging the country and placing scaling ladders against the city's towers—as I will do if I'm not accorded my rights. I call the gods to witness that despite my doing the honorable thing in everything, I'm being robbed of my rights by ungodly fraud!" He returned his gaze to Jocasta. "There, Mother, I have stated my case on its merits, without resorting to fancy words."

"Your argument is sensible," said Jocasta, nodding, before looking to Eteocles. "And your response, my son?"

Confidently returning his mother's gaze, Eteocles produced a wry smile. "If everyone was unanimous on what constitutes honor and wisdom, men would never disagree," he began. "But fairness and equality don't exist in this world beyond the words. There is really no such thing. For instance, Mother, I will tell you this quite openly—I would ascend to the rising of the stars and the sun or dive beneath the earth, if I were able to do so, to win the power of a monarch, foremost in all divine things. Therefore, Mother, I will never yield this blessing to another but will keep it for myself. Besides, what foul disgrace it would be to glorious Thebes if I should hand my scepter over to him through fear of Argive might. He should not, Mother, have attempted reconciliation with armed force. Still, if he chooses to live here on other terms, he may. But I will never willingly let go of the scepter! Never will I become his slave when I can be his master! Never!" He glanced back at

Polynices. "Bring on fire and sword! Harness your steeds, fill the plains with chariots! For I will never give up my throne. If we must do wrong in life, to do so for a kingdom is the fairest cause."

While Polynices silently fumed, Jocasta sighed and said, "Eteocles, my son, suppose I put before you two alternatives? One is to rule, the other is to save this city. Do you still say 'rule'? Will you see all Thebes a captive and her women brutally raped for the sake of your scepter? And you, Polynices, you have shown little sense in coming to lay waste to your own city. If, on the other hand, your army is defeated, how can you return to Argos? Oh, my children, lay aside your deadly dispute, I pray you!"

"Mother," Eteocles responded irritably, "the time for negotiation has passed. Your good intentions are useless, for we shall never be reconciled, unless on the terms already named—that I keep the scepter and be king of this land. So stop your tedious warnings, and let me be." Returning his burning glare to Polynices, he snarled, "As for you, either get yourself outside these walls or die!"

"And who will kill me?" Polynices snapped back.

"You are very near him. Yes, very near. See this sword arm?" He shook his right arm in his brother's face.

"I see it. Whoever kills me will meet the self-same fate."

Eteocles laughed. "Relying on the truce that saves you, you've become a boaster."

"One last time, I call on you to return my scepter and share the kingdom."

"I have nothing to return. It's all mine. Go!"

"I'm being driven from my city."

"And I'll kill you, to boot!"

Polynices looked to the ceiling and called to the heavens: "O, Father, can you hear what I'm suffering?" Perhaps, he thought, his father might lift his curse from the grave should he be aware of Eteocles's treatment of him.

"Don't mention our father," Eteocles bellowed. "Get yourself back to Argos!"

"I'm going. But thank you, Mother. To you, at least, I bid farewell."
Briefly, Polynices embraced his mother.

"I'm born to sorrow," wailed Jocasta. "Endless sorrow!"

"I'll prepare to meet you before the walls," said Polynices, as he
brushed past his brother, heading for the door, "and deliver your death."

"My own thoughts exactly," Eteocles crowed.

"My sons, what are you doing?" cried Jocasta.

But Polynices had departed, and without another word Eteocles
turned and strode after him. They left Jocasta alone and in tears, convinced that soon one of her sons would be dead, and fearful that Thebes would before long be a city in ruins and her people would be in
chains.[62]

14.

SEVEN GATES, SEVEN CHAMPIONS

Once Polynices arrived back at the Erythrae camp after the failed peace negotiations between his brother and himself, King Adrastus ordered the army to march at dawn the next day. Its invasion of Theban territory was now unstoppable. As the army marched, Adrastus's brother Mecisteus would march with it. Mecisteus had remained at Erythrae to await the outcome of the peace parley that he had helped set up. With the failure of that meeting, Mecisteus persuaded his elder brother to permit him to remain with the army and join the campaign against Thebes. He not only brought one more chariot to the army, he also brought an experienced head when it came to war.

Mecisteus's strategic advice influenced the line of march that Adrastus now chose to make. Instead of taking the direct route to Thebes from Mount Cithaeron straight up the Plataea Road across the exposed plain, when the army moved out from its Erythrae campsite and tramped down onto the plain it turned sharply right and marched along below Mount Cithaeron to the east. It would then turn north. Marching along the eastern edge of the Theban Plain, it would make for the Teumessus Hills.

By taking this roundabout route, Adrastus would avoid having to make camp on exposed flat terrain in the middle of the plain, which would invite attack. Adrastus's own scouts were telling him that Eteocles was staying put in Thebes, either daring the Argives to advance on his city, or through fear of battle. To mask the Argive army's movements, patrols would be sent out to capture Theban scouts, keeping

Eteocles guessing on which route they were taking. If the army went unchallenged as hoped, it would reach the town of Teumessus, which occupied high ground in the homonymous hills. The town was just one day's solid march northeast of Thebes via the Chalcis Road.

The use of this route east and north bypassed Thebes and was also intended to surprise and unsettle the Thebans. To increase that surprise and cover his march, as the army headed east, Adrastus sent his cavalry ranging up the Plataea Road in search of Theban scouts. Sure enough, they encountered a group of scouts who had dismounted to water their horses, and the Argive cavalry swept down on them. Every Theban scout but one was killed. Their horses and the lone survivor were taken east to the marching Argive army, the horses to be added to Argive cavalry mounts, the scout to be questioned.[63]

As the army marched, the infantry spread out, with the baggage train trundling along behind them. The cavalry led the way, with the chariots rolling along on the flanks and in the rear to protect against enemy cavalry attack.[64]

The captured Theban cavalryman was interrogated by Adrastus and the Seven once the army halted at noon to make their overnight camp. This frightened fellow revealed that as he and his comrades of the scouting party had departed Thebes that morning, hundreds of heavily armed troops had arrived at the city. These men were mercenaries, recruited by Eteocles's agents in Phocis and farther afield at the city of Phlegra in Thrace. The Minyan ancestors of the Phlegrans had historic links with both Thebes and Mycenae as settlers, but it was Eteocles's gold that had brought these men to the city, not any thoughts of shared history.[65]

The mercenaries would bolster the Theban army that Eteocles was now finally calling to arms. His own men came from the capital and from towns and villages throughout the lands controlled by Thebes. Townsmen and farmers who now laid down their tools and took up their arms were not professional soldiers and few had previously seen battle. The knowledge that the experienced mercenaries were on their way to him had given Eteocles the confidence to rebuff the peace initiatives of both Tydeus and Polynices. He genuinely believed that he could withstand an assault by the Argive army, despite knowing that his forces would be outnumbered. He even appeared confident that he could defeat his brother and his Argive friends.

It was only when the remaining residents of Teumessus came flooding down the Chalcis Road to Thebes with all they could carry, push, or pull that Eteocles realized the line of advance being employed by the invading army. Meanwhile, Adrastus allowed the captured Theban scout to live. He would be brought along with the army as a prisoner in case he might prove useful later in the campaign.

As the army crossed the hills and approached Teumessus, Adrastus unleashed the leading division of foot soldiers, whose position in the march had been determined by a draw of lots before the army resumed its march that morning. Hundreds of men gleefully descended on the town, looting and destroying it. This obviously delighted the troops involved and whetted the appetites of the remainder of the army for some of the same.[66]

At the camp the army made outside the now-devastated Teumessus, once all troops had arrived, Adrastus called a meeting of the Seven outside his newly raised tent. He announced that the following day, the army would reach and encircle the walls of Thebes after a march of twelve and a half miles, which would take some five hours. He then called on Polynices to describe his hometown Thebes and its defenses to his comrades one last time before they launched the assault. This would allow any lingering questions to be addressed, ensuring that every commander was certain of his role and responsibilities.

As Adrastus and Mecisteus joined the members of the Seven, eight men formed a broad circle around Polynices, who drew his sword. With this, he drew a shape in the earth before them—the head of a spear with the sharp end pointing north. This was Thebes.[67] Polynices went on to point out the seven gates in the high wall surrounding the city. The eastern and western sides of the town were bounded by rivers—the

Dirce to the west, the Ismenus to the east, with a third stream, the Strophia, entering the town from the north. In the east and the west, the city wall lined those rivers, with the waterways making assault difficult from these directions.

Along the city's southern wall, facing the plain and opening onto the Leuctra Road, Plataea Road, and Tanagra Road, were three gates. Near the wall's southwest corner stood the Hypsistan Gate, named for the nearby Sanctuary of Zeus Hypsistus. Next came the Electra Gate, named for Electra, sister of King Cadmus, founder of Thebes. Toward the southeastern corner of the wall stood the Fountain Gate—which would a decade later be renamed the Homolid Gate. Of the gates of Thebes, these three were the easiest to assault. But all seven gates would have to be blockaded to prevent Thebans escaping the city and to prevent supplies and reinforcements getting into Thebes.

In the western wall, opening to the Dirce River, was the Neistan Gate, named for Neis, son of Theban ruler Zethus and nephew of King Amphion. This was also known as the Onca Gate, because the Sanctuary of Athena Onca was located just to the south of the gate, within the city. In the northwest, the Boreas Gate, named for the god of the north wind, opened to a ford over the Dirce and the road west to Thespiae. In the central north of the wall there was the Ogycian Gate, the city's oldest, named for Ogycus, a chieftain of the local Ectene tribe that had united with Cadmus at the time of his invasion of Boeotia and settlement of Thebes. Not far away, in the northeast wall, the Proetid Gate, named for long ago Theban native Proetus, opened onto a ford across the Ismenus, with the Chalcis Road leading away from it.[68]

As King Adrastus explained to the Seven, before the army made the final advance on Thebes, the members of the Seven would draw lots to determine which gate would be assigned to them and the men of their division for the coming assault. That night, in the warm air of a long summer evening, all the troops of the army sat in their divisions on a hillside as a formal religious ceremony led by Amphiaraus and presided over by King Adrastus took place below them.

The members of the Seven came to this ceremony armed, dressed in their helmets and armor, and carrying their shields—shields they'd had made or modified for the campaign against Thebes. First, from Amphiaraus's own upturned plain bronze helmet they drew pottery shards gathered from the ruins of Teumessus, shards onto which alpha to eta had been scratched by the Prophet. This would dictate the order of a second draw later in the ceremony. Tydeus drew the alpha shard, Polynices the eta shard, with the other five taking the letters in between.

Amphiaraus then proceeded to cut the throat of one of the huge black bulls that had been brought with the army from Argos. He then allowed the animal's blood to drain into his own upturned circular convex shield. The plain leather face of this shield, stretched over a frame of curling bronze, was without adornment of any kind, which was typical of the unpretentious Prophet, who shunned any outward display of greatness. "Amphiaraus's reputation doesn't rely on the show of seeming to be the best," it was commonly said, "but on his being so!"[69]

Once the shield was almost brimming with the dark blood, it was lifted up by attendants. One by one, in the order dictated by the draw of shards, the members of the Seven stepped up to the blood-filled shield. Tydeus was the first. He wore bronze greaves on his lower legs. Thick leather arm-protectors decorated with bronze ran up his arm from wrist to elbow. The body armor over his tunic took the form of a bronze cuirass molded to the shape of his chest and back and strapped in place. His bronze helmet was of the classic Argive type, open at the face but with broad cheek-pieces to protect the sides of the face. Normally, a wooden crest-holder ran along the top of the helmet from front to rear, with this holder sprouting a large crest of horsehair, usually natural white or black. Defying tradition, and typically for the flamboyant Tydeus, he wore not one crest on his helmet, but three.

The design on Tydeus's large round shield was simple and practical. On a black background representing the night sky spread polished bronze stars that were riveted to the shield's bronze underframe. In the middle of the shield, a shining circle of polished bronze represented a full moon. But there was more. From the bottom of Tydeus's shield hung long leather strips, weighed down by a small bronze bell at the bottom of each strip. This leather curtain provided some protection for his legs against missiles, while the tinkling bells added a novel and unsettling note to the threat he posed opponents.

As Amphiaraus held out his own upturned helmet, Tydeus again reached into it, withdrew a piece of broken pottery, and handed it to Amphiaraus. The Prophet loudly read the name inscribed on the shard, for all the army to hear, "Tydeus has drawn the Proetid Gate."

A roar arose from the men of Tydeus's division, who would join him in attacking Thebes's Proetid Gate, which sat opposite the ford in the Ismenus on the Chalcis Road and was the nearest to the army's present camp. Amphiaraus dipped a silver cup into the bull's blood, then handed it to Tydeus, who placed one foot on the body of the slain black bull and raised his blood-filled cup the heavens. Amphiaraus then led him in repeating the oath that the Seven had first sworn at Argos the previous year:

"By the blood of the sacred bull and in the sight of the gods, ever faithful to my fellow champions, the men who follow me, and the gods, I vow to destroy Thebes to the last stone, or to spill my life's blood in the attempt, the gods willing!"

Once Tydeus had loudly declared his oath and drunk down the contents of his cup, Amphiaraus added a caution. The way the blood of the bull had initially flowed, he said, had indicated to him that it would be fatal to Tydeus to cross the Ismenus River. He must wait outside the city, on the river's eastern bank. This brought a grimace from Tydeus and a groan of disappointment from his men.

Capaneus had drawn second place, and now the massive man, the tallest in all the army, came forward and took his turn at drawing a gate. Like Tydeus, he wore body armor, while from the sides of his helmet jutted two white plumes, like giant feathers. The long, oval shield on his left arm had seen plenty of past service. It bore the image of an unarmed man carrying a burning torch, and from the figure's mouth came the inscribed words "I will fire the town." In Capaneus's belt there was an ornate torch.[70]

"Capaneus has drawn the Electra Gate," Amphiaraus announced.

The men of Capaneus's division cheered their approval, as others looked disappointed—many considered this the main gate of Thebes, and it was a prize in the minds of the troops. The big man recited his oath to destroy Thebes then drank down his cup of blood, wiping his bloodied lips with the back of his massive hand. Then Capaneus turned to the men on the hill, raised his torch, and roared, "With or without the will of Zeus, the city will be sacked by me!"[71]

The entire army roared in response to this, with many men vocalizing their personal war-cries. With their voices still filling the air, Capaneus withdrew, allowing Eteoclus to step forward to take his turn at drawing a gate. Eteoclus's armor and helmet were similar to those of his predecessors, while the design on his large round shield was that of a man, clad in armor from head to foot, who climbed a ladder set against a defensive tower. It was with the assault on Thebes in mind that Eteoclus had dictated this design to the artist who had rendered it in Argos.

Eteoclus drew his shard and handed it to the Prophet, after which Amphiaraus announced, "Eteoclus has drawn the Neistan Gate."

The men of Eteoclus's division cheered and hooted before their commander took his oath to destroy or die, then downed the contents of a bloody cup. Inspired by Capaneus, and knowing that the war god Ares was a patron deity of Thebes, Eteoclus then loudly also vowed, "Not even Ares himself will hurl *me* down!"[72]

Yet another roar filled the air.

Hippomedon, another big man, now strode to the fore, intense and ready for the fight. His helmet and armor varied little from the champions who'd come before him, but his round shield bore the design of the Typhon, the fire-breathing snake of myth that had been vanquished at Delphi by the god Apollo. The black background to this curling serpent was overlaid with painted smoke and fire. Intertwined bronze snakes circled the rim of the shield, increasing its protective strength. This also added to the shield's weight. An ordinary man would struggle to carry this burden far, but to the powerful Hippomedon it was as if the shield were as light as a feather.

"Hippomedon draws the Ogycian Gate," Amphiaraus announced after the champion had drawn his shard, and his men voiced their approval—there was much prestige in being assigned the city's oldest gate.

Hippomedon, too, gave voice to his vow and drank a cup of blood, then withdrew amid resounding cheers to permit another member of the Seven to take his turn.

The long-haired Parthenopaeus had drawn fifth place, and he followed Hippomedon to reach into the upturned helmet to select his gate. Shorter, slighter than the men who'd come before him, the youngest member of the Seven still had some growing to do. But he had spared no expense in preparing his arms. His shield, of the figure-eight Mycenaean style, was so large that, when he set its bottom rim on the ground in front of him, just his helmeted head could be seen. Rendered in painted bronze sheet on the upper face of the shield was a depiction of the Sphinx. On the bottom half spread the supine figure of a man pleading for his life, again in painted bronze, representing a Theban victim of the Sphinx. This was Parthenopaeus's jest at the expense of all Thebans, proclaiming that, like the Sphinx, a woman, this son of a famous female warrior would slaughter all men of Thebes who crossed his path.

Parthenopaeus came to the draw carrying a spear seven feet long, its head decorated with gold. Resting the spear against his shoulder to free his right hand, he removed a shard from its receptacle and handed it to the Prophet.

"Parthenopaeus has drawn the Boreas Gate," called Amphiaraus, and the men of the young warrior's division cheered.

The pretty-faced youth raised his gold-tipped spear in his right hand, then, instead of taking the formal vow to destroy Thebes or die in the attempt, he declared, "Honoring this spear more dear than any god, I swear by it to destroy the town of Cadmus, in spite of Zeus!"[73] Still with his foot on the bull's carcass, he jabbed his spear into the ground, accepted his cup. and drank down his portion of the beast's blood.

His vow brought a widespread gasp of shock, followed by an admiring roar.

Amphiaraus had sixth place. Oldest member of the Seven, the most experienced in war, one of the heroes to have taken part in the legendary Hunt of Calydonian Boar, and revered as a seer with a direct line to the gods, he drew out the penultimate shard. "I draw the Fountain Gate," he proclaimed, and the men of his division voiced their loud approval before he recited the formal blood oath and drank his cup of bull's blood.

Finally, Polynices stepped up, wearing his Corinthian helmet and bearing a new design on his Boeotian shield. This design, in gold, showed a woman, representing Justice, leading a fully-armed man, representing Polynices. There was an inscription emanating from the woman's mouth: "I will bring home the banished man."[74]

Because only one shard remained, it was a foregone conclusion which gate Polynices would draw, but Amphiaraus announced it anyway. "Polynices goes against the Hypsistan Gate."

Polynices's men cheered, and then, as the Seven drew their swords, raised them to the heavens, and stood with one foot each on the slaughtered bull, the entire army joined them in a martial roar.

The captured Theban scout had heard the Argive army roar time and again at their hillside assembly. Once the men returned to camp after dark, the prisoner overheard his guards, men from Capaneus's division, talking and drinking with comrades from several other divisions.

From these discussions the Theban learned that Capaneus would be leading his troops against the Electra Gate, Hippomedon would go against the Ogycian Gate, and Polynices would attack the Hypsistan Gate. There was also reference to a burning torch and the arrogant confidence of Tydeus, who was considered an outsider by some men of Argos despite having married a daughter of their king.

All this euphoria over the following day's assault on Thebes, followed by much drinking of wine in camp, saw most men of the Argive army fall into a deep sleep. Even some sentries nodded off. The Theban prisoner, who was only chained by the wrists, saw his opportunity to escape, and, in the early hours of the morning, with his guards asleep, he warily crawled from the camp, which had no perimeter walls, then set off at a lope across the hills, heading southwest toward Thebes.

15.

CHAMPION VERSUS CHAMPION

H aving returned from his failed mission to Colonos, Creon was at his house in Thebes in the mid-morning when he was informed that a Theban scout who had escaped from Argive custody was at his door. When he had the man brought in, he found the fellow covered with perspiration and dust and still wearing his Argive chains.[75]

The scout had feared that the irascible young King Eteocles would have him executed for allowing himself to be captured by the enemy. Creon, the king's uncle, would, the scout hoped, give him a more reasonable reception. "Your Excellency," said the scout breathlessly, "the Argive army spent last night at Teumessus."

"I am aware of that," Creon returned. "What more can you tell me?"

The man continued. "I overheard the enemy's plans. They will be marching on Thebes as we speak, and intend to encircle the city."

"Tell me all you know," Creon urged. "Which city gate has been allocated to each of their seven champions?"

The escaped prisoner named the gates drawn by Polynices, Capaneus, and Hippomedon.

"And the other members of the Seven—what gates did they draw?" Creon asked.

The man gulped, then proceeded to invent the gate assignments of the remaining four members of the Seven, because he had only overheard details of the first three. Failing to mention Eteoclus, of whom he was quite ignorant, he claimed that the seventh gate had been assigned to King Adrastus. When Creon asked what shield designs each of the Seven carried so that they could be identified in battle, the escapee began by saying that the shield of Amphiaraus was blank.

"That," said Creon, "has long been known. What of the others?"

The man, who had not seen the shields of any of the Seven, then reeled off a series of inventions. Parthenopaeus, he said, had an image of Atalanta wounding the Calydonian boar with an arrow. That made sense, but it wasn't correct. He gave the burning torch of Capaneus to Tydeus. A shield emblazoned with the chariot and horses of Poseidon was his description for Polynices; for reasons known only to him, the scout, possibly a native of Potniae, connected the Potniae shrine of Poseidon to the Theban-born prince. And in the full flow of invention, the scout attributed a shield covered with a hundred vipers to King Adrastus, which was close but not altogether correct—the king's shield bore the device of the snake-headed Gorgon.

Creon knew all this to be untrue, as he now revealed to the embarrassed escapee. "We had a spy in the Argive army's ranks, pretending to be a Theban defector," he said. "That man reached us several hours ago, after running all the way from the camp at Teumessus. Last evening, while with the enemy army, that man witnessed the assignment of gates to the Seven and memorized the designs of all their shields—designs that do not comport with your information."[76]

Bravery in venturing escape he would always commend, but Creon abhorred lies that could cost lives. Unimpressed, he sent the man away to have his chains removed, ordering the fellow to thereafter be armed and sent to the city wall to join the other defenders of Thebes. Creon himself went in search of Eteocles, taking with him the spy from the Argive camp. He found the young king, who was not yet thirty years of age, in his armor and energetically marshalling troops by the Proetid Gate, assisted by Creon's own son Megareus.

"I've been looking everywhere for you, King Eteocles," said Creon. "All around the watchtowers and sentry posts."

There was a wild look in Eteocles's eyes as he answered. "And I've been anxious to see you, also, Creon, ever since I found the peace terms unsatisfactory in my meeting with Polynices."

"We have intelligence, from inside the Argive camp." He nodded toward the spy. "The enemy is on the march and will reach us before the day is out. They intend to draw a ring of troops around the city."

"In that case, I must lead out our troops."

Creon looked incredulous. "To where? Are you so young that your eyes are blind to what is happening?"

"To where? Across the entrenchments, for immediate action!"

"Our forces are small compared to theirs. And the Argive warriors are of no mean repute."

Eteocles emitted a nervous laugh. "Never fear, I'll soon fill the plain with their dead."

"I wish it were so, but it won't be that easy."

"Trust me. I won't keep our forces within the walls. Or do you have a better plan?" His tone was sarcastic.

"Victory is entirely dependent on making the right decision," Creon replied, remaining calm. "I would consider every plan before venturing everything in a battle outside the walls in broad daylight, outnumbered as we are."

Eteocles pulled a discomfited face, then said, "Suppose we let them encamp outside the city and then fall on them in the night?"

"A good idea, provided that in the event of being repulsed you can successfully withdraw to the city."

"Night equalizes risks. In fact, it favors a daring act."

Creon countered: "The dark of night is a terrible time to suffer a disaster."

"Well, shall I fall on them when they sit down to their supper?" Eteocles suggested disdainfully.

"That might cause them a scare, but it's a victory we want."

"What if our cavalry makes a sortie against their army while it's still on the march?"

"Their infantry is fenced all around with chariots."

Eteocles threw his hands in the air with frustration. "Then what do you expect me to do? Surrender?"

"No, no. But form a wise plan."

"What scheme is wiser than mine?" Eteocles demanded, glaring at his uncle and standing with hands on hips.

"They have seven chiefs to lead their companies and storm our gates. Choose seven chiefs yourself to set against them at the gates—our very bravest men. And under them appoint captains to share the burden of command."

Eteocles's eyes lit up. "It shall be done!" he declared. "Who are their champions? Name them at once."[77]

Creon motioned for the Theban spy to speak, and the man correctly named each gate and its chosen attacker from the Seven. For each member of the Seven, Eteocles now nominated an opposing Theban warrior. Tydeus was the first name to be mentioned.

"Against Tydeus I will post Melanippus, the valiant son of Astacus," Eteocles pronounced after a moment's thought. "Nobly born, abhorrer of bombast and rhetoric, he holds honor dear." There was an added edge to his choice of opponent for Tydeus, one that typified Eteocles, who had made a fine art of sarcasm. Melanippus was the name of the brother that Tydeus had allegedly murdered at Calydon years before. In the Theban army's ranks, once this assignment became known, it would be said with a laugh that the dead brother was coming back to haunt Tydeus.

"The Electra Gate fell to tall Capaneus," the spy went on. "That fellow boasted 'With or without the will of Zeus, by me the city will be sacked.'"

"He challenges heaven?" Eteocles exclaimed. "What insanity! Against him, I'll send a slow-speaking man with a fiery spirit, and tall as a tower—Polyphontes. Who's next?"

"Eteoclus, with a man scaling a tower on his shield, was next. He drew the Neistan Gate, proclaiming, 'Not even Ares himself will throw me down!'"

"Here is the man to send against him," said Eteocles, putting his arm around the shoulders of his assistant. He smiled at Creon. "Your son Megareus will command at the Neistan Gate."

Creon smiled back. But it was not a happy smile. Creon had fathered several daughters and three sons, including his youngest boy Lycomedes, who was not yet ten. Every one of his children was precious to him. But he knew that he could not keep his middle son out of the firing line; in war, every man is expected to do his duty to his country and his countrymen. The youth was well liked by the Theban elite. The older nobles called him Young Menoeceus because in looks and manner he reminded them of his grandfather Menoeceus, father of Creon and Jocasta. Knowing he had a reputation to live up to, the youth had developed a strong sense of duty. But he was inexperienced and naïve. Worse, to Creon's mind, by making Megareus one of Thebes's seven champions, Eteocles was putting him in mortal danger. Why not choose Haemon, his older, more experienced brother? It seemed almost as if Eteocles were giving Megareus this appointment to spite Creon for arguing against his battle plan.

"You will bring us back two captives, Young Menoeceus," said Eteocles with a grin. "One will be Eteoclus, the other will be the fellow scaling the tower on his shield."

"Yes, Majesty," a beaming Megareus proudly replied.

"Go on," said Eteocles to the spy. "Who is next?"

"Next, to the Ogycian Gate," the spy continued, "comes Hippomedon."

"Oenops's trusty son Hyperbius shall face him," Eteocles decreed. "A fine figure of a man, and fearless. They are well matched, and there is an old enmity between the two. All Hyperbius has ever asked of me was an opportunity to serve, and I gladly give it to him. Continue . . ."

"At the Boreas Gate, Parthenopaeus, the waif from Arcadia, cub of the huntress. A pretty boy, but with a savage temper."

"We have a champion for the churlish Arcadian, too. No braggart, just a strong hand. It will be another son of Oenops, Actor, brother of Hyperbius. Who's next?"

"Before the Fountain Gate comes a mighty and majestic man, the prophet Amphiaraus."

"A famously just man," Eteocles remarked, nodding, "courageous, god-fearing, with the gift of prophecy—but consorting with blasphemers! He will fall, if it's the will of Zeus, dragged down with his bad confederates. Against him I will send valiant Lasthenes, mature and wise, a man who has remained youthfully fit. He's quick of eye, and sure of hand. And last of all? Where shall we find my brother Polynices?"

"Last of all, Majesty, Polynices goes against the Hypsistan Gate, bearing Justice on his shield."

"Justice? I will give him Justice. I will go to meet him myself."

"Is that such a good idea?" Creon asked.

"Who has a better right? King to king, brother to brother." Suddenly agitated, Eteocles looked down at his bare legs. "My greaves! Fetch me my greaves!"

"You want to kill your own brother?" said Creon. "One child of Oedipus murdering the other? If evil must come and he must die, let it be free of shame. Or else it will go to the grave with you. Only honor lives on after us. Change your mind, while you have time. Seek the grace of the gods. Make offerings, and send another to the seventh gate."

"What are the gods to me?" Eteocles was wide-eyed now. "I think the hour for offerings has long passed."

"Don't go to the gate," Creon urged, putting a restraining hand on his nephew's arm.

"Say no more," Eteocles returned, removing Creon's hand. "My mind is made up."[78]

Then from the top of a Proetid Tower came a warning shout. A sentry was pointing up the Chalcis Road. He called down to say that he could see dust rising in the direction of Teumessus and the glint of sun on a mass of white shields in the distance.

Eteocles frowned. "White shields?"

"White Argive shields," Creon replied, "sporting the motif of a running wolf, no doubt—symbol of Apollo Lykeios, lord of the wolves, patron deity of Argos. The wolf is at our door, Eteocles."[79]

"To arms! To arms!" Eteocles cried, sounding panicky. "Lead out our troops. Form them up in two lines outside the walls."

Creon looked aghast. "Did we not agree that we would defend the city from within the walls?"

"No, no, we must defend the city outside the walls! The enemy cannot be allowed to reach the gates!"

Creon didn't reply. He saw much of the unstable Oedipus in that man's second son. For eleven years, ever since Eteocles had ascended the Theban throne, Creon had been his strong right arm, often moderating Eteocles's actions but never opposing them outright. He knew Eteocles better than the young king knew himself. Just as youth can be wasted on the young and wealth squandered by the undisciplined, power can dissipate in the hands of the unwise; Eteocles was all of these things, young, undisciplined, and unwise, but Creon had succeeded in guiding him up to now. In this instant, with the fate of his city at stake, Creon was forced to decide whether to back his nephew, or defy him.

Seeing Creon's hesitation, Eteocles exploded with rage. "I am your king. Do as I say!"

16.

FIRST BLOOD

H eld back by its lumbering baggage train, the Argive army had made slow time as it advanced down the Chalcis Road from Teumessus through the heat of a hot midsummer's morning. As midday approached, the distant walls of Thebes finally became visible to those in the marching column, and the spirits and pace of the army lifted.

At the predawn conference with his officers, where sacrifices had produced good omens and the day's watchword had been passed around, Adrastus had given the Seven their marching orders. Now, as the force came up to the city, it was obvious that the Theban defenders had formed two defensive lines in front of the seven gates of Thebes, with their small cavalry force in seven detachments behind them to provide support. Although for now Thebes's chariots remained within the city, Eteocles had essentially won the argument over battle strategy with Creon. Or, more accurately, Creon had given in to Eteocles.

As a result, between two and three thousand troops had been deployed outside the city, as Eteocles had wanted all along. As many as ten thousand women, children, and old men from Thebes and surrounding towns and villages filled the city itself, along with visitors fearful of being caught by the invaders. Among those visitors was a party of Greek women from Phoenicia who Eteocles had promised to escort to Delphi to consult the Pythia.[80]

A separate military force, made up entirely of the recently arrived mercenaries from Phocis and Phlegra, had been arrayed in two lines around the Sanctuary of Heracles at the southeast corner of the city, close by the Fountain Gate. This sanctuary consisted of a stone altar in a grove of laurel and olive trees on the bank of the Ismenus, the stream that flowed along the eastern edge of the city. This was distinct from the Sanctuary of Apollo Ismenius, which was on a rise inside the southwest corner of the city wall. There was also a spring in the grove that was used as a water fountain for the city, and this gave rise to the name of the nearby Fountain Gate. This was the same fountain where Oedipus had washed blood from himself after he first arrived in Thebes. As a consequence, while old-timers called this the Melia Fountain, later generations of Thebans referred to it as Oedipus's Fountain.[81]

The mercenary force, made up of hundreds of soldiers of fortune, many of them mature men who had also brought their sons into their ranks, linked up on the left flank of the Theban infantry that formed double ranks in front of the Fountain Gate. That Theban force in turn linked up with Theban defenders outside the Electra Gate, which linked with the troops outside the Hypsistan Gate. This created a pair of solid lines of close-packed infantry south of the city between the Ismenus in the east and the Dirce to the west. In the north, defenders of the Boreas, Ogycian, and Proetid Gates had also linked up. The defenders of the Neistan Gate in the west of the city were on their own, being isolated from their comrades at the other gates.

The men in the Theban front line were the city's best troops, mostly men in their twenties and thirties whose round shields proudly hung on their walls at home. Older men, as well as archers and boys, filled the second line. All wore jackets sewn with bronze mail and simple helmets and carried round shields. Most had a sword on their hip, and in their right hand all spearmen carried a seven-foot-long spear, which they would use as a jabbing, stabbing weapon. The horsemen behind them, who were helmetless but were equipped with small shields, each carried a number of darts—small spears that were hurled, like the larger javelin.

Elements of the attacking army began to peel away from the advancing column. Eteoclus's division, led by escorting chariots, crossed the Dirce River and marched to the Neistan Gate in the west of the city. Three divisions concentrated around the northern gates; three other divisions marched down the eastern flank of the city to the southern gates. The baggage train and escorting cavalry, led by Adrastus and Mecisteus in their chariots, trundled south to the village of Potniae, where Adrastus established his main camp and headquarters. The last remaining residents of Potniae, women, children, and old men, were only now abandoning their homes and fleeing into the city with all they could carry, herding their animals before them. The Theban troops of the defensive line there had to part to let these civilians through so they could reach the southern gates.

With these movements under way, it became clear to Argive commanders that the Thebans would remain fixed in their defensive lines. Encouraged by this and with the Argive infantry divisions forming close-packed serried ranks behind them, the Argive chariot force went on the offensive, charging along in a line parallel to the opposition lines. Each chariot had a two-man crew: a driver, in armor and helmet, with, behind him and to his right, a noble, who was well armored and wore a helmet with a flowing horsehair plume. Each noble had a large shield on his left arm, with which he had to defend both himself and his driver from incoming missiles, be they flying arrows, darts, javelins, or sling-stones.

For their harrying runs before the walls of Thebes, these chariot-borne warriors left their spears with their armor-bearers and went into the attack armed with darts. A dozen or more throwing darts filled a leather quiver attached to the right side of the chariot. Three to four feet long, with a metal tip, these darts were equipped with a leather thong a foot or so from the bottom, which provided greater ballistic throwing power.

That afternoon, led by their champions, one hundred and fifty Argive chariot teams ran back and forth in front of the gates to which they had been assigned, with a little over twenty at each gate. In the case of Tydeus, he ranged along the eastern bank of the Ismenus, flinging darts and insults from his chariot with equal intensity. He stayed east of the river not so much because of the ill omen voiced by Amphiaraus the previous evening, but because the Theban defenders of the Proetid Gate were lined up on the opposite bank. Behind the chariots of Tydeus, the infantry of his division, spearmen from all over Greece, formed up in close-packed ranks and awaited the order to join the attack, standing with the bottom of their spears on the ground and the tip pointing skyward. From a distance, these thousands of spears looked like a forest of dead trees.

As the speeding chariots followed each other in a lethal line outside the gates, their warriors launched darts at the stationary Thebans before turning to make a fresh run back in the opposite direction. As darts came flying into their ranks, the frontline Thebans could only raise their shields and pray. From behind them, the archers in the second line let loose arrows that rose above their heads to fall like a light rain on and around the chariots. Most fell uselessly to earth. The others were fended off by the shields of the chariot-borne warriors. The Theban cavalrymen, confined behind their infantry, threw their own darts at the passing chariots from the backs of their stationary, unsettled steeds, but with little effect.

Once the Argive chariots had expended all their darts, they returned to their own waiting infantry divisions, where the nobles stepped down to be replaced by slingers. The chariots then returned to the attack, and soon deadly small and oval sling-stones, which couldn't be seen until the last moment by their targets, were whirring into the Theban lines from the chariots, often striking men in the face—taking out the eyes of some, who dropped their shields and staggered away, clutching at their wounds, creating gaps in their line. After the Argive slingers had used up all their store of deadly ammunition, the chariots returned to collect their nobles for yet another run with a fresh supply of darts.

At the southern gates, the pressure of these missile attacks told. By the time of the latest chariot run, Theban men there began to break away from their lines and run back to the nearest gate to find safety behind the city's walls. The more men who deserted their positions, the more who followed. Before long, the southern defense lines had disintegrated, with the exception of the mercenaries before the Sanctuary of Heracles. These tough, proud professional soldiers from Phocis and Phlegra would never retreat—certainly not without orders to do so and not from a place sacred to the heroic warrior-god Heracles. They had no intention of budging. That was to prove their undoing.

Because they stood their ground while the Thebans ran, the mercenaries left themselves exposed and unprotected on their right flank. Amphiaraus, leading the chariot attack on this southern front, saw this and immediately realized he could exploit the weakness. Calling to the waiting men of his infantry division, he led an all-out assault on the mercenary position. As the division's trumpeter lifted his long, thin instrument to his lips and sounded "Charge," Amphiaraus's driver Baton pulled their chariot to a halt. Amphiaraus jumped down to the ground with a long spear in his right hand and his plain white shield on his left arm.

"Form up behind me!" he bellowed to his division.

His foot soldiers came running on the double to join their commander and the other nobles who had dismounted from their chariots to participate in the attack. The spearmen came in a rush with shields bearing the emblems of numerous cities—among them the dove of Sicyon, Corinth's Pegasus the flying horse, and the inverted "V" of Sparta. Once the infantry had swept past the chariots, the charioteers pulled their vehicles back to await further orders.

Amphiaraus, the oldest member of the Seven, ran at the flank of the Phocians and Phlegrans with his lengthy fair hair splaying out from beneath his helmet. He hit the mercenary front line with the fury of a tornado. To his men, it was almost as if he didn't fear death. In fact, Amphiaraus, after so many unsuccessful attempts to thwart Fate, had come to accept that as a result of the Pythia's prophecy, he would die fighting beneath the walls of Thebes. As a consequence, he was determined to make that death as brave, glorious, and memorable as possible so that men would still be talking about it long after.

Bellowing their war cries, the men of Amphiaraus's division followed close on his heels. They outnumbered the mercenaries by at least three to one. This, combined with the exposed flank, the mercenaries' determination not to take a backward step, and Amphiaraus's mercurial example, enabled Amphiaraus's men to mow the Phocians and Phlegrans down like grass before the scythe. Thebans would talk with disdain of this swift destruction of the mercenary force that Eteocles had paid so handsomely to come to their aid, describing it as nothing less than a rout.[82]

A few of the mercenaries, very few, finally gave way and ran through the trees of the sanctuary to the Fountain Gate, to be admitted to the city before the gate closed. The scene of carnage left on the battlefield south of the city wall as a result of the Seven's initial assault made even the most resolute of the city's defenders shudder: discarded weapons and shields, headless bodies, decapitated heads in helmets, corpses missing arms and legs, even severed hands still holding swords.[83]

Amphiaraus and his men pursued the fleeing survivors; but a rain of arrows, darts, and stones fell on them from the gate towers and the wall, launched by defenders who had swiftly repositioned themselves. With the attackers being felled or grievously wounded by missiles all around him, Amphiaraus ordered his men to fall back under cover of their shields and regroup. The Phocians and Phlegrans, meanwhile, had been destroyed as a fighting force and would contribute little more to the defense of Thebes.

Adrastus, seeing the Theban defense crumble outside the southern gates, sent orders to the members of the Seven at the other gates to press home the attack and drive all defenders from outside the walls, thus securing the encirclement of the city. Very much aware of the prediction from Amphiaraus that Tydeus would perish if he crossed the Ismenus, Adrastus dispatched his brother Mecisteus to lead the assault at Tydeus's Proetid Gate, with Tydeus under orders from his father-in-law to stay east of the river.

Mecisteus, who had hungered to be involved in the attack on Thebes ever since it had been first mooted a decade earlier, eagerly sped his chariot up the eastern side of the city, accompanied by a protecting troop of cavalry. There, he dismounted and prepared to lead Tydeus's troops into the attack, choosing a hundred men to join him in going against the Theban line. They aimed for a narrow front at the river ford, where the Ismenus and its banks were at their lowest. Tydeus' men would gladly follow Mecisteus, brother of their commander in chief, with the same ardor as they displayed for Tydeus.

Naturally, Tydeus was hugely frustrated to have his command taken from him in this way. When a trumpet sounded and Mecisteus led the chosen men from his division splashing across the shallow ford toward the lines of Theban troops opposite the Proetid Gate, Tydeus ran his chariot back and forth along the eastern bank of the stream, all the time yelling threats and imprecations at the Thebans, just as a horse champs at the bit.[84]

Melanippus, eldest son of the noble Astacus who had been senior adviser to Oedipus, Creon, and Eteocles over the years, was the champion designated by Eteocles to defend the Proetid Gate. Like Mecisteus, Melanippus was middle-aged, but he was younger and fitter than the opposing general, along with being highly respected by his men. As the Argive troops came wading across the stream in an attempt to drive him from his position, Melanippus picked out Mecisteus in the lead—probably from a Gorgon's-head design on his shield, the motif of the Argive royal house—and made directly for him.

There in the stream, with water washing around their lower legs, Mecisteus and Melanippus squared off against each other and did mortal combat, shields raised, spears at chest level and projecting out by the edge of their shield. Around them, Mecisteus's men struggled to climb the bank on the western side of the river and come to grips with the Thebans, who thrust their spears down in their faces. Soon, Argive bodies were floating away down the stream, whose waters began to color red with blood.

From his chariot, Tydeus lost sight of Mecisteus in the ebb and flow of battle as, time and again, Thebans pushed the Argives back into the river. After the fighting in the Ismenus had lasted half an hour, Tydeus saw the Argives falling back. Reining in his horses, he called to the nearest men, as they flooded past him, "What's occurred?"

"It's too difficult!" cried one soldier, who had lost his spear and sported a bloody facial wound. "A man can't fight while wading a river."

"Where is Mecisteus?" Tydeus demanded.

"Mecisteus has fallen," yelled another, who had cast away his shield, passing the chariot.

"Mecisteus, fallen? How can that be?"

"Felled by Melanippus," advised another retreating soldier breathlessly. "The Theban, too, was wounded, but not enough to prevent him from leading the enemy rush."

"Who saw Mecisteus fall?" Tydeus demanded of the passing throng.

"I did," called yet another man, who had lost his helmet. "Melanippus dragged his body back toward the wall, where we couldn't retrieve it."

"And they're firing flaming arrows at us from the towers," a fifth man cried, sounding panicked. Sure enough, arrows dipped in pine resin and set alight were arcing over the heads of Theban fighters. Most arrows landed in the stream, although several men were struck and caught alight. Comrades had to douse burning friends in the Ismenus.[85]

"Mecisteus felled and in their hands?" Tydeus exclaimed. "This can't be!" Raising his spear, he called to the troops behind him, who awaited their turn to go into action. "You sons of Argos, before being riddled by their fire, what's stopping you falling on their gates with all your might and vigor? The whole of you, spearmen, horsemen, and charioteers! With me! With me!"[86]

This call to arms had the desired effect. Bareheaded cavalrymen dismounted and prepared to act as infantrymen, charioteers jumped down to the ground and armed themselves with throwing darts, and untested infantrymen of this division came at the run with their spears. A trumpet sounded the charge, and with hundreds of fresh, yelling soldiers behind him, Tydeus splashed across the stream and up the far bank, in defiance of the prophecy from Amphiaraus that if he crossed the Ismenus he would die.

The impetus of this charge drove the Theban line back toward the gate. Fighting like a veritable machine, with the triple crest on his helmet rippling and with the tuneless peal of the bells dangling beneath his shield, Tydeus sent every enemy soldier who appeared in front of him reeling away with savage spear wounds. His example encouraged all around him, and soon the Argives had forced the Theban defenders back to the gates. Now Tydeus and his men began launching darts at the top of the towers, killing several archers, who toppled from their lofty perch and fell to the ground. Other archers fled in fear, abandoning the battlements atop the towers.

From a narrow opening between the two tall wooden gates, a man in glittering helmet and armor emerged. This was Eteocles, the Theban king. He was preceded by two tall soldiers with large shields, who quickly flanked him once he was in the open. It was their job to use their shields to protect their king from missiles, even at the peril of taking a hit themselves. Locating Melanippus among the throng of close-packed Theban fighters, Eteocles saw from his eyes that his most mature general had been exhausted by the intense fighting, and he was covered with blood. But it was not his own; it was the blood of Argives. In all other respects, Melanippus seemed unharmed.

"Melanippus, if you continue to hold honor dear," Eteocles called, "you will lead a counterattack at once, and dispatch the Calydonian!"

"Yes, Majesty!" came the reply. Urged on by their young king, and with bloodied Melanippus at their head, the Thebans made a determined rush at Tydeus and his Argives, driving them back toward the Ismenus. At the same time, more archers ascended the towers and began firing down into Argive ranks. When Eteocles saw that he had prevented a rout, he withdrew back inside the city and hurried to the

Ogycian Gate close by, where other Thebans were under pressure from Hippomedon and his men.[87]

Tydeus was forced back by the crush of his retreating men. And then a grinning Melanippus was before him. "Now," cried Melanippus, "prepare to meet your death at the hands of a champion, dwarf-head!"[88]

"Dwarf-head?!" Tydeus thrust his spear toward the Theban, who parried the blow with his shield.

Melanippus maintained his grin. "Yes, dwarf-head."

"Now see how a true champion fights, old man," Tydeus retorted.

Tydeus's men held their ground near him. Melanippus's men did the same. Greek fighting men knew not to interfere in a one-to-one fight between two commanders. This was a matter of honor. The duo's fight was on the dry land west of the Ismenus, and this enabled Tydeus to use his footwork to advantage as he danced around the more lead-footed Melanippus. Both men made feints. Melanippus's spear-point glanced off Tydeus's shield several times. Tydeus ducked and weaved, and then, using his shield to push aside his opponent's shield just a fraction, he created an opening through which he slid his spear, plunging it into Melanippus's throat. Melanippus, dropping his spear and letting his shield arm fall lower, staggered backward, then fell on his back. He lay there, blood spurting from his neck, looking up in disbelief. Tydeus stepped up, a triumphant look on his face, and towered over his fallen adversary, preparing to deliver the coup de grâce.

"Now who is a dwarf-head?" Tydeus snarled. "Prepare to lose *your* head."

But his pause to gloat cost him dearly. In focusing on Melanippus's face, Tydeus failed to see that his opponent had drawn his sword. With one last effort, Melanippus thrust this sword upward. The blade entered Tydeus's body beneath the bottom of his armor, below the navel. Pushing as far and as hard as his fast-ebbing strength would allow, Melanippus then gave his sword a twist and drew it sideways.

Now it was Tydeus's turn to stagger back. Letting go of his spear, he reached down and tried to push his bloody entrails back into his belly as they sagged out through the rent in his abdomen. Two of his soldiers, stripping the shield from his left arm, carried him to the stream and then across it. Behind them, Thebans cheered as they secured Melanippus, their fallen general.

"Leave me here, where I can witness our victory," Tydeus gasped to his men. "Return to the fight. And bring me the head of Melanippus!"

So, the two men sat him in the shallows, with his back against the eastern bank of the Ismenus, and rejoined the struggle. As the battle raged on, a messenger rode quickly to King Adrastus at Potniae with the news that his brother Mecisteus was believed killed and Tydeus had been seriously wounded. Quickly overcoming the shock of the news, Adrastus ordered Amphiaraus to hurry to the Proetid Gate and take charge there. In his absence, Adrastus would take personal command of the troops assigned to attack the Fountain Gate.[89]

Away galloped Amphiaraus in his chariot. It didn't take him long to reach the scene of the fighting outside the Proetid Gate. Jumping down from his chariot and ordering his driver Baton to pull back and await further orders, the Prophet hurried to where Tydeus half sat, half lay in the water at the riverbank, his sword now in his right hand, his left hand clutching his midriff as his lifeblood flowed away in the waters washing around him.

"What did I tell you about not crossing the Ismenus, fool?" Amphiaraus growled as he reached his cousin-in-law and dropped to one knee beside him. "You bring me to these walls, but you could not even follow the omens when I strive to keep you alive." Amphiaraus had never much liked Tydeus. In fact, he blamed Tydeus for drawing him into this war, for bringing him to these walls where it was forecast that he himself would soon die. He would have blamed Polynices equally for his predicament, but it was Tydeus who now sat before him and was the recipient of his baleful glare.

"Just bring me the head of Melanippus," Tydeus weakly replied.

Without another word, Amphiaraus rose up, entered the water, and strode off across the river to rally the Argive troops at the far bank. The fighting now was over the body of Melanippus; the Theban general had died from the throat wound inflicted by Tydeus. Led by Amphiaraus, once again the Argives drove the Thebans back, forcing them to leave the body of their commander where it lay. Expressionless, Amphiaraus looked down at the dead son of Astacus, then thrust the head of his spear into the ground and unsheathed his sword. With a single two-handed blow, he separated the man's head from his body. Sheathing his sword once more, he pulled his spear from the ground, then jabbed the end into the neck region of the skull. With the head of Melanippus on the end of his spear, Amphiaraus returned to Tydeus.

"Your trophy," said the Prophet, depositing the head on the river-bank beside Tydeus.

Tydeus turned his head to look into the lifeless eyes of his now-dead adversary. Slowly, with difficulty, he raised his sword. Then, finding the last of his strength, he brought the razor-sharp sword down on the skull of Melanippus, neatly cleaving the top from it and exposing the dead man's brain. Tydeus knew that he was dying. He had seen men with a wound such as his live for hours, but eventually, even when the wound was bandaged and the blood ceased to drain from his body, they died. Letting his sword drop into the water, Tydeus reached over, scooped a handful of brain matter from Melanippus's skull. Dragging it free, he thrust it into his mouth, and swallowed. Looking up at the horrified Amphiaraus with blood and gore dripping from his mouth, Tydeus smiled a crazy smile.[90]

17.

THE SUPREME SACRIFICE

Unable to locate Eteocles, who was not at his chosen command, the Hypsistan Gate, Creon climbed the steps to the heights of the Cadmea to obtain an overall picture of the fighting around the city. As he ascended, the sounds of battle, death, and maiming were clearly heard from all quarters beyond the walls.

There at the hilltop citadel, Creon was joined by his king, who sent his bodyguards to stand out of earshot at the palace door. Eteocles explained to Creon that he had been around all the gates, terminating panic and stiffening resistance. He revealed that at the Proetid Gate he had learned that Melanippus was dead and his opponent Tydeus had been severely wounded.

"If Tydeus dies, Calydon is safe," Creon remarked.

"But Thebes is not," Eteocles returned. "While Polynices lives, the threat to us all remains."

"Despite the losses at the sanctuary, we are meeting the threat."

Eteocles shook his head. "There is still much that remains undone, Creon. If I suffer any mischief, you must see to the marriage between my sister Antigone and your son Haemon."[91] This would ensure that Antigone had a legal protector for many years to come, long after Creon's passing, husbands being the guardians of their wives under Greek law.

"It will be done," Creon replied, nodding soberly.

"And this commandment I lay upon the city, and you—should my cause prevail, never give Polynices's corpse a grave in Theban soil. If some friend of his should bury him, let death be that person's reward."

"As you command."

"One thing remains for us to do—to ask the prophet Teiresias if he has anything to tell us regarding heaven's will. Let no man say that Eteocles did not do everything in his earthly power to save his city. Teiresias has reason to reproach me, for I've long scorned his prophetic art, even to his face. I'll send your son, Little Menoeceus, to fetch the seer here in your name. Teiresias will come with your boy, for he'll readily talk to you."

"Very well," Creon agreed.

So, a messenger was sent to the Neistan Gate, where the defenders were commanded by Creon's son Megareus, also known as Little Menoeceus. The message summoned the gate commander to bring the prophet, who had first alerted Oedipus to his true parentage and murder of King Laius, to the palace.

As the afternoon was turning to evening and fighting continued to rage at all seven gates of Thebes, the blind old prophet climbed the wooden steps to the Cadmea. Teiresias had his cornel wood staff in his right hand. The boy who had previously served as his guide and attendant had grown to adulthood and was no longer at his side: that youth was now one of the soldiers fighting and dying to defend Thebes. In the boy's place, Teiresias's teenage daughter Manto was his crutch, while Megareus, teenage son of Creon, served as his guide. Megareus was adorned in rich armor and a shining crested helmet. Neither they nor the sword at his side had ever seen battle prior to this day.

"My knees grow weary," Teiresias complained to Megareus and Manto as they paused him at the bottom of the palace steps. "I can scarcely keep up this pace."

"Take heart, Teiresias," called Creon from the top of the steps, where he and Eteocles stood waiting. "You have reached your moorings."

"I have arrived?" asked the old man with relief. "So, why, Creon, did you summon me so urgently?"

"The struggle for Thebes is great, old man. Eteocles, our king, has gone in full harness to meet the enemy's champions." As Creon said this, he scowled threateningly at the prophet's daughter Manto, who could clearly see that the king was present and his uncle was lying. Shaking his head at her, Creon put a finger to his lips, then said to Teiresias, "But Eteocles has bidden me ask you the best course for our city."

Beside Creon, Eteocles smiled amusedly at his uncle's blatant untruth. Folding his arms, the king remained silent and proceeded to listen to what transpired.

The blind Teiresias, unaware that Eteocles was taking in every word, rested on his staff. "If this had been for Eteocles that I'd been summoned," he began, "I would have sealed my lips and refrained from any response. But I will speak to you because I know you have a genuine desire to learn from me. This country, Creon, has long been cursed—ever since Laius went against the will of heaven to father a child, resulting in the unfortunate Oedipus becoming his own mother's husband. The sons of Oedipus treated him shamefully. They exasperated the poor, suffering fellow. So he, stung by suffering and disgrace, vented awful curses against them. And because I left nothing unsaid or undone to prevent this, I incurred the hatred of the sons of Oedipus. Well, let me tell you, death at each other's hands awaits them, Creon. And the many heaps of slain, some Argive, some Theban, will create great lamentation in the land of Thebes."

Creon glanced at Eteocles beside him. For a man who claimed not to believe in the power of Teiresias's gift of foresight, the young king looked decidedly shaken by this prediction.

"Alas for you, poor city," Teiresias went on, spreading one hand before him, "you are being involved in the brothers' ruin—unless I can persuade one man."

Creon frowned. "One man? Which man?"

"The best course was for no child of Oedipus to become either citizen or king of Thebes. But evil has had the mastery over good. Still, there is one other way to secure safety." He suddenly paused, seeming to have a change of heart. "But it's unwise of me to say anything. It would be too painful for those whose privilege it would be to supply their city with the saving cure. Farewell. I will away, if need be to share my doom at the hands of the attackers, just like all the other citizens of Thebes." He turned to walk back the way he had come, and his daughter turned with him.

"Stay, old man!" Creon called with alarm. "Tell me what can save Thebes and its citizens."

Slowly, Teiresias turned back in Creon's direction. "Though you wish to know it now, you will soon wish you didn't possess the answer to that question."

Creon scowled with impatience. "I wouldn't wish to save my country? How can that be?"

"You are still eager to be told? Very well, then you will hear my prophetic words. But first, where is Young Menoeceus, the youth who brought me here?"

"My son Megareus? He's by your side still."

"Have him depart, far from my voice."

"My son won't reveal anything he hears here."

"You wish me to tell you in his presence?"

"Yes, of course. He'll be happy to hear how the city can be saved. We both will."

Teiresias shrugged. "Then, since you demand to hear it, here is the substance of the oracle that I've received—which, if you follow it, will save the city that Cadmus built. Your own son Menoeceus must be sacrificed for your country."

For a moment, Creon was dumbstruck. Finding his voice, he demanded, "What does this mean? What are you saying, old man?"

"This is what you must do to save your country."

Creon turned away, putting his hands to his ears. "I shut my ears! I never heard!"

"Ha!" Teiresias laughed. "The man is changed. Now he withdraws his faith."

Creon waved him away. "Go in peace. It's not your prophecy that I need."

"Truth cannot be ignored just because it brings you woe."

First looking at his son Megareus, who stared back at him in shocked dismay, Creon began to come down the steps. "Keep your silence," he said threateningly to Teiresias. "Don't reveal your prophecy in the city."

"You want me to act dishonestly? No! I will not hold my peace."

Reaching the step immediately above the old prophet, Creon looked down at him and said, plaintively, "Then, what would you have me do? Kill my child?"

"That's for you to decide." There was the faintest of smiles on the blind man's lips. "It's for me to speak. Nothing more."

Creon's eyes narrowed. "From where came this curse on me and my son?"

"This youth must offer his lifeblood because of Ares's ancient grudge against Cadmus. If you do this, you will win Ares as an ally. Your son Haemon's betrothal debars him from being the victim. But this tender youth, consecrated to the city's service, might rescue his city by dying."

"Might. . .?"

"It is for you to choose one of these alternatives—either save the city or your son. That's all I have to say. Come, now, daughter, lead me home. It's a fool who practices the diviner's art, for if he makes an adverse pronouncement he makes himself disliked by those who seek him out; yet, if through pity he deceives those who consult him, he sins against heaven. Bright Apollo should have been man's only prophet, for he fears no man."

As Teiresias shuffled away with his daughter, Creon looked up at Eteocles, who had heard it all, and who now smiled back down at him with a look of amusement on his face. Eteocles found Teiresias a tiresome quack, but he knew that many of his countrymen believed in the old man's prophecies. He also disliked his uncle's influence over Theban affairs, even though that influence had kept Eteocles on his throne. It pleased Eteocles that Creon now found himself in this gut-wrenching bind. The young king opened his hands wide, as if to say that this affair was for Creon to resolve. Turning away and entering the palace accompanied by his bodyguards, he left father and son together.

Creon had already made his decision. Stepping down and pulling Megareus into an embrace, he said, softly, "I'm an old man and ready to die to save my country. But you, my son, must up and fly before the whole city learns of this. Teiresias will go to the Governors and around the commanders of the seven gates telling of his prophecy. If you delay, you will die."

"Where can I flee, father?" Megareus asked, still in shock. "To what city?"

Now Creon held his middle son at arm's length and looked him in the eye. "Fly to wherever is furthest removed from this land."

"Name a place, and I'll do as you bid."

"Go west. After passing Delphi, go first to Aetolia. From there, to the wild Thesprotians of Epirus."

"To the mountains?"

Creon nodded approvingly. "Good, you follow me exactly. I'll supply you with the money from the palace."

"It's a good plan, father. Come, let's away."

Father and son hurried to fulfill the escape plan. Creon filled a purse with gold, and the pair hastened to the Neistan Gate. There, the father kissed his middle son and embraced him one last time, before Megareus climbed the wooden ladder to the top of a Neistan tower. There, the pair agreed, the young man would await nightfall, after which he would slip out the gate, sneak by the Argive troops stationed beyond the western wall, and then flee west.[92]

But the idealistic, duty-bound Megareus had no intention of escaping. He feared that in doing so, he would be known as a coward to all who spoke his name from that day forward and would be destined to live in shame for the rest of his life, in exile far from the people and the city he loved. Instead, Megareus chose to make the sacrifice required by Teiresias and so save his people. Better to be remembered for your sacrifice, he reckoned, than your cowardice. Sending away the men with him, he climbed up to stand on the edge of the tower with his sword in hand. Holding on to the tower's wooden roof with his left hand, he took one last look out over the city of his birth. And then, with tears running down his cheeks, Megareus slit his own throat. Heavily did his body fall to the ground outside the tower. The son of Creon had voluntarily made the ultimate sacrifice. Now it was up to the god Apollo to keep his part of the bargain and save Thebes.

18.

THE THUNDER OF ZEUS

At Potniae, the king of Argos stood in the twilight, looking morosely toward the southern city walls. Despite the early Argive success against the mercenaries from Phocis and Phlegra and the fact that the Thebans had eventually been driven back inside all their gates and the city had been sealed off, the day had not gone well for Adrastus. His brother Mecisteus was dead. And the latest report from Amphiaraus at the Proetid Gate confirmed that the king's son-in-law Tydeus had also now died from his wound.

To prevent the Argives from giving their fallen generals funeral rites, the Thebans had succeeded in dragging the bodies of both Mecisteus and Tydeus to the base of a Proetid Tower. There the pair still lay, stripped of their weapons and armor, eerily lit by a funeral pyre that the Thebans had lit outside the gate for their general Melanippus, whose corpse and mutilated head had been retrieved in one last rush to secure his body and that of Tydeus. Any Argive foolish enough to try to reach those bodies would have been an easy target for the archers in the towers above.

With the daylight fading, Adrastus called for a cessation of the assault, withdrawing his troops to the three Argive camps that had sprung up—a large one at Potniae for the southern divisions and another on the Chalcis Road for the northern divisions, with a smaller one west of Thebes opposite the Neistan Gate. Adrastus then summoned his six remaining generals to dinner and a conference at his Potniae headquarters. Polynices and Capaneus only had to come a short distance from their southern commands, while from the northern gates in their chariots came Amphiaraus, Hippomedon, and Parthenopaeus. From the Neistan Gate in the west came Eteoclus.

It was a gloomy meeting, with Tydeus and Mecisteus sorely missed. Apart from Parthenopaeus, none among the Argive commanders had wanted war more than those two. And for their reward, they were the first to die. When Amphiaraus told the others about the funeral pyre outside the Proetid Gate, Eteoclus said that there was also a funeral pyre outside his gate in the west. His men had told him that a Theban officer had fallen from a gate tower after appearing to take his own life. A little while later, wailing women had rushed out the Neistan Gate, and they had begun to strip, wash, and bind the officer's body.

Much later, Adrastus would learn that the Theban officer in question was Megareus, son of Creon, and that the wailing women were the young man's mother Eurydice, sisters Henrioche and the red-headed Pyrrha, and their female servants. Out of respect for the women, Eteoclus had pulled his men back and allowed the women to do their work, as they gathered shields of dead Argives and Thebans and fired a pyre, where they cremated Megareus. No one in the Argive camps was aware that Megareus had killed himself to fulfill the prophecy of Teiresias.

Both armies had by this stage lost two commanders, but the overall numbers were still very much in the Argives' favor. Adrastus sent his six generals away with orders to launch an all-out assault on all gates when the sun rose the next morning. Adrastus was taking personal charge at the Fountain Gate, and the six remaining members of the Seven all prepared their forces at their respective gates. At dawn the commanders led the Argive chariots in a preliminary attack outside all seven gates.

Once again, the chariots raced up and down outside the city, first sending showers of darts and then of sling-stones at the gate towers and the battlements around them, softening up the defenses before the infantry went against the gates with the aim of breaking their way into the city. The new day, the surviving members of the Seven were convinced, would bring them victory.

E teocles spent the night at the Cadmea. With the dawn, he heard the rumble of chariots on the plain. Emerging from his palace in full armor, he was flanked by his bodyguards and other attendants. Of Creon there was no sign: he was in mourning for his dead son. Above, the sky was dark and ominous. A storm was brewing, figuratively and literally. Below, the men of Thebes silently manned their battlements, waiting for the renewed Argive infantry assault.[93]

Standing there atop the steps, Eteocles could see clouds of dust being raised by the Argive chariots as they charged back and forth before the southern gates of Thebes. He could hear the pounding of hooves. He could even hear the grind of chariot wheels on axles. And then he heard the war cries of the warriors in the chariots. As they yelled, the warriors clashed their swords on their shields. Among them, Eteocles knew, was his brother Polynices. Behind the chariots, emerging through the yellow dust, marched the infantry divisions, their men close-packed with shields touching, slowly heading for the gates. These foot soldiers, too, clashed their weapons on their shields. It sounded like five thousand thunderclaps.

In the city, a line of fearful wailing women climbed the wooden steps to the Cadmea. Hundreds of them—mothers, daughters, and sisters of the citizen soldiers of Thebes—flooded around the base of the steps below Eteocles. All of them dropped to their knees and, reaching out to their king, beseeched him to save them.[94]

"The city is surrounded on every side!" cried one wife of the Spartoi.

"We have prayed to the blessed gods that they will protect us as the chariots rattle around our walls," said another woman.

It is said that, no matter what the religion, it is the women who are the most devout. And so it was said in these times.

"Yes, I prayed to Pallas," said a third woman.

"I prayed to Poseidon, lord of the horse and the wave," added another, "begging him to use his trident to destroy the enemy horde."

"We have prayed to Ares and Hera," said an older woman. "And to Aphrodite, mother of our race, asking her to be a wolf to the Argive wolves, and a wolf-slayer!"

An elderly, white-haired woman called up to Eteocles, "Should mother and matron and maiden and bride be hauled by the hair, like a horse is led by the forelock, with a ripping of clothing as they go to their ruin? Should the unwed bride be raped like the reaping of unripe corn?"

Eteocles's face was dark with rage. "Oh, you intolerable pack! You hags!" he called down to them as he paced back and forth. "Do you think this will help the city? Will it inspire a bold resistance in our beleaguered troops? Good times or bad, may I never again live with a woman. The courage of a woman is submissive, rash, beyond reason. And when she's timid, she's an added plague to home and fatherland! Whoever they may be—man, woman, or some despicable being halfway between them both—whoever from this moment fails in most strict obedience to my orders shall publicly be stoned to death!"

Death by stoning was the traditional punishment for treason throughout Greece. This threat from Eteocles caused the female wailing to cease and to be replaced by pale-faced shock, as a greater fear of Eteocles than of the enemy outside the walls took hold of the women. In all the years he had been on the throne, Eteocles had never before revealed the depth of his disdain for women, and homosexuals.

"Go, remain indoors, and don't get in the way of our plans," the king commanded. When the women remained frozen where they were, he bellowed, "Now! Didn't you hear? Or do I speak to the deaf? Deaf females at that!"

"Son of Oedipus," said one woman in reply, "you cannot blame us. Fear grips our hearts. We are doomed!"

Many other women timidly voiced their agreement.

"Do you think a seaman panics and rushes from bow to stern to save his ship in a storm?" Eteocles asked. "Bloody sacrifice, offerings to oracles, these are men's matters. When the needs of war put all things to the test, your business"—he cast his gaze around the throng—"is submissive silence and to stay indoors. Calm your wild thoughts. This is all caused by excessive fear."

"In submissive silence?" asked one woman, whose cheeks were wet with tears. "My fears are my master, and my tongue runs away with itself."

Seeing resistance to his will, the king cunningly changed his tack. "Then, if I cannot command you, let me entreat you. With good grace, do as I ask you, and go home!"

"Have you personally begged the gods to help this city?" one woman called. It was strongly rumored in Thebes that Eteocles never curried favor with any deity because he believed the gods had cursed his father and his family.

Eteocles sighed, then said, "This I confirm by solemn oath: I have vowed to the gods, 'I will bedeck your sacred shrines and hang the forecourts of your sanctuaries with spoils rent by our spears—the garments of our foes.' So, pray that this will come to pass. I meanwhile will get myself to my post. At the seven gates I have appointed six men of might and mettle, with myself at the seventh. All are equipped to achieve greatness, and none need to be convinced of the need to fire their souls."

With that, Eteocles, followed by his entourage, hurried off down the steps to the city. The women slowly followed, talking worriedly among themselves as they descended beneath a blackening sky. They would do as Eteocles had instructed and go to their homes and bar their doors. But few had any faith in the young king, nor even liked him. Their fears only strengthened once they reached the bottom of the Cadmea steps, for they could hear the sounds of the chariots outside and the sound of sling-stones hitting the towers and battlements like winter hail. With many of their number in tears, the women bustled away to their homes.

Once the Argive chariots had completed their softening-up runs to release darts and sling-stones at the Theban walls, they pulled back.

Their warriors dismounted to take up spears and head up their infantry divisions. The trumpets of all the divisions sounded, and, with their generals in the lead, the foot soldiers of every division charged their respective gates at the double, emitting a ferocious roar. Overhead, the clouds were growing ever darker. Thunder rumbled in the distance. The gods, many a soldier in this battle thought, were unhappy. But unhappy with which side?

Young Parthenopaeus, son of Atalanta, led the Argive attack at the Boreas Gate, which lay near the tomb of Amphion, builder of the city's walls. Commanding the Theban defenders at this gate was Actor, one of the sons of the Theban Governor Oenops. Under cover of their raised shields, Parthenopaeus and hundreds of his men clustered outside the gate, bashing the wood of its two bronze-reinforced doors with the hilts of their swords, to no avail. Applying no science to their efforts, the Argives attacked the gates of Thebes with more spirit than knowledge.[95]

The Argives' sole tactic appeared to be to attempt to break through the gates with brute force. The attackers hadn't come with battering rams or siege engines on wheels—that sort of siege engineering was centuries away. It hadn't even occurred to them to manufacture scaling ladders to go over the walls, or to bring materials to light fires at the base of the gates. Meanwhile, the defenders above were raining darts, arrows, sling-stones, and pieces of broken rock down on the attackers, causing numerous casualties. Once they ran out of stones, the desperate and determined Thebans resorted to breaking off and using the battlements' decorative top layer of stone coping.

To underestimate your opponent is among a general's worst failings. The overconfident Adrastus and the Seven had fallen into this very self-made trap, and they were paying the price for their mistake. Only once young Parthenopaeus reached his assigned gate did he form a plan of assault. "Bring fire and picks!" he ordered.[96]

So, the picks used for camp-building were brought up and passed through the ranks, beneath the cover of shields, to the men in front.

Other men brought armfuls of firewood, and a burning torch. The wood was also passed forward, and heaped in front of the gates. With colleagues around them covering them with their shields, several men began digging beneath the stones on either side of the gate. Parthenopaeus himself took a turn with a pick. His primary plan was to dislodge the lower stones and then remove those above them, until the gateway's frame gave way, causing the gates to collapse. It was a workable plan, but it would take time. A lot of time.

Parthenopaeus's second plan, burning the gates, couldn't be accomplished while the men working with the picks were so close. So the firewood remained unlit. Meanwhile, numerous Argive attackers were being killed or injured by the rain of missiles from above. Wounded men were being regularly passed back beneath the shields, with reinforcements from the rear being called forward to take their places.

One of the defenders atop a Boreas Gate's tower was a Theban citizen named Periclymenus. He claimed to be a descendant of the god Poseidon, and because Periclymenus was a large, physically powerful man with an equally powerful temper, no one disputed his claim. Periclymenus had arrived at the Boreas Gate before dawn that morning, driving a wagon filled with broken stones that he had carried to the top of the gate tower to use as ammunition against the Argive attackers, and these stones, too, were causing injury and death as Periclymenus hurled them down.

After the Theban spy had revealed the designs on the shields of each member of the Seven and their gate assignments, Creon had sent these details around the towers. Now, looking down from the top of the Boreas Towers, Periclymenus could see, amid a sea of white Argive shields bearing the wolf motif, a Mycenaean figure-of-eight shield with the images of a Sphinx and a supine man. Periclymenus recognized this as the shield of Parthenopaeus of Arcadia.

Having identified his prime target, big Periclymenus raised stones from his diminishing stockpile and heaved them down at the image of the Sphinx. Some stones bounced off the shield, but several eventually broke it. Then the shield sagged under the weight of the cascade of stones. Parthenopaeus sank to his knees, injured. The young general's men pulled him from the face of the wall and passed him back through the shielded ranks. Periclymenus soon saw Parthenopaeus being carried away from the wall by four men. There was no mistaking who he was. The handsome, clean-shaven face and the long blond hair, bloodied as they were, could only belong to the son of Atalanta.

Grinning from ear to ear, Periclymenus turned to Actor, Theban commander at the Boreas Gate, and proclaimed, "I have split open the head of the cub of the huntress! I have killed Parthenopaeus!"[97]

It was a premature claim. Parthenopaeus was suffering from a concussion so severe that he couldn't stand; nor could he see straight, and he was vomiting. As he was returned to his camp for medical attention, command of the Argive troops attacking the Boreas Gate devolved to one of the captains under Parthenopaeus, who decided to try his chief's second plan. Setting alight the wood at the base of the gateway's double wooden doors, he and his men withdrew.

Attackers at all the other gates, under sustained missile fire from above, were experiencing similar difficulties. At the Electra Gate, the men led by Capaneus were falling all around their raging commander. Leaving the assault, Capaneus took his chariot back to the Potniae camp. There he loaded a long wooden ladder onto the chariot—he had made it from a fir tree he'd cut down while the army was camped on Mount Cithaeron. Taking the chariot back to where his troops were still struggling against the Electra Gate, he dismounted and, with his shield raised, carried the ladder on his right shoulder through the crowd of men at the gate, who parted to let him through. In the black clouds above, lightning flashed, followed within seconds by thunderclaps close by.

"Not even the awful lightning of Zeus will prevent me from utterly destroying this city!" Capaneus bellowed. Ignoring missiles from above that glanced off his shield and the shields of soldiers who were trying to cover him, he placed the ladder against the tower.[98]

His armor-bearer then handed him his famous torch, which was already alight. Made from bronze with an ivory handle, this torch's large bowl was filled with highly flammable pine resin. Holding his massive oval shield above him with his left hand and with the torch in his right hand, Capaneus climbed the ladder. Once he neared the top, he fought off defenders in the tower by pushing fire into their faces, then set alight the tower's timber rafters and thatched roof.

To cheers from Capaneus's men below, the roof and woodwork were soon ablaze, and every Theban defender fled the burning summit of the tower. This brought a cessation of missiles against the Argive troops at the gate. Torch still in hand, a grinning Capaneus waited on the ladder as flames engulfed the tower. His plan was to climb into the tower once the flames subsided, followed by his men, and from there open the gate from the inside. Suddenly there was an almighty flash of lightning, accompanied by a deafening thunderclap. The lightning had struck Capaneus! Blackened from head to foot by this strike, Capaneus was catapulted from the ladder—spinning like a wheel, according to some observers. He was dead before he hit the ground. Still burning, his torch lay beside his crumpled body at the foot of the tower. His terrified troops fled the scene in panic.

From atop a tower of the nearby Hypsistan Gate, King Eteocles had witnessed this. Returning to the ground, he hurried to the Boreas Towers, whose summit was by this time fully ablaze, with flames reaching into the dark sky.

"Zeus struck Capaneus down with a thunderbolt!" one of his men said, as awestruck Theban soldiers crowded around their king on his arrival.

Eteocles, who had demonstrated time and again that he had little time for the gods, was unimpressed. All he was interested in was again manning the top of the Boreas Gate tower so that it could be defended. But now the gods seemingly came to his aid, for the heavens opened and rain began to sheet down, quickly extinguishing the flames. This enabled Eteocles to send gate commander Polyphontes and a party of his men up to the top of the scorched tower. The same downpour also put out the fire at the Boreas Gate.

As the rain fell thickly all around Thebes, King Adrastus rallied the frightened men of Capaneus's division and ordered all Argive forces to pull back from the gates, stationing them in lines out of missile range in front of all seven gates, until the rain should stop and conditions underfoot dry out. There the bedraggled Argive troops stood, soaked by the rain, with the equally wet defenders of the city watching them from their walls and towers, as both sides waited for someone to make the next move.

And then, after the storm passed and the rain finally did stop, all seven gates opened. Charging out of them came the chariots of the Theban nobles, including Creon's eldest son Haemon. Thebes had far fewer chariots than the Argive army—forty or fifty, but in a single mass they were a formidable sight. Nonetheless, the wet ground was against them. Churning up mud, they labored to make several runs back and forth in front of the Argive lines, with their warriors launching a shower of darts.

Seeing the lines hold against the missiles, the commanders of some Spartoi chariots made the daring choice to charge into the Argive front line in an attempt to break it. This saw Argive spearmen being thrown into the air by the impact of charging chariots. In several cases, bodies fell between wheel and chariot, and the wheels came off the vehicles. Argive soldiers surged onto the wrecks, killing drivers and commanders and capturing their horses. Within minutes, the breaches in the Argive lines were repaired and once more became solid. The sacrifices of the Theban chariot crews had been for nothing.[99]

With Argive troops yelling obscenities at them, the rest of the Theban chariots turned and raced back to their starting points within the city, and the gates closed behind them. A token display of defiance from Eteocles, it had achieved nothing either tactically or strategically—other than a brief elevation of Theban morale.[100]

19.

ONE ON ONE

The thunderstorm had passed. With blue sky replacing the earlier black heavens, sunshine streamed over the saturated battlefield. Eteocles was below a tower of the Hypsistan Gate when his uncle Creon approached him. Taking the king aside, Creon urged a plan upon him—a plan, he said, that would deliver Thebes from peril, one way or another, if Eteocles had the courage to put it in motion.

It was late morning when Eteocles appeared on the top of a tower at the Hypsistan Gate, climbing up onto the parapet so that he could be clearly seen. First requiring silence from his own men and then that of the nearby Argive troops, he called, loudly, "You captains of Greece and chieftains of Argos assembled here and you men of Thebes, don't put your lives on the line for Polynices or for me! There's no point in continuing this conflict. You must not lose your lives here. The earth has been sown with enough dead already."

This generated a buzz of conversation in all quarters.

"Men of Argos!" Eteocles called anew, "I myself excuse you from this risk. For I will engage my brother in single combat. And if I slay him, I will possess my throne without a rival, and you, men of Argos, you must return to your land. But if I come off the worst, I will bequeath the city to him."[101]

Deciding a battle by putting up a single champion from each side was an age-old resolution to war, and Eteocles's proposal brought an even more spirited swell of conversation.

Now, from the Argive ranks immediately opposite, Polynices burst forth. "I accept the challenge!" he called.

And all the troops on both sides shouted their approval.

"Then send three representatives to agree on a truce and the terms of our single combat, bound by sacred oath," Eteocles responded.

Before long, the Electra Gate opened. Unarmed and carrying olive branches, Eteocles's uncle Creon and the elders Astacus and Oenops, representing the king and Governors of Thebes, emerged and walked down the Plataea Road toward the Argive lines. As they solemnly tramped toward the attacking army, they passed the heaped bodies of attackers and defenders that lay outside the gate, along with discarded shields and weapons. Behind the trio came several priests, leading three sheep. At the same time, Amphiaraus, Hippomedon, and Eteoclus, representing King Adrastus and Polynices, approached from the opposite direction, also unarmed and toting olive branches and likewise followed by priests.

The two parties met on the road in the middle of the battlefield. There, watched in silence by the men of both armies and from afar by Eteocles in his tower and by Adrastus and Polynices from the king's chariot behind their army's lines, the six ambassadors proceeded to agree to terms and exchange sacred oaths for a truce during which Eteocles and Polynices would engage in single combat.

The truce was to commence at once and last until after the outcome of the fight between the brothers was known. That fight would take place right where they were meeting, in the open beside the Plataea Road, at dawn the following day. The men from both armies could come, unarmed, to witness it. Only the two participants could come armed. Should Eteocles be the winner, the Argive army would pack up and go home, with Eteocles recognized as the undisputed king of Thebes. Should Polynices be victorious, he would be hailed the undisputed king of Thebes and his army would march back to Argos, with a victorious Polynices paying his troops a bounty from the treasury of Thebes.

The priests then slaughtered the three sheep and committed the carcasses to a fire they built there on the plain. Closely watched by the ambassadors, the priests consulted the flames, then pronounced the omens they believed they portended.

"There is a damp reek in the air," said the unhappy chief priest for the Argive side. "This is a bad omen."

"However," said the chief priest for the Theban side, "note the two tongues and forks of fire, and the tapering flame. This gives decisions on two points, being both a sign of victory and of defeat."[102]

"Well," said Creon, who had lost his son Megareus to this short, bloody war, looking at Amphiaraus with eyes reddened from weeping for his favorite son, "do we proceed with the challenge, or do we not?"

Amphiaraus, who had lost his relative Mecisteus the previous day, hesitated. There was the bad omen to consider. On the other hand, for one side the outcome of the challenge would mean victory and for the other defeat, so there was an equal chance that Polynices would be the victor. And if Polynices, the taller, stronger brother, was victorious, the war would be over. Uppermost in the mind of Amphiaraus was the prediction of the oracle at Delphi that he himself would die here beneath the walls of Thebes. If this challenge went ahead, the army of Argos would march away and there would be no more fighting beneath the walls whichever way it ended. Perhaps then Amphiaraus would have thwarted the prophecy. For Amphiaraus, the need to save his own life was paramount, and there could be only one answer. "We shall proceed," he announced, sounding almost relieved.

So the ambassadors withdrew and the men of both sides were informed that the challenge was to take place at sunrise the following day. The Argive troops returned to their camps.

As the first golden streaks of the rising sun appeared in the eastern sky, the three southern gates of Thebes opened and the defenders came filing out to witness the fight between the champions of Thebes and Argos. From their camps on three sides of the city came the troops of the besieging Argive army, the infantry and cavalry on foot and their officers in their chariots. All came without their armor, helmets, or weapons, wearing tunics and cloaks in the early-morning chill.

A tense silence hung in the air as the thousands of men formed a vast circle beside the Plataea Road beneath the brightening sky. The Thebans created a half-circle on the city side; the Argives completed the circle by sitting and standing on the outer side, with their officers drawing up their chariots behind the circle and then moving to stand at the forefront of the spectators' ranks. Eteocles then came out the Electra gate in his chariot accompanied by his charioteer, and Polynices arrived in his chariot from Potniae. Wearing glittering armor, both men dismounted and walked through the spectators to the circle. They were followed by their charioteers and armor-bearers carrying their helmets, shields, and spears.

When the brothers came to the circle, they stood facing each other with a space of perhaps fifty yards between them. Neither man flinched. Both had come resolved to win. On Polynices's side, Adrastus came to him to offer words of support, followed by the remaining members of the Seven—Amphiaraus, Hippomedon, Eteoclus, and, with his head swathed in a bandage and aided by his charioteer, young Parthenopaeus.

Adrastus kissed his son-in-law on both cheeks, then handed Polynices his shield. Adorned with the figures of Justice and himself, it was scuffed from days of battle beneath the Hypsistan Gate. "Polynices," said the king, "it rests with you to set up an image of Zeus as a trophy and to crown Argos with great renown."

Hippomedon stepped up and placed Polynices's Corinthian helmet on his head, then tied the leather chin-strap tight. Eteoclus handed Polynices his spear.

On the other side of the circle, Creon gave Eteocles a shield that sported the charging boar, one of the symbols of Thebes. "We both know what we must do this day," Creon told his nephew. "Now you are fighting for your city. If you are victorious, the sovereign's scepter will remain within your grasp."[103]

Astacus placed Eteocles's helmet on his head, and Oenops handed him his spear.

From the other side of the circle, King Adrastus called, "Thebes, is your champion ready?"

"He is," Creon responded. "Is your champion ready, Argos?"

"I am ready!" Polynices declared.

The two brothers stepped forward and stood, on the inner perimeter of the man-made circle, facing each other, shields raised, spears in their right hands. Polynices was stone-faced. He had overcome the shock of losing his brother-in-law and best friend Tydeus and the astonishment of seeing Capaneus killed by lightning. In the night, he had wrestled with the ethics of killing his own brother to reclaim his crown. He had won that fight. Polynices had the capacity to be single-minded, and that was what he now became. He focused on outwitting and defeating a foe; no more, no less. Across the patch of earth that separated them, Eteocles was equally focused. He had absolutely no compunction about killing his elder brother. In fact, he was looking forward to it. Once Polynices was out of the way, Eteolces's rule would be unchallenged.

Slowly, the two men began walking toward each other. And then, suddenly, Eteocles ran at Polynices, and the spectators erupted with a full-throated roar that continued as long as the brothers' duel lasted. The fight began with dashes and feints, as both men peered over the top of their shields, and continued with each brother warily testing the other, looking for a weakness, an opening.

Both men were targeting the throat, aiming at the jugular, to inflict a lethal blow. Young, fit, and agile, both men had excellent reflexes. What each was looking for was a gap between shield and body when the other moved to make a strike.

After much parrying, Eteocles made a bold overhand thrust. Just in time, Polynices placed his shield in the way. The force of Eteocles's blow meant that his spear-tip lodged in Polynices's shield, and, as Eteocles tried frantically to pull his weapon free, he took his eyes from his opponent. This was the opportunity that Polynices had been waiting for. Seeing an opening, he thrust forward with his spear, past the edge of Eteocles's wavering shield, driving it into Eteocles's side. A roar went up from the watchers, combining the exhultation of one side with the horror of the other.

When his brother, looking shocked, involuntarily sagged onto one knee, Polynices closed in for the kill. Letting go of his own spear and discarding his shield, which was now weighed down by Eteocles's embedded spear, Polynices drew his sword from the scabbard on his left hip.[104]

But Eteocles was not finished. As Polynices advanced to deliver the coup de grâce, with his sword now held in two hands to take off Eteocles's head, Eteocles drew his own sword, and, in the very instant that Polynices swung his blade at his sibling's neck, Eteocles drove his blade up between his elder brother's legs. The tip of Eteocles's sword went so far up through his body, it pierced Polynices's heart. Polynices had exposed himself to the exact same mortal blow as his brother-in-law Tydeus.

Too late, Polynices realized that he, too, was a dead man. "Come join me in the Shades," he gasped to his brother before, as Eteocles withdrew his sword, falling, dead, on top of Eteocles. Not that Eteocles would live to celebrate his brother's defeat; he was drowning in his own blood and would soon also draw his last breath.

The watchers raised a new cry, with each side urging their champion to get up. But neither man rose. Creon and Amphiaraus came forward, and each knelt beside his champion and checked for signs of life. Both men shook their heads. Eteocles and Polynices had fulfilled the wish—and the curse—of their late father Oedipus by killing each other.

Now Creon raised his right hand, giving a signal. What followed was the idea of Eteocles, who had already demonstrated his lack of respect for the sanctity of sacred vows. But Creon not only had agreed to it, he now executed it.

From beneath tunics and cloaks, the soldiers of Thebes produced short swords and daggers that they had hidden by order of Eteocles, and with a roar they rushed on the unarmed Argive troops, in contravention of the truce agreed by both sides the previous day. At the same time, the waiting chariots of Thebes came charging out of the southern gates with their crews fully armored and armed.

What followed was a rout. Many Argive soldiers were killed on the plain. Others were chased back to the camp at Potniae, where they had run to arm themselves. Many survivors kept running, fleeing all the way to Mount Cithaeron before they were safe from pursuit.

"The truce! The oaths!" Argive soldiers cried as they were cut down.

But the Thebans would no doubt later excuse their act of treachery by saying that the truce had ended the moment that Eteocles and Polynices had died. Theban troops had orders to seek out and kill the Argive officers, with the members of the Seven at the top of their execution list. The three remaining sons of Astacus hunted down the last, unarmed members of the Seven in their chariots and dispatched them. Ismarus ran down and killed Hippomedon. Leades ended the life of Eteoclus. And Amphidicus was easily able to overtake and slay the wounded Parthenopaeus, who was barely able to hang on in his careering vehicle, let alone avoid Amphidicus's spear.[105]

Amphiaraus succeeded in reaching his chariot, in which he and his charioteer Baton attempted to make their escape. Periclymenus, the man who had wounded Parthenopaeus the previous day, had set his sights on killing the Prophet, and he gave chase in his chariot. Feeling naked with neither weapons nor protective armor, Amphiaraus was wild-eyed with fear as the Pythia's prophecy that he would die outside the walls of Thebes seemed about to be realized. Yet, unwilling to give in to his fate and driven by the basic human instinct to survive, he urged Baton to save them both.[106]

As the two chariots sped away from the battlefield and raced across the plain, Periclymenus gradually overtook Amphiaraus. As he came up behind his target and was about to launch his spear into Amphiaraus's back, an earthquake shook the area. A long, narrow crevasse opened in the plain right in front of Amphiaraus, and into the gaping hole in the plain plunged the chariot. Amphiaraus, Baton, and their horses fell to their deaths, while Periclymenus's charioteer managed to just avoid the crevasse and pull away to one side of it. The myth would grow that Zeus himself had opened this hole in the ground and swallowed Amphiaraus, sending him directly to the Underworld.[107,108]

King Adrastus was also able to run as far as his own chariot, his unarmed bodyguards giving their own lives to permit their king to live. He reached the vehicle, only to find that one of his two horses had been seriously wounded by the darts of the Theban charioteers. Unhitching his famous white horse Arion from the chariot's yoke, Adrastus mounted up and, riding bareback, successfully made his escape south to Mount Cithaeron on the steed he claimed had been given to him by Heracles, a steed that easily outran the Theban chariots that attempted to chase it down. Of the leaders of the Argive army, King Adrastus was the only one to escape and survive. Every member of the Seven perished there outside Thebes.

Perhaps a thousand men of the Argive army perished with the Seven, either during the assaults on the gates or when the Thebans treacherously fell on them following the mutual deaths of Polynices and Eteocles. Theban losses, combining the dead mercenaries from Phocis and Phlegra with those Thebans who were killed during the conflict, were as heavy as those of their opponents, if not more, even though Thebes was victorious. This battle spawned the Greek phrase "Cadmean victory," meaning a victory that brings destruction to the victors. For not only had Thebes suffered grievously in repelling the Argive invasion, the war between Argos and Thebes was not yet over.[109]

THE FIGHT OVER BODIES

With the death of Eteocles, the Governors of Thebes elected Creon to serve as regent of Thebes until Eteocles's son Laodamas came of age and could be crowned king. Creon immediately issued a proclamation that neither Polynices nor any other member of the Argive army should be given funeral rites or cremated. All were to be left where they had fallen, to rot or be consumed by wild dogs. Any person who disobeyed this commandment was to be put to death.

All through the siege of Thebes, Antigone and her sister Ismene had been confined by their uncle and guardian Creon to rooms on the top floor of his house in the city. Now Creon permitted the sisters to join their mother in washing and binding the body of Eteocles, which was then cremated with full rites outside the city on a pyre made from discarded Argive shields and the wreckage of Argive chariots. The female members of the families of all the other Theban dead similarly located their men and placed them on pyres outside all seven city gates.[110]

Jocasta, made bereft by the deaths of both her sons at the hands of each other, and embittered because she was forced to leave Polynices lying on the battlefield as a result of her brother's decree, went back up to the palace on the Cadmea. There she strung a length of cloth from a rafter and, this time, succeeded in hanging herself.

Just as Creon was keeping the promise he had given to Eteocles about preventing funeral rites for his brother, Antigone, sister of Polynices and Eteocles, was intent on keeping the promise she had given to Polynices at Colonos that she would ensure he received those rites. In the night, she went outside the city with a servant, searching for the body of her eldest brother so that she could wash, bind, and cremate it, in defiance of Creon's order. Creon had set watchmen among the Argive dead to ensure that his decree was observed, and these men sat at small watch-fires around the battlefield.

By the early morning, several of these watchmen had nodded off to sleep, enabling Antigone to locate the body of Polynices among the many hundreds of Argive corpses, only for there to be an earth tremor, a successor to the quake on the last day of the fighting around Thebes. The tremor woke the watchmen, who, spotting Antigone, seized and arrested her, taking her to Creon at the Cadmea.

Flying into a rage at his niece's defiance, Creon had her taken to a large tomb outside the city, where she was thrown inside. Creon then ordered the entrance bricked over. His son Haemon, who was engaged to marry Antigone and had strong feelings for her, came to save her, despite his feelings never being returned by Antigone. Too late, Haemon discovered that Antigone had hanged herself inside the tomb, emulating her mother's fate. Shattered, Haemon fell on his sword, killing himself. His mother Eurydice, already grieving for the loss of her son Megareus, who had taken his own life to fulfill the prophecy of Teiresias, was so distraught when she learned of the death now of her eldest boy that she, too, committed suicide. Now Creon, who had lost his two eldest sons and his wife in a matter of days, was feeling the same pain of loss that his decree had caused others.

Meanwhile, King Adrastus of Argos had crossed Mount Cithaeron and reached the Attic city of Eleusis, which lay at the western extremity of Athens's power. While ordinary soldiers of the Argive army who had fled from the carnage at Thebes tramped home to restart their former lives, Adrastus was joined at Eleusis by officers who had also escaped. Adrastus, incensed by the decree of Creon that prevented the provision of death rites to the men from Argos, made offerings with his officers to the goddess Demeter at her shrine at Eleusis in hopes of the gods' intervention.

At Athens, King Theseus learned of this, and he came to Eleusis driving a chariot drawn by four white horses. Like Adrastus, Theseus was enraged by the decree of Creon, which he considered unjust and unholy, and he sent a cavalry force galloping to Thebes to immediately secure the bodies of the fallen Argives. Theseus followed at a slower pace with a convoy of wagons for the dead. After Creon resisted the Athenian demand, there was a short, sharp skirmish outside Thebes in which the Theban troops were routed by the Athenian cavalry.

Creon was captured in this melee; but when Theseus arrived, he declined to draw his sword against him. Instead, the pair sat down to agree to a treaty via which the bodies of the opposing dead were repatriated to their own people.[111]

King Theseus returned to Eleusis with the Argive corpses. But one body had eluded Theseus. In defiance of his grandfather, Maeon, son of Haemon, had recovered the body of Tydeus outside the Proetid Gate. Maeon hadn't forgotten that Tydeus had spared his life following the cowardly ambush at Potniae, and he had full rites performed for the Calydonian prince, then cremated him. Maeon interred Tydeus's ashes beneath a mound outside the Proetid Gate, beside the Chalcis Road.

The site of Tydeus's last resting place lay beside the tomb of Melanippus, the Theban champion who had killed him, and the Tomb of the Children of Oedipus, which contained the remains of Eteocles and Antigone.[112]

By the time King Theseus returned to Eleusis with the bodies of the fallen, the mothers, wives, and daughters of the dead fighting men from Argos had arrived at the city after walking for many days all the way from Argos with ashes on their heads, bloody scratches on their faces, and their clothes ripped, in accordance with Greek mourning ritual. Funeral pyres were raised outside Eleusis for the now-rotting dead, with the recovered bodies of five members of the Seven prominent— Polynices, Hippomedon, Capaneus, Eteoclus, and Parthenopaeus. Under Greek law, the dead could not be brought inside cities, so bodies had to be cremated and interred outside their boundaries.

Evadne, the wife of Capaneus, was so distraught at his death that she threw herself on the fire to be with her husband. Like him, she was consumed by the flames. It was a distressing ending to a noble episode—the recovery and burial of fallen Argive fighters—in which Athenians took great pride.[113]

Once the ashes were interred at Eleusis, King Adrastus and his people sadly returned to Argos. But the antagonism toward Thebes over the treacherous, dishonorable way the war had been brought to a conclusion did not die. It would give birth to a new Argive campaign against Thebes, led by the sons of the Seven.

21.

THE OFFSPRING SUCCEED WHERE
THEIR FATHERS FAILED

Ten years after the defeat of the Seven, a new army assembled at Argos. The sons of the Seven had vowed to avenge their fathers, and they came together to go against Thebes, which, with the death in old age of the crafty, duplicitous Creon, was now ruled by the son of Eteocles, Laodamas, who was aged around twenty by this time.

These sons of the Seven, now mostly aged in or close to their twenties, were called the Epigoni (Offspring) by the Greeks. Aegialeus, son of King Adrastus, was chief among the agitators for the new campaign, along with Thersander, eldest son of Polynices. Thersander had married Demonissa, a daughter of Amphiaraus, and she had borne him a son, Tisemenus, grandson of Polynices and great-grandson of Oedipus. Another who was keen to go against Thebes was Diomedes, son of Tydeus, who like his father had a glib tongue. But it was said by his detractors that unlike his father, Diomedes was not so skilled in combat.[114]

Aegialeus, Thersander, and Diomedes sent to the oracle of Delphi for a prophecy that would strengthen their campaign, and the Pythia replied that the Offspring would only conquer if Alcmaeon, eldest son of Amphiaraus the Prophet, was the first through the gates of Thebes. But Eriphyle, widow of Amphiaraus and mother of Alcmaeon, forbade either of her sons from participating, fearing they would die in the campaign and she would be left without any male relatives.

So, in return for allowing her sons to join the campaign, Aegialeus, Thersander, and Diomedes offered Eriphyle the cloak of Harmonia, a garment in which Polynices had wrapped the necklace of Harmonia when he smuggled the boar-tusk casket out of Thebes. Eriphyle already had the necklace, and, now tempted by the cloak of the bride of Cadmus, she agreed to allow her sons Alcmaeon and Amphilocus to join the second campaign against Thebes. It should be remembered that both boys had sworn to murder their mother should Amphiaraus fail to return from the first war against Thebes, but neither had taken any step toward fulfilling their vow.

These five sons of the Seven were joined by Sthenelus, son of Capaneus, and Polydorus, son of Hippomedon. Medon, son of Eteoclus, also joined the Offspring. Promachus, son of Parthenopaeus, was another recruit. He was as yet well short of coming of age so was brought into the group to demonstrate that every one of the Seven was represented by their offspring. These sons of the Seven were joined by Euryalus, the son of Mecisteus and nephew of Adrastus. In this way, every one of the leading men who had fallen in the quest of the Seven against Thebes was represented.[115]

To meet the prophecy of the Delphic oracle, the Offspring elected as their leader Alcmaeon, son of Amphiaraus, and, like their fathers, they all made sacred vows to take Thebes. As part of these vows, they swore to send to the Temple of Apollo at Delphi the finest of the spoils from a conquered Thebes. The Argive army of the Offspring assembled under the aegis of old King Adrastus, who would accompany the Offspring on the campaign and lead the Argive army in the same way that he had led the army of the Seven. This force was not as large as that which had accompanied the Seven a decade earlier. Apart from troops from Argos and Sicyon, the force included a contingent sent by Mycenae and Arcadia and formal contributions from each of Corinth and Megara, with which Adrastus had sealed treaties.

As part of the preparations, women of Argos worked through the night, weaving vests for the city's soldiers, while artisans toiled to make new chariots and helmets, the latter sporting expensive purple plumes for the officers.[116]

When the Argive army marched on Thebes, it took the same route as the Seven to Mount Cithaeron, collecting contingents along the way. Once over the mountain, the force followed the advice of Adrastus in continuing to mimic the same route as that taken by the Seven, skirting along the eastern fringe of the Theban Plain to the Chalcis Road northeast of Thebes, laying waste to every Theban village it came upon en route.

The Governors of Thebes had known the Argives were preparing for a fresh war with them, so they increased the height of the city wall with additional layers of bricks. But Laodamas, the young king of Thebes, became convinced, as his father had been before him, that the way to beat the Argives was in a battle in the open, outside the city. With his confidence boosted by the fact that the Theban army he assembled actually outnumbered that of the Offspring, Laodamas led the Theban army up the Chalcis Road to confront the invaders. He found the Argive Army camped in the foothills of Mount Hypastus, near the village of Glisas. This was just under a mile from Teumessus, which had been destroyed by the Seven during their campaign. Boldly, Laodamas encamped his army within sight of the Argive force.

The Battle of Glisas was soon fought just outside the village, to the right of the Chalcis Road. In the battle, King Laodamas sought out Aegialeus, son of King Adrastus, whom he saw as his equivalent in rank. In their one-on-one fight, Laodamas killed Aegialeus. Another member of the Offspring to fall in the fighting was the boy soldier Promachus, son of Parthenopaeus, who was no match for grown men.

But Laodamas was in turn killed by the Argive commander, Alcmaeon. With the death of their king, the Theban forces lost both their commander and their will to win. With the Theban army routed, survivors fled back to Thebes. The Offspring chose to remain at Glisas to give funeral rites to Promachus and Argive officers who had fallen with him. Their ashes were subsequently interred in a mound built on the battlefield. The body of Aegialeus was not included in this ceremony. King Adrastus, devastated at losing his son and heir, planned to take Aegialeus home to Argos for cremation.

The victorious Argive force then marched on Thebes. As it approached, emissaries came out of the city to discuss a truce. It turned out that the elderly seer Teiresias had ordained that the people of Thebes must abandon their city. The Offspring agreed to allow those Thebans who wished to do so to evacuate the city, on the condition they leave behind their gold and Manto, daughter of Teiresias. A portion of that gold would be sent to Delphi, to thank Apollo for the Argive victory predicted by his oracle, while Manto would be sent to act as slave to the Pythia. These conditions were accepted by the Thebans.

Many people of Thebes departed in two wagon convoys. Knowing that King Theseus offered sanctuary to refugees, one group, having fallen out with Teiresias, went south to Attica, where they founded a settlement, Hestiae, under Athenian rule.

The other group went west with Teiresias. En route to Thessaly, this convoy led by Teiresias stopped for water at the Tilphussa spring in the foothills of Mount Tiphosium, just to the south of Lake Copais in Boeotia. Teiresias passed away shortly after drinking from the spring, which his people became convinced had been poisoned. These refugees continued on to Mount Homoloe in Thessaly in western Greece, south of Tempe and north of Ossa. There, they founded a settlement, Homoloea.

The seven gates of Thebes were left open by her people, and, fulfilling the Pythia's prophecy, Alcmaeon was the first man to enter the conquered city. The Argive army followed. Once inside the walls, the troops hailed Thersander, son of Polynices and grandson of Oedipus, as the new king of Thebes. Diomedes, son of Tydeus, had defied his critics by fighting skillfully and bravely, and, in congratulating his friend Thersander and their fellow Offspring, he was to declare: "We boast ourselves as even better men than our fathers. We took the seven-gated Thebes, though the wall was stronger and our men were fewer in number."[117]

The Argive army then looted the city and pulled down its walls before setting off for home. It had reached Megara when the aged King Adrastus fell ill. He died there from a combination of grief for his lost son Aegialeus and old age. As a consequence, Aegialeus was cremated and interred outside Megara and Adrastus was succeeded as king of Argos by his eldest grandson Diomedes, son of Tydeus. Diomedes would reign as king of Argos for decades before being succeeded by Cyanippus, son of Aegialeus and another grandson of Adrastus.

Following the return of the army to Argos, the Offspring commander Alcmaeon went through with the murder of his mother Eriphyle, as he'd vowed to his father a decade earlier that he would. Alcmaeon, driven mad by this matricide, went into hiding in remote Arcadia, taking the necklace and cloak of Harmonia with him. There he was ambushed and killed, for the necklace and cloak, by local leaders.

Statues of the members of the Offspring would be erected at both Argos and Delphi. Manto, the daughter of Teiresias, was sent to Delphi by Thebes's new king Thersander with part of the loot from Thebes, as promised to Apollo at the campaign's outset. However, the Pythia released Manto from her bondage at Delphi's Temple of Apollo, on the condition that she marry the first man she saw after leaving the sanctuary at Delphi, which she did. That husband, Rhacius, went on to lead the establishment of the city of Caria in Asia Minor. Ocnus, the son of Rhacius and Manto born in Caria, in turn migrated to Italy, where he established a settlement that he named after his mother—Mantua.

Thersander, who had achieved what his father had failed to do in becoming king of Thebes, worked tirelessly to build up Thebes, even succeeding in enticing back many refugees who had fled the city. Those who came from Homoloea entered via the Fountain Gate, no doubt to make offerings of thanks at the adjacent Sanctuary of Heracles or the altar of Apollo Ismenus, or both. As a consequence, the Fountain Gate thereafter became known as the Homolid Gate. Thersander even expanded Thebes's power and influence, among other things taking the town of Erythrae, in the foothills of Mount Cithaeron, from the control of the city of Plataea.

When the Trojan War erupted several decades later, Thersander sailed with a force of Theban warriors to join King Agamemnon of Argos and Mycenae on the plain outside Troy, only to be waylaid and killed at Mysia in Asia Minor on the way. From Argos, several other members of the Offspring joined the siege of Troy. Among them were Tydeus's son Diomedes, and Sthenelus, son of Capaneus. Cyanippus, son of Aegialeus, who'd been too young for the second war against Thebes, grew to manhood in time to also go to the Trojan War. He would be one of the Greek warriors who hid inside the famous Trojan Horse, surviving the war to later succeed Diomedes as king of Argos.

Over the coming centuries, Thebes rebuilt its walls and its army, becoming the most powerful city-state in Greece, even defeating the armies of the mighty Sparta in several famous battles. The Theban army was by that time centered around an elite permanent force of three hundred called the Sacred Band, whose men were all homosexual partners—which would have appalled the earlier King Eteocles – fierce fighters who led Thebes to victory in battle after battle. Thebes's reign ended in the fourth century BC with the defeat of the Greek states by Philip of Macedon and his son Alexander, the future Alexander the Great, when the Sacred Band was wiped out. After Thebes revolted against Macedonian rule, Alexander had six thousand Theban men put to death and the thirty thousand remaining residents sent into slavery in 335 BC, then ordered the city razed to the ground. He permitted just a single house to remain standing, the home of Pindar the poet. Later generations would rebuild Thebes, and during the Byzantine Empire it would be famous for its silks, not its soldiers.

Today, almost nothing remains of the ancient city. The walls have long gone, but the rocky Cadmean hill still rises steeply from the Theban Plain, although it is no longer crowned by its formidable citadel. A modern city (Thiva) of 22,000 friendly people occupies the original Thebes footprint and also spreads south and northwest of it. There is no sign of most of the famed seven gates. Just one, the Electra Gate, has been located by modern archaeologists. Nor is there any hint that here, more than three thousand years ago, the Seven went against Thebes in one of the most famous and complex military adventures of all time.

———————

Did all this really happen? Was the story of the *Seven Against Thebes* and the later victory of their sons historical fact? Although all the ancient dramatists and poets put their own words into the mouths of the characters, with some classical authors such as Euripides and Statius demonstrably fictionalizing aspects of the story for their own dramatic purposes, and with most writers of the time attributing various aspects of the tale to the actions of the gods, the Greeks and Romans were convinced that the basic story was true. Some felt that it equaled or even bested the story told by Homer in his *Iliad* about the siege of Troy.

Pausanias, after visiting Thebes in the second century AD, was to say, "This war between Argos and Thebes was, in my opinion, the most memorable of all those waged by Greeks against Greeks in what is called the Heroic Age." It's hard to disagree with him.[118]

AFTERWORD

SOURCES AND INTERPRETATION

W̲e know from the Greek biographer Plutarch, himself a native of Chaeronaea in Boeotia, who wrote in the first and second centuries AD and served for a time as a priest of Apollo at the oracular shrine at Delphi, that a number of earlier Greek and Roman historians whose work has not survived had written about the campaigns of the Seven against Thebes and the Offspring, all treating these events and the individuals involved as factual.

Writing the biography of the Athenian king Theseus, Plutarch tells of the mission of Theseus and Adrastus to secure the bodies of the fallen heroes after the Seven's assault on Thebes. He notes that while the playwright Euripides, one of our sources for the lives of Oedipus and his family, had the Thebans handing over the bodies through fear of Theseus's force of arms, "the greater part of the historians write" that the handover was part of a negotiated treaty, as described by the third-century BC Greek historian and biographer Philochorus. Statius, writing four centuries later, told of a military clash taking place between Athenian and Theban troops before the treaty, although he describes a skirmish rather than a full-fledged battle.

We know from archaeological evidence that the cities and towns mentioned did exist when and where described in the classical Greek histories, poems, and plays that told of Thebes, Oedipus, and the Seven. Thebes, famous in classical times as the birthplace of the Greek god of wine Dionysus and the hero-god Heracles/Hercules, and the home of the poet Pindar, is considered by some anthropologists and archaeologists to be Europe's oldest continuously occupied town. Traces of the Cadmea and ancient religious sites have been unearthed in and around Thebes. But much remains open to question about ancient Thebes.

For example, did Thebes genuinely possess seven gates in antiquity? Homer stated quite emphatically in his *Odyssey* that Thebes was "seven-gated," and the Greek dramatists Aeschylus and Euripides both allotted seven gates to the city in their works. Certainly, when the Greek geographer Pausanias wrote about a visit to Thebes in the second half of the second century AD, he saw and described the city's seven gates and gave their locations and histories.

According to Greek myth, the early Theban king Amphion, son of the gods Zeus and Antiope, had the walls and seven gates of Thebes built while he played his lyre. The foundations of a circular Electra Gate tower were located early in the twentieth century. But the existence of all seven gates at the time of *Seven Against Thebes* has never been proven—or disproven—by archaeology as recent as American digs at the site by Pennsylvania's Bucknell University between 2012 and 2017.

Numerous roads from all points of the compass terminated at Thebes. Yet the fifth-century BC Athenian playwright Sophocles, in his plays about Oedipus and Thebes, spoke only of the City Gate, a single gate on the road into Thebes that was watched over by the Sphinx in Oedipus's time. But that doesn't necessarily deny the existence of other gates. Aeschylus spoke of the City Gate and wrote in detail about all seven gates of Thebes, meaning the City Gate was a familiar name for one of those seven—most likely the Electra Gate, considered by many the main entrance to Thebes from the south.

A single point of entry to a city the size of Thebes would have been highly impractical and very unlikely. The other Thebes of antiquity, in Egypt (later known as Luxor), had more than a hundred gates. Admittedly, its population was much greater than that of the Greek Thebes, but farmers daily bringing their produce to market would have faced a massive, time-consuming bottleneck if forced to use a single gate.

Numerous gates providing entry from all directions would seem logical. In the nineteenth century, historians identified the potential locations of all seven gates to the ancient Thebes—three in the southern wall, one in the northern wall, two in the west, and one in the northern part of the eastern wall. In addition, these seven gates were linked to six roads. The road between Thebes and Plataea was considered the main road to Thebes in ancient times. Other roads led to Leuctra, Tanagra, Acraephnium, and Thespiae. A sixth road went northeast to the port of Aulis on the Euripus Strait. Aulis was the crossing place for the three-mile journey to the important city of Chalcis on the island of Euboea. Although this highway to the coast from Thebes terminated at Aulis, it was always known as the Chalcis Road.

While a single roosting place was given to the Sphinx by Sophocles, he doesn't tell us its specific location. Was it west, east, north, or south of Thebes? Not that this mattered to ancient storytellers, because they would have rationalized that the winged Sphinx could, like an eagle, soar on the winds to cover all roads to Thebes and then swoop down on its prey. Apollodorus's *Library* names the Sphinx's hiding place as Mount Phicium (Phikion), which lay some distance away, between Argolis and Arcadia, and seems unlikely, although the Sphinx may have originated there.

Of course, the Sphinx was a fictional beast, but most ancient myths are likely to have been inspired by actual events involving mere mortals. Plutarch tells us, in relating the biography of Theseus (who was to play an important part in the lives of Oedipus and his family during the time of the Seven), that a host of murderous highway robbers notoriously operated on Greek roads at the time of Oedipus and the Sphinx.

In fact, when Theseus, as a young man, set off to travel from his birthplace of Troezen (southeast of Argos) to Athens (home of his father Aegeus) to claim his birthright, his mother Aethra, along with his maternal grandfather and tutor Pittheus, begged him to travel by sea to avoid the deadly highway robbers. But Theseus boldly went by road anyway, following the Saronic Gulf, seemingly hoping for an opportunity to show off his martial skills against highway robbers.[119]

Similarly, on the road in the Crommyonian district between Corinth and Megara, Theseus was attacked by—and overcáme—several well-known brigands. Most famously, he killed Phaea, a female highway robber. Plutarch tells us that Phaea was nicknamed the Sow because of her cruelty and foul manners. A later heroic Greek myth that grew around Theseus would turn Phaea into an aged hag who owned a rampaging giant boar called the Crommyonian Sow, which Theseus supposedly killed. This myth would make Theseus's killing of Phaea, a lone woman brigand, which would have been considered far from heroic, into a heroic act as the story was retold down through the ages. One of the other myths surrounding Theseus had him capturing the huge Marathonian bull owned by an old woman on Crete, and this may have led to the morphing of bandit Phaea the Sow from woman bandit to boar-owning hag. Alternatively, some later storytellers simply confused or conflated the two tales.

In the same way, it is possible that the myth of the riddling Sphinx was based upon another female brigand. In this case she would have been a bold and clever woman with a talent for inscrutable riddles, who bore the nickname of the Sphinx and terrorized travelers to Thebes from her hiding place in the hills. The propaganda of Oedipus once he was king of Thebes would have subsequently spread the story that the Sphinx was real, in the same way that the female brigand Phaea the Sow in Theseus's life story was mythologized into a real female boar. This is a possibility I canvass at one point in this book.

Historians generally believe that the kings and royal families in the stories about Thebes really did exist and that the battles and sieges described are likely to have occurred. It's only when the Greek gods are shown as influencing events that the story goes from historical probability to myth. Remove the causational influence of the gods from the story—this god brought pestilence, or that god caused a hole to open in the ground beneath a warrior, for example—and something approaching historical fact can be arrived at. However, the role played by the religious beliefs and practices of the protagonists cannot and should not be discounted, as these influenced their actions.

The story of the Seven going against Thebes inspired countless generations of Greeks and Romans. The stories of Oedipus and the subsequent quest of the Seven against Thebes was handed down verbally for hundreds of years by poets (the traditional tribal storytellers) before appearing in written form in four Greek plays that we know of, written between 750 and 500 BC, but which have not survived to modern times. One of those four Cyclic plays, as they are called, the original *Thebaid*, which told the history of Thebes, has frequently been attributed to Homer. The lost plays are believed to have strongly influenced later classical Greek playwrights.

In the fifth century BC, the Greek playwright Aeschylus wrote *Seven Against Thebes* as the third in a series of plays telling the story of Oedipus and the war between his sons, with which he won first prize in a playwriting competition. Of those three plays, only *Seven Against Thebes* survives in its entirety.

Other Greek playwrights, Sophocles and Euripides, and the historian Apollodorus also covered the story, or elements of it, in their works, as did the later Roman writers Seneca and Statius in the first century AD, and even Julius Caesar a century earlier—his play about Oedipus hasn't survived. Statius, writing late in the first century, certainly used the earlier Greek plays as source material and may have also used Greek histories that no longer survive.

Seneca's play about the life of Oedipus, an obvious attempt to show Seneca's cleverness, was probably the most inept of all the classical accounts of Oedipus. Not only did Seneca's version occasionally digress from the story being unfolded, eliminating suspense, but Seneca had ancient Greeks talking about the Parthian shot a thousand years before it was invented. Worse, Seneca had Queen Jocasta dating King Laius's death to just ten years prior to Oedipus's learning the truth about Laius's murder, after which Oedipus abdicated in favor of his sons Polynices and Eteocles, who subsequently agreed to share the throne. This would have made the boys around nine and eight years of age, respectively, at the time—much too young for what the pair did in the wake of Oedipus's abdication (Eteocles taking the throne for himself, and Polynices fleeing alone to Argos, where he gained sanctuary, married the king of Argos's daughter, and fathered a son before embarking on the Seven's mission against Thebes).

Those events indicate a period of some twenty years between the death of Laius and Oedipus's self-discovery and abdication, during which Oedipus's children were born and grew to maturity. Seneca seems to have confused the time between Laius's death and the abdication of Oedipus with the ten-year period between the initial Seven-against-Thebes campaign and the campaign of their sons, the Epigoni.

Seneca's contemporary Statius, the author who dealt with the Seven against Thebes in the most detail in Roman times, was, like the earlier Sophocles, sympathetic toward some of his female characters in his telling of the story. He was said to have been close to his own wife and stepdaughter, and he seems to have imagined how they would have acted had they sought to recover and cremate his body when he wrote of the attempt of Antigone and Argia to recover the body of Polynices.

Statius often goes into fine detail in his *Thebaid*, even naming the childhood nurse of the wives of Polynices and Tydeus as well as the herald sent by Theseus to Thebes, plus numerous soldiers on both sides of the conflict. It's possible that Statius obtained these details from Greek histories that are no longer extant; but, with none of the surviving Greek sources naming any of these lesser figures, it's likely that Statius invented them.

Statius's timings frequently raise suspicions as to their authenticity. For example, he placed King Theseus's defeat of the Amazons when they invaded Attica in the weeks between the death of Oedipus and the arrival of the Argive women in Athenian territory in quest of their dead from the siege of Thebes. The legend of this Attic War between the Amazons and Theseus, which some modern historians doubt ever took place, was set decades before the Seven went against Thebes, when Theseus was younger and an associate of Heracles, who'd been dead for some years by the time of the Seven.

Statius had Polynices and Tydeus marry the daughters of Adrastus as soon as they reached Argos, which is unlikely, then march against Thebes three years later. The pair's sons from these marriages were among the Offspring who conducted the second Argive campaign against Thebes, ten years after the first. Using Statius's chronology, these sons would have only been twelve by the time of the Offspring's campaign. Most authorities agree that the Seven could only have gone against Thebes some ten years after Polynices and Tydeus sought sanctuary at Argos; a hiatus as brief as three years would have been impossible.

The missions of Creon and Polynices to Oedipus at Colonos, which feature in earlier Greek accounts, go unmentioned by Statius. He gives Tydeus a violent temper, but this doesn't accord with any other source—Euripides merely describes Tydeus as expert in the science of war, but not so well versed in the skills of debate and negotiation. If Tydeus had a violent temper, why wasn't he enraged when Adrastus chose to support Polynices's campaign against Thebes before going against Calydon on Tydeus's behalf? In fact, Tydeus meekly accepted that decision. The Tydeus that comes across from the Greek sources is a vain young man who was supremely confident of his military skills. And in contrast to the very serious Polynices, Tydeus seems to have had a more lighthearted, pragmatic attitude to the mission of the Seven, frequently lifting the spirits of his brother-in-law, with whom he had become close.

Statius gives Arion, Adrastus's stallion, a coat of golden hair and a red mane, while most other sources describe Arion as possessing a white coat and a black mane (Homer gave him a green mane). Statius also describes Theseus of Athens seeming to kill Creon outside Thebes, while all other accounts have Creon ruling as regent of Thebes until Laodamas came of age and ascended the throne.

In describing the events that took place at Nemea early on the march of the Seven to Thebes, Statius has the army running out of drinking water by the time it reaches Nemea, and King Adrastus, supposedly ignorant of where there might be water in the area, sending the Seven in search of a water source, after which the episode with Hypsipyle and the baby Ophelles takes place. This defies logic. Nemea, part of Adrastus's kingdom, was just two days' slow march from Argos. Adrastus would have been fully aware that fresh water was available from the Nemea River on his route, the main road to Corinth, and would have sent scouts ahead to identify campsites, with the army likely to have camped beside the river on the second night of the march. Plus, there is no other report of drought in Argolis that could have dried up water sources at this time.

Most importantly, Statius ignored the earlier Greek source Euripides, who, in his *Hypsipyle*, tells us that Amphiaraus the seer went to Nemea in quest of sacred water for use in religious offerings that he would make on behalf of the army—not for drinking water. While several of Euripides's plot twists, particularly in his *Phoenician Maidens*, were clearly invented, some of his details appear to have come from historical sources, and his explanation of the quest for water at Nemea is much more logical and credible. For instance, both Adrastus and Amphiaraus would have been fully aware that there was a well sacred to Zeus at Nemea, and that it was watched over by the priest Lycurgus, who seems to have been newly elected to the role. Incidentally, some scholars have described Lycurgus as king of Nemea, but Nemea was a town subject to the city of Argos and would not have had a king of its own. As the priest of Zeus, Lycurgus would have been considered the headman of Nemea.

There is great melodramatic detail in Statius's account of the funerary games for Ophelles at Nemea. This information is not repeated by other sources, with the Greek writer Apollodorus several centuries earlier providing a much more credible list of the winners in these games. Statius goes on to give detailed descriptions of six contests in the games. Yet we know the Nemean Games consisted initially of seven contests. In his fanciful account, he also distributes quite expensive prizes—from armor to a female slave—to the first three place-getters in each event.

Multiple reliable sources tell us that only the winners of Pan-Hellenic games events were recognized, not other place-getters, and these victors were all presented with a simple crown as their prize. That crown was usually of laurel; but in the case of the Nemean Games, victors were awarded a celery crown, in memory of the place where Ophelles was killed by the snake.

And while Statius mentions that the twin sons of Hypsipyle took part in the chariot race at these games, he fails to mention the games' seventh event, the Hoplitodromos race, which several other sources tell us was jointly won by the sons of Hypsipyle. This suggests that Statius invented most of his Nemean Games story. Several other sources have the sons of Hypsipyle happening to turn up at the house of Lycurgus when the Seven are there, implying that the reunion with their mother was coincidental. However, with so many volunteers from around Greece marching in Adrastus's Argive army, it's highly likely that the brothers were actually in the army's ranks, attracted by thoughts of adventure and loot. Like others of noble birth in the army, they subsequently competed in Ophelles's funerary games.

Adding to doubts about the authenticity of much of Statius's epic is the fact that the Greek funerary rites he describes were actually the much later Roman rites of his own era. He also attributes to the Greeks of fourteen hundred years before his day military aspects from his own time, such as the Roman legionary cohort and the wedge formation. He also claims that Ismene was engaged to a soldier named Atys, which no other source supports, and says Parthenopaeus's mother Atalanta was still alive and in contact with her son at the time of the Seven, while all other indications are that both she and her husband Hippomenes were dead by then.

Statius's book of verse about the Seven going against Thebes, his *Thebaid*, was a best seller after publication in Italy in AD 92 and was studied in Roman schoolrooms, with young Romans devouring the detail-laden depictions of athletic contests and heroic battles. He seems to have written for sensation and sales. He was nonetheless a gifted poet and a strong later influence on Chaucer and Dante. Occasionally, his details ring true—the thunderstorm at the time of Capaneus's death and the subsequent rain, for example. But, overall, with many elements either provably wrong or uncorroborated by other ancient authors, his *Thebaid*, which is also laced with the involvement of the gods, must be considered largely a work of fiction.

All the ancient Greek and Roman authors used much the same characters, although the ultimate fates of the leading figures in the story vary in different accounts. Euripides, writing *The Phoenician Maidens* a generation after fellow dramatists Aeschylus and Sophocles wrote their plays, names Adrastus, king of Argos, as one of the Seven, and assigns him to the attack of one of the seven gates of Thebes, omitting Eteoclus from the Seven. The Roman Statius later followed his example, despite ignoring other details provided by Euripides. Most importantly, Euripides actually contradicted himself and named Eteoclus as one of the Seven in another of his plays, *The Suppliants*, with his description of Eteoclus in that work mirroring that of Aeschylus in the earlier *Seven Against Thebes*.

We don't know in which order Euripides composed his plays. It's possible that he wrote *The Phoenician Maidens* first, using a historical source that spoke of Adrastus commanding Argive forces at one of the gates during the assault on Thebes. There is an element of truth in this, for it is clear that Adrastus took over command of the attacking forces at one of the seven gates after the death of Tydeus. Perhaps, after being reminded that Aeschylus had named Eteoclus as one of the Seven, Euripides subsequently added Eteoclus to the Seven when he wrote *The Suppliants*, taking his description of Eteoclus from *Seven Against Thebes*.

With Euripides correcting himself to include Eteoclus in the Seven and with two earlier detailed Greek sources on the Seven (Aeschylus and Sophocles) both naming Eteoclus as one of the champions while putting Adrastus in command of both the Argive army and the overall operation against Thebes, this personnel scenario seems to be the most consistent, the most corroborated, and above all the most logical, and is the one I have followed.

Euripides also allocated different gates to four of the Seven from those provided by Aeschylus in *Seven Against Thebes*, and gave shield designs and weapons to the Seven that mostly differed from Aeschylus. These discrepancies could be explained as the youthful exuberance of a novice writer—Euripides started writing plays at the age of eighteen. I have chosen to explain Euripides's information as a false report from the escaped prisoner he describes in *The Phoenician Maidens* and have remained faithful to Aeschylus's *Seven Against Thebes* for the majority of the martial details regarding the Seven. One of Euripides's most glaring differences in this respect is that he gives the flaming torch and the compulsion to burn Thebes to the ground to Tydeus, despite the fact that all other sources, including illustrations on classical Greek jars that survive to this day, make Capaneus the pyromaniac, not Tydeus.

Notably, Euripides never served as a soldier, unlike Aeschylus and Sophocles. Aeschylus heroically served as a common soldier in the famous Battle of Marathon, where the Athenians defeated the invading Persian army; one of Aeschylus's two brothers died in that battle. Sophocles was one of ten generals elected annually at Athens, and he commanded troops in battle. The lack of military knowledge on the part of Euripides shows in some of his battle descriptions. For example, he has Amphiaraus in a speeding chariot as the arriving Argive army floods to the walls of Thebes, and in that chariot he also places live sacrificial sheep! Hardly a likely scenario, and certainly not one described by any other source.

Euripides was prone to basic error—he makes Polynices younger than Eteocles, when all other sources make him the elder of the brothers. He also appears to have changed some details to suit his dramatic purposes. For example, he kills off Eurydice, mother of Megareus, in childbirth and has Megareus's aunt Jocasta suckle and raise him, which enables Euripides to present a dramatic scene involving Jocasta as the youth goes knowingly to his death. Other sources not only have Eurydice outliving her son, they also say she cremated him.

Yet Euripides should not be dismissed entirely. For example, he calls the southeastern gate of Thebes the Fountain Gate, while Aeschylus calls it the Homolid Gate. As Pausanias informs us, this gate only took the name Homolid several decades after the Seven's assault on Thebes. At the time of the Seven, this gate was still being called the Fountain Gate. Euripides must have become aware of this fact from a source such as a Greek history that was extant in his time, or from a personal visit to Thebes.

No detailed makeup of the Argive army that King Adrastus led against Thebes is provided by ancient sources. The Theban poet Pindar tells us that three thousand men were in the army's ranks when it departed Argos, and a total of five thousand is probable once all contingents had joined the force en route to Thebes. Apart from natives of Argolis and Nemea and a large contingent from Sicyon (which Adrastus also ruled), indications from various ancient sources are that adventure-seeking volunteers came from Arcadia, Calydon, Sparta, Thessaly, and as far away as the island of Lemnos in the northern Aegean, while Aeschylus tells us that some men in this Argive army came from Thebes itself—one of them on a spying mission.

The fact that Adrastus was revered in Colonos strongly suggests that volunteers also came from there. Plus we know that, ten years after this, Argos had formal alliances with Megara, another place where Adrastus was revered, and Corinth, with both cities contributing troops to the Argive army led against Thebes by the Offspring. So it's highly likely that contingents from Megara and Corinth marched with Adrastus and the Seven—if not via a formal alliance, then as a result of volunteers joining the Argive army from these cities.

In my account I have drawn upon all the extant classical plays, poems, histories, and geographies for the broad story but have followed the account of Sophocles, who wrote a series of three plays about Oedipus, to arrive at the fates of Oedipus and Antigone. For Jocasta's fate, with most playwrights having her live well past Oedipus's abdication and playing a part in the events of the siege of Thebes, I have followed

Euripides, having Jocasta survive her attempt to hang herself described by Sophocles to play a leading role in the last-ditch peace negotiations just prior to the siege of Thebes. But Euripides has Jocasta later kill herself with a sword, following the violent deaths of her sons and eldest daughter, while other sources say she hanged herself. Considering Jocasta's earlier attempt to hang herself, a second successful use of the same method rings true.

Incidentally, Pausanias, one of history's first travel writers, who provides credible firsthand descriptions of Thebes and the topography of the settings of the *Seven Against Thebes* story, wrote that he believed that Oedipus didn't marry Jocasta, and that the mother of his four children was Euryganeia, Jocasta's little-known sister. This would have turned Oedipus's children Polynices, Eteocles, Antigone, and Ismene into Jocasta's nieces, nephews, and grandchildren, not her children. Pausanias gave as his only source for this belief the *Oedipoea*, a lost poem of the Cyclic quartet by the obscure Greek poet Cinaethon.

As Pausanias's writings show, he was a devout pagan. In fact, the modern historian Paul Cartledge describes him as "eminently pious." It's likely that the story of the incestuous relationship between Oedipus and Jocasta, a story that every other classical author on the subject vouches for and which I have followed, did not sit comfortably with Pausanias. In fact, it seems to have offended Pausanias's religious sensibilities to accept that Oedipus impregnated his own mother, and he chose to believe Cinaethon's lone, more decorous explanation for the couple's relationship. Scholars today tend to accept that Jocasta was both the mother of Oedipus and of his children.[120]

The story of the later campaign of the Epigoni, or Offspring, the sons of the Seven, comes from Apollodorus and also from a fragment of Aeschylus's play *Epigone* discovered as recently as 2005. In addition, Euripides ends his play *The Suppliant Women* with a reference to the Offspring going against Thebes and succeeding where their fathers had failed. In *The Iliad*, written before Aeschylus's *Seven Against Thebes*, Homer makes mention of two of the Offspring, the sons of Tydeus and

Capaneus, by that time middle-aged men, describing them as two of the leading Greek warriors taking part in the siege of Troy.

The story of King Oedipus, with his complex relationships, solving the riddle of the Sphinx, unwittingly killing his own father and marrying his own mother, has fascinated and inspired great writers and thinkers down through the centuries. In the 20th century, psychoanalyst Sigmund Freud used the term "Oedipus complex" to describe a child's sexual infatuation for their own parent, while the term "Jocasta complex" is used to describe a mother's lust for her own son. However, neither of these usages accurately reflects the source material. Neither Oedipus nor Jocasta knew they were related or lusted after each other prior to their wedding. Oedipus was given Jocasta in marriage without having met her, with neither of them knowing at the time that they were related. It would be many years after Jocasta bore Oedipus four children that she and Oedipus learned the truth about his parentage, a discovery that horrified them both.

The dialogue I use throughout this book is based on the extant works of the Greek playwrights, poets, and historians. Sometimes I've had to modernize the often-Elizabethan language used in English translations to make it intelligible to modern readers. Occasionally I've abridged it, for the playwrights of old would put scene-setting story exposition into their dialogue, telling their audiences things that modern readers already know. Very occasionally, where no ancient source provides it, to advance the narrative I have created dialogue based on known elements of the story exposition in the ancient plays, poems, and histories.

Often, however, the dialogue very closely follows that in classical texts. Sophocles, rated in his own lifetime as Greece's greatest dramatist, being awarded that mantle on Aeschylus's death, was a brilliant wordsmith comparable to, and a forerunner of and model for, William Shakespeare. When, in *Oedipus Rex*, Sophocles has Oedipus interrogating his brother-in-law Creon; the messenger from Corinth; the shepherd whose job it was to cast him into the wilderness as a baby; and his wife Jocasta, the crisp, realistic dialogue often reads like exchanges between prosecutor and witnesses in a modern courtroom drama.

Like Shakespeare, Sophocles had great insight into human nature, and through his dialogue in *Oedipus Rex* and *Oedipus at Colonos* we see Oedipus's mind unraveling as he is racked with guilt, shame, bitterness, and paranoia. But for all of Sophocles's genius, his *Oedipus Rex*, today by far his most famous and revered work, was in his own day beaten into second place in a drama contest by a play written by an otherwise insignificant nephew of Aeschylus, none of whose work has survived.

Because Greek dramatists always limited the number of speaking parts in their dramas and used the anonymous Chorus to play a number of supporting roles, I occasionally spread existing dialogue among several characters known or expected to be present. In this way, I give a voice to Ismene, for example, who could not be expected to remain mute when she was with Antigone at the very last emotional meeting between the two sisters and their brother Polynices.

This book commences with the girls' father Oedipus as a young man. Classical sources fail to give us Oedipus's motivation in going to Thebes in the first place. His route from Delphi to the three-way crossroads in Phocis, where he had his bloody confrontation with King Laius, intersected with roads to Daulia and Plataea. His stated intention was to escape to a place where he could never fulfill the prophecy of patricide and incest and to do so by navigating by the stars.

Corinth, where Oedipus was raised, was a maritime city, with the sea god Poseidon as its patron deity. This suggests that Oedipus had some experience aboard ships as a boy, when he would have been taught to navigate by the stars. Were Oedipus to have traveled on the Daulian road, it would have taken him to Orchomenus, Chaeroneia, and the coast. Having acquired a boat, he would have been able to sail far away, as he planned.

Why, then, after killing Laius and three of his four companions in an outburst of violent rage, did Oedipus turn away from the road to Daulia and the coast, instead taking the road to Plataea, and from there taking the turn to Thebes, toward the deadly Sphinx? Was Oedipus aware of the existence of the Sphinx? Perhaps he wasn't. He went along the road and right into her jaws. We know that no recent traveler to Thebes before Oedipus had lived to tell of the Sphinx and its riddle. Yet King Laius not only knew that the Sphinx was killing all who attempted to enter Thebes, but he was on his way to ask the Oracle of Delphi how to deal with the beast. What's more, the Sphinx had permitted Laius and his party to pass out of the city, as she apparently only threatened those who attempted to enter Thebes. This suggests that word of the horrible deaths inflicted by the Sphinx on people trying to reach Thebes had been spread abroad by people who left Thebes, and Oedipus should have been aware of this danger. But how much credence would he have put in it?

I have Oedipus taking the road that ultimately led him to Thebes in pursuit of the lone witness to his multiple murders, planning to also eliminate him and so keep his crime secret, after which he would continue his journey to escape by sea. It's possible that he dismissed the stories of a Sphinx attacking travelers on the road to Thebes as fantastical inventions. The final alternative, as previously mentioned, was that the Sphinx was actually a female highway robber; and Oedipus was afraid of no woman!

NOTES

CHAPTER 1. OEDIPUS AND THE RIDDLE OF THE SPHINX

1. Oedipus was described as tall by all ancient sources. His tawny beard is described by Euripides in *The Phoenician Maidens*. His dress at this time, including the broad-brimmed hat and sheathed sword, is shown on an ancient Greek vase depicting Oedipus with the Sphinx. Apollodorus, in *The Library of Apollodorus*, describes Oedipus as driving a chariot, but all other sources put him on foot and dressed to maintain a low profile.

2.–5. Sophocles, *Oedipus Rex*.

6. Apollodorus names Polyphontes as the steward and says that he killed one of Oedipus's chariot horses, which is contradicted by other Greek sources that put Oedipus on foot, not in a chariot. According to Apollodorus, the king of Plataea interred the remains of Laius.

7. Apollodorus says that Oedipus killed two men. Sophocles and other earlier Greek sources agree that he killed at least four.

8. Sophocles, *Oedipus Rex*.

9. Based on Sophocles, *Oedipus Rex*.

10. Homer, *The Iliad*, describes Thebes's wide streets.

11.–12. Based on Sophocles, *Oedipus Rex*. Throughout this work, where Sophocles and other dramatists use the anonymous Chorus to represent the senior Spartoi, I have spread the Chorus's dialogue over Astacus and Oenops, senior Theban Spartoi.

CHAPTER 2. OEDIPUS LEARNS THE TRUTH

13. The entire exchange and all that follows is from Sophocles, *Oedipus Rex*.

14.   Again, where Sophocles uses the anonymous Chorus, I have used Oenops and Astacus.

15.   Apollodorus, *The Library*, tells of Teiresias's cornel wood staff.

16.   Sophocles, in *Oedipus Rex*, has Oedipus use two brooches from Jocasta's garment to stab himself in both eyes at once. This would have involved removing one brooch, putting it down, removing the other, then picking up both, in left and right hands, and simultaneously stabbing himself in both eyes. Try it—not with a real sharp object, obviously. It's time-consuming, messy, and counterintuitive. It's much more likely that, in the passion of the moment, Oedipus rapidly stabbed himself in both eyes with one brooch. For background on Jocasta's fate, see the Afterword.

CHAPTER 3. POLYNICES AND ETEOCLES: BROTHERS AT WAR

17.   Dialogue based on Sophocles, *Oedipus Rex*.

18.   No ancient author tells us how the brothers decided the order in which they would take turns on the throne. I suggest that the ultra-competitive Eteocles would have initiated this spear-throwing contest as a decider.

CHAPTER 4. TYDEUS AND POLYNICES: THE BOAR AND THE LION

19.   Euripides, in *The Suppliants*, describes this meeting between Adrastus, Polynices, and Tydeus.

20.   Apollodorus names the ten relatives Tydeus was variously accused of murdering.

21.   Apollodorus describes the shield designs of Polynices and Tydeus, the foreparts of a lion and a boar.

CHAPTER 5. THE KING'S PROMISE

22.   Dialogue in this chapter is based on what we know took place at the palace during this time, from all sources.

CHAPTER 6. RECRUITING THE SEVEN

23.   Statius, *The Thebaid*, has Argia pestering her father to lead the war against Thebes to reinstate her husband, even making a cloak for Polynices to wear on campaign.

24. This chapter's dialogue is based on all we know from all sources of the Seven's recruitment.

25. The necklace and its use by Polynices as a bribe is described by Sophocles in *Oedipus Rex, Oedipus at Colonos,* and *Antigone.*

26. These insults addressed to young Parthenopaeus come from Aeschylus's *Seven Against Thebes.*

27. The description of Eteoclus is taken from Aeschylus, *Seven Against Thebes,* and Euripides, *The Suppliants.*

28. Various fathers including the god Ares were attributed by classical sources to Parthenopaeus, but Apollodorus and Pausanias (in his *Descriptions of Greece*) agree that it was Talaus, which would have given him royal blood and made him acceptable to Adrastus.

29. The bull's-blood oath is described by Aeschylus in *Seven Against Thebes.*

CHAPTER 7. ON THE MARCH: TRAGEDY AND DISCOVERY AT NEMEA

30. Homer, in *The Iliad,* tells of the failed mission of Polynices and Tydeus to collect recruits from Mycenae.

31. Pausanias describes the parting of Amphiaraus from his sons in detail, including the fact that Alcmaeon was naked.

32. Pindar, *Odes,* and Statius both number the army at three thousand men at this point.

33. Statius gave the horse a coat of golden hair and a red mane. Other ancient sources describe Arion as a white horse with a black mane.

34. Apollodorus says Amphiaraus's charioteer was called Elato by some older sources, but Baton was his most commonly given name.

35. Euripides, *Hypsipyle*—see Collard and Croft, *Euripides Fragments.*

36. Statius turns the snake into a huge dragon, which the members of the Seven have to combat in the style of Jason and his Argonauts. Earlier more reliable sources describe a snake biting the child. Poisonous vipers are common in Greece.

37. Verbatim from Statius, who also describes Tydeus pushing Lycurgus back with his shield.

38. Euripides, *Hypsipyle.*

39. Apollodorus provides the details of the winners of the funerary games' events. He fails to mention the Hoplitodromos, and says there was a long-jump, which there wasn't. In Statius's suspect account, which can be considered mostly fiction, Adrastus loaned his two chariot horses, including the magnificent Arion, to Polynices, who added them to his own pair of horses. But Arion was unaccustomed to a strange driver, and both ran faster than the rest of the team and veered off course—or so the story goes. And then Polynices was jolted from his chariot, flying out the back and landing in the sand, without injury. In Statius's suspect version, Polynices's driver-less chariot was the first to cross the finishing line, with Amphiaraus, using a team of four snow-white horses, close behind, and it was Amphiaraus who was declared the winner.

In Statius's *Thebaid*, the first three place-getters in each event were given expensive prizes by Adrastus. But Statius well knew that only the victor in pan-Hellenic games received a prize, and that prize was always a simple crown. Winners of Olympic Games events were awarded an olive crown. Delphic Games winners received a laurel crown. Winners of the later Nemean Games were always awarded a crown made from fresh celery. The Isthmian Games, held at Corinth, initially awarded its winners a crown woven from pine branches, although by Statius's time this had been replaced by a crown of dried celery, apparently as a salute to the Nemean Games.

Statius also gave his imagination free rein when he described the games' sprint event. Statius wrote that Parthenopaeus was so fleet of foot, he could catch his own shadow! He went on to write that a fellow competitor, a young Spartan, tugged Parthenopaeus's long hair as they reached the finishing line, holding him back sufficiently for the Spartan to breast the line fractionally ahead. When Parthenopaeus complained to Adrastus of foul play, the king ordered the pair to rerun the race, with a large space dividing them. This time, went Statius's fictional story, Parthenopaeus won.

40. Pepin, *The Vatican Mythographers*, describes the victory of the brothers and the maternal reunion that followed.

41. Ibid; and Statius, who devotes an entire chapter to the Lemnos episode.

42. This reunion is based on Pepin, Apollodorus, Statius, and Hyginus. In addition, "The Cyzican Epigrams," Mackhai, *Select Epigrams*, describes a temple at Cyzicus where Euneus and Thoas are depicted showing their mother the Golden Vine as proof of their identity.

43. Apollodorus; and Statius.

44. Sophocles, *Oedipus at Colonos*; and Plutarch, "Theseus."

45. Euripides, in *The Phoenician Maidens*, sent Tydeus on this mission while still living at Argos; but Apollodorus more credibly sends Tydeus to Thebes when the advancing Argive army was camped on Mount Cithaeron.

CHAPTER 8. CREON'S KIDNAP ATTEMPT

46. Sophocles describes the scene in *Oedipus at Colonos*, inclusive of Oedipus's wafting white hair. Much of his dialogue is reproduced here verbatim from that source. Sophocles doesn't name the two men with Creon, but it's extremely likely his sons accompanied him.

47. Sophocles attributes these words to the anonymous Chorus. Xenon is Greek for host, and guest, and he was indeed both a host to Oedipus in Colonos and a guest in his house there.

48. All from Sophocles, *Oedipus at Colonos*.

CHAPTER 9. POLYNICES'S MISSION TO OEDIPUS

49. All dialogue in this meeting and the one that follows is from Sophocles, *Oedipus at Colonos*.

CHAPTER 10. AMBUSH: TYDEUS'S PEACE EMBASSY TO THEBES

50. Apollodorus writes of Tydeus's peace mission to Eteocles. Homer, in *The Iliad*, also tells of this mission, the fifty assassins, and their leaders, sent to ambush Tydeus on his way back to the Argive camp from the meeting. Both tell of the contests in which Tydeus challenged Theban champions.

CHAPTER 11. THE DEATH OF OEDIPUS

51. The trip to Colonos, and the dialogue, is from Sophocles, *Oedipus at Colonos*.

CHAPTER 12. IN THE ARGIVE ARMY'S CAMP

52.   I have used this campfire episode to explain several aspects. Firstly, the deeply superstitious nature of Greeks of the time and the fact that it was in campfire discussions that news and gossip were commonly exchanged, along with the sometimes-competing myths that grew around Oedipus and Theseus even while they were still alive. I also wanted to demonstrate that some Argives would have dismissed the story of Oedipus and the Sphinx as mere Theban propaganda, at the same time illustrating how the story of the Sphinx may well have developed from a real-life female highway robber named the Sphinx, such as that encountered by Theseus in the same era and which was subsequently romanticized into a mythical beast.

53.   Verbatim from Euripides, *The Phoenician Maidens*.

54.   Plutarch, "Theseus," tells both the mythical story of Phaea and the widely circulated story that she was actually a female highway robber.

55.   Apollodorus relates the story of Atalanta and Hippomenes. He gives the latter the name Melanion, which means "By Ares," relating to the myth that he was fathered by the god Ares. This was possibly a nickname of Hippomenes. Ovid, *Metamorphoses*, and Theocritus, "Idyll," both refer to him as Hippomenes.

56.   Apollodorus details the attempt to ambush Tydeus. The grove at Potniae meets the description of the ambush's location.

57.   Dialogue from Statius. His *Thebaid* names a number of otherwise unknown attackers, but only Maeon and Polyphontes are named elsewhere. Statius also placed Tydeus's mission well before the Argive army even departed Argos, but Apollodorus places it more credibly when the army was camped on Mount Cithaeron and within two days' march of Thebes.

CHAPTER 13. JOCASTA'S PEACE CONFERENCE

58.   Homer, *Iliad*.

59.   Euripides, *The Phoenician Maidens*, says Jocasta sent a message to Polynices to summon him to this peace conference with his brother. With Mecisteus known to be competing at Oedipus's funerary games, he would have been ideally placed to carry that message from Jocasta.

60.   Pausanias describes this house where I have placed the truce parley. Euripides is vague about the meeting's location but has Creon at the palace and ignorant of the meeting's location in the city until after it took place. Creon then searches throughout the city to locate Eteocles once he left the meeting. Euripides has Oedipus still alive, but all other sources have Oedipus dead by this stage, as Sophocles spells out in *Oedipus at Colonos*. Euripides also places the Argive army now right outside the city's walls at this time, but this is much too premature for their arrival. And with the invading army supposedly right on the city's doorstep, Euripides has Theban watchmen permitting Oedipus to enter and wander the city, without a Theban escort and armed with a sword! An invited peace envoy from an enemy army besieging a city would have arrived unarmed and carrying an olive branch. And he would have been escorted to and from the meeting place, not left to wander around as a potential assassin, arsonist, or spy.

61.   Euripides, *The Phoenician Maidens*. He gives a mother's disappointment in her son's marriage the ring of truth. Perhaps he'd had a similar experience with his own disappointed mother; he never married, and reputedly disliked women.

62.   Ibid.

CHAPTER 14. SEVEN GATES, SEVEN CHAMPIONS

63.   Euripides, *The Phoenician Maidens*, tells of this Theban soldier who was taken prisoner; he would have to have been a cavalry scout.

64.   This formation for the advancing Argive army is described by Euripides.

65.   Pausanias tells of these mercenaries recruited by Eteocles.

66.   Euripides is the lone ancient source to say that the Argive army advanced via Teumessus. Other sources give no indication of the army's route. It's possible that Euripides was relying on a now-lost Greek history for this route, which is credible, because later, says Pausanias, the Offspring would also attack Thebes from the direction of Teumessus. This suggests that the Offspring deliberately adopted the identical route of attack that their fathers had used before them.

67.   Such a briefing on Thebes and its defenses would have been necessary so that each member of the Seven would know his task in the operation, and Polynices, who was born and raised in Thebes, was uniquely able to impart this information.

68.   Details of the seven gates from Pausanias.

69.   Aeschylus, *Seven Against Thebes*, describes this ceremony in detail, inclusive of this quote about Amphiaraus. He also gives the order of the draw and the equipment details of the Seven. Some details, such as Amphiaraus's undecorated shield, are corroborated by Euripides in *The Phoenician Maidens*.

70.   Capaneus's helmet, shield, and torch are depicted on a fourth century BC amphora held by the J. Paul Getty Museum, California. The shield design is from Aeschylus, *Seven Against Thebes*.

71.-74.   Aeschylus.

CHAPTER 15. CHAMPION VERSUS CHAMPION

75.   Euripides, *The Phoenician Maidens*, tells of the escaped prisoner and the information he imparts to Creon.

76.   Aeschylus, *Seven Against Thebes*, tells of the Theban spy in the Argive army's ranks and the information he brings Creon. Aeschylus says the spy ran all the way from the Argive camp—12.5 miles. This is credible, remembering that, several hundred years later, the Athenian warrior Philippides would run all the way from Marathon Beach to Athens following the Battle of Marathon, to inform Athenian leaders that the Persians had been defeated. This was close to twice the distance of the run from Teumessus to Thebes. Admittedly, Philippides did drop dead from exhaustion after delivering his message! Today, in the modern marathon race, athletes run 26 miles (42 kilometers), in emulation of Philippides's run.

77.   Euripides, *The Phoenician Women*, gives this exchange.

78.   Aeschylus, *Seven Against Thebes*, gives these assignments and the accompanying comments from Eteocles and the spy.

79.   Both Aeschylus and Euripides refer to the Argive troops' white shields, and Aeschylus describes Apollo as "lord of the wolves."

CHAPTER 16. FIRST BLOOD

80.   Pausanias was told by the people of Thebes about these mercenaries and their assignment and the alternate names for the fountain.

81.   Euripides based his play *The Phoenician Maidens* around these female visitors who were caught up in the war.

82.   Pausanias tells of the rout of the mercenaries.

83.   *Seven Against Thebes.*

84.   Various sources describe arrows being used by the defenders, and the fiery torch that Capaneus would use in the attack. Scholars believe Capaneus used incendiary pine resin in his torch. Euripides, in his *Medea*, describes a plant-based chemical used at this time to create fires that were impervious to water.

85.   Tydeus's call to arms from Euripides, *The Phoenician Maidens*.

86.   Ibid., for Eteocles rallying the troops here after Tydeus and his men had emptied the tower with javelin fire. He also tells of the soldiers whose task it was to shield their king.

87.   Statius, *Thebaid*.

88.   Aeschylus, *Seven Against Thebes*, uses "dwarf-head" as a Theban insult directed at Tydeus.

89.   This explains Euripides's belief that Adrastus was in command at "the seventh gate."

90.   Apollodorus provides this horrific scene.

CHAPTER 17. THE SUPREME SACRIFICE

91.   This scene and the dialogue that follows are taken from Euripides's *The Phoenician Maidens*. According to Euripides, Teiresias had returned the previous day from helping the sons of Cecrops I of Athens defeat Thracian invader Eumolpus. However, these leaders and events were from an entirely different period in Greek history, and Euripides clearly inserted them here as a fictional flourish, perhaps to show off his historical knowledge.

92.   Euripides has Megareus's mother Eurydice die in childbirth while delivering him, with the boy subsequently suckled and raised by Creon's sister Jocasta. This was apparently a dramatic device by Euripides to permit an

emotional scene with Jocasta, an existing character, rather than introduce Eurydice, a new character. Other sources agree that Eurydice not only outlived her son, she cremated him.

CHAPTER 18. THE THUNDER OF ZEUS

93.   The later lightning strike during this morning's fighting, recorded by all sources, reveals a dark sky with an electrical storm approaching, bringing rain, as Statius describes.

94.   The scene and dialogue are taken from Euripides, *The Phoenician Maidens*.

95.   *Description of Greece.*

96.   Euripides, *The Phoenician Maidens*.

97.   This claim was propagated by Euripides. Apollodorus and Pausanias have Parthenopaeus surviving these wounds and later, more credibly, being killed by Amphidicus, as described in the next chapter.

98.   Multiple sources tell of the thunderbolt that knocked Capaneus from the ladder and killed him. Euripides speaks of the Electra Gate tower being scorched by the fire started by Capaneus's torch and of how Eteocles sent his men back into it once the fire was extinguished—by rain from the storm.

99.–100. Euripides describes this Theban chariot sortie.

CHAPTER 19. ONE ON ONE

101.-103. Euripides, for the dialogue and the negotiation details.

104.   Statius wrote that the tip of Eteocles's sword went so far up through his body, it pierced Polynices's heart. This is supported by an Etruscan funerary relief from the second century BC, predating Statius by some three hundred years and today in the Museum-Lapidarium of Maffei. It depicts Eteocles on one knee, still with his shield on his left arm, but devoid of his spear and now with his sword in hand, ready to thrust it up into his brother. Polynices, having discarded his shield, stands over his brother and is about to cut Eteocles's throat with his sword.

105.   See Note 97 for comment on differing versions of Parthenopaeus's death. Some sources give Amphidicus the name of Asphodicos.

106. The fifth-century Theban poet Pindar, in writing of Amphiaraus's wild-eyed flight in his *Odes*, would say: "Amid divinely sent panic, even the children of gods flee."

107. All classical sources agree that Amphiaraus was swallowed by an opening in the earth, with many attributing this to the intercession of Zeus. We can interpret this hole as caused by an earthquake, which is supported by a reference by Euripides in *The Phoenician Maidens* to an aftershock within a week or so of the original quake. The Thebes area has long been a major seismic activity zone. As recently as July and September 2021, earth tremors shook Thebes and surrounding areas. That July, 160 tremors were recorded around Thebes. On September 2, 2021, a major shallow earthquake measuring 4.0 on the Richter scale occurred just one kilometer east of Thebes and was felt as far away as Chalcis and Athens, where it caused considerable alarm. The location of this quake was very close to the sites of the ancient villages of Harma and Mycalessus, which, historically, claimed to be where Amphiaraus was swallowed by a hole that opened in the earth.

108. Later, a small pillared enclosure would be built to memorialize Amphiaraus, to the right of the Plataea Road between Potniae and Thebes. Amphiaraus would be revered for generations to come by many Greeks. Even Thebans would declare him a good man who, to their minds, fell in with bad company. Besides, the fact that Zeus had supposedly intervened to claim Amphiaraus would impress many a superstitious Greek for centuries to come. This monument to Amphiaraus could still be seen thirteen hundred years later. Some Thebans would claim that this was where Amphiaraus died, but it was more likely the location of the fight between Polynices and Eteocles and the unholy betrayal of the Argive army. Two villages on the Chalcis Road to Thebes's northeast, Harma and Mycalessus, would both claim that Amphiaraus and his chariot were swallowed up in their vicinity, indicating that Periclymenus chased Amphiaraus up the Chalcis Road for some distance. As mentioned in the previous note, seismic activity in this area continues to this day.

109. "From that time," Pausanias wrote, "a Cadmean victory meant one that brings destruction to the victors."

CHAPTER 20. THE FIGHT OVER BODIES

110.   Pausanias.

111.   This treaty was, according to the third century BC Greek historian and biographer Philochorus, "the first treaty that ever was made for the recovering of the bodies of the dead."

112.   Years later, a monument of three worked stones would be placed over Tydeus's last resting place, almost certainly by his son Diomedes once he became king of Argos, and thought to represent the three crests on Tydeus's helmet. Pausanias, on his visit to Thebes in the second century AD, would be shown this monument to Tydeus by Thebans, and would reflect on how Homer, in his *Iliad*, referred to "Tydeus, who at Thebes is covered by a heap of earth." The grave of one other leading figure in the venture of the Seven against Thebes existed at the time of Pausanias's visit, that of Amphidicus, the man who had killed Parthenopaeus. It was right next to the Fountain of Oedipus, outside the southeast corner of the city wall.

113.   "It is our boast," the Greek historian Herodotus, in *The History*, would quote the later Athenians as saying, "that we went out against the Cadmeans [Thebans], recovered the bodies, and buried them at Eleusis in our own territory."

CHAPTER 21. THE OFFSPRING SUCCEED WHERE THEIR FATHERS FAILED

114.   Homer, *The Iliad*, wrote of Diomedes, when talking about Tydeus: "His son can talk more glibly, but he cannot fight as his father did."

115.   On the advice of the people of Thebes, Pausanias also added Polynices's sons Timeus and Adrastus to the list of the Offspring, although young Adrastus would only have been ten or eleven by this time. In addition, the first-century Roman writer Hyginus would add Tiesmenes and Biates to Offspring ranks, claiming that they were further sons of Parthenopaeus, which, considering Parthenopaeus's youth at the time of his death, was highly unlikely. Tiesmenes is actually thought to have been a half-brother of Parthenopaeus, while Biates is otherwise unknown.

116. The dramatist Sophocles dedicated a play to this campaign, calling it *The Epigoni*. That work didn't survive to modern times, but in 2005 several brief excerpts were discovered: "And the helmets are shaking their purple crests, and for the wearers of breastplates the weavers are striking up the wise shuttle's songs that awakens those who are asleep . . . And he is gluing together the chariot's rail." *Independent on Sunday*, 17 April, 2005.

117. Hyginus, *Fabulae*.

118. Pausanias.

AFTERWORD: SOURCES AND INTERPRETATION

119. I had an uncle-in-law like Theseus, a soldier who chose to attract the attention of highway robbers. A captain with Britain's Royal Marine Commandos who was at one time in charge of all British commando training, Frank McGhee deliberately took a back road while on holiday in Phuket, Thailand, in hopes of being attacked by a notorious local band of muggers who disguised themselves as women. Sure enough, the gang held up Frank, a diminutive Scotsman, and his wife Helen. Using his unarmed-combat skills, Frank went to work. After a flurry of action, he had the robbers disarmed and running for their lives, nursing bruises and broken bones. "Now, Helen," said Frank to his wife, dusting off his hands, "let's go to dinner."

120. Cartledge, *Thebes*.

BIBLIOGRAPHY

BOOKS

Aeschylus, *Aeschylus, Sophocles, Euripides, Aristophanes, 'The Plays of Aeschylus'* (G. M. Cookson transl.). Chicago, University of Chicago, 1952.

Apollodorus, *Gods and Heroes of the Greeks: The Library of Apollodorus* (M. Simpson transl.). Amherst, University of Massachusetts Press, 1976.

Boardman, J., J. Griffen, and O. Murray, *The Oxford History of the Classical World*. Oxford, Oxford University Press, 1986.

Cartledge, P., *Thebes: The Forgotten City of Ancient Greece*. London, Picador, 2020.

Collard, C., and M. Cropp, *Euripides Fragments: Oedipus-Chrysippus, Other Fragments*. Cambridge, MA, Loeb Classical Library, 2008.

Dando-Collins, S., *Rise of an Empire: How One Man United Greece to Defeat Xerxes's Persians*. Nashville, John Wiley and Son, 2013.

Euripides, *Aeschylus, Sophocles, Euripides, Aristophanes, 'The Plays of Euripides'* (E. P. Coleridge transl.). Chicago, University of Chicago, 1952.

Herodotus, *The History*. Chicago, University of Chicago, 1952.

Homer, *The Iliad of Homer* and *The Odyssey*. Chicago, University of Chicago, 1952.

Hyginus, *Hygini Fabulae*. London, Ontario, Scholars Choice, 2015.

Mackhai, J. W., *Select Epigrams from the Greek Anthology*. London, Longman Green and Co., 1890.

Ovid, *Metamorphoses* (D. Raeburn transl.). London, Penguin Classics, 2004.

Pausanias, *Description of Greece* (W. H. S. Jones transl.), Cambridge, MA, Harvard University Press, 1985.

Pepin, R. E., *The Vatican Mythographers*. New York, Fordham University Press, 2008.

Pindar, *The Complete Odes* (A. Verity transl.). Oxford, Oxford World's Classics, 2008.

Plutarch, *The Lives of the Noble Grecians and Romans, 'Theseus'* (J. Dryden transl.). Chicago, University of Chicago, 1952.

Roman, L., and M. Roman, *Encyclopedia of Greek and Roman Mythology.* New York Facts on File, 2010.

Seneca, *Four Tragedies and Octavia, 'Oedipus'* (E. F. Watling transl.). London, Penguin, 1966.

Sophocles, *Aeschylus, Sophocles, Euripides, Aristophanes, 'The Plays of Sophocles'* (R. C. Jebb transl.). Chicago, University of Chicago, 1952.

Statius, P. P., *The Thebaid: Seven Against Thebes* (C. S. Ross transl.). Baltimore, Johns Hopkins University Press, 2004.

Theocritus, *Antique Gems from the Greek and Latin.* Whitefish, MT, Kessinger, 2005.

Warry, J., *Warfare in the Classical World.* London, Salamander, 1980.

NEWSPAPER

"Extraordinary Discovery Unlocks Secrets of the Ancients," *Independent on Sunday,* London, 17 April 2005.

INDEX